Managing
FOR
Value

STEFAN BÖTZEL & ANDREAS SCHWILLING

Managing FOR Value

CAPSTONE

First published 1999 by
Capstone Publishing Limited
Oxford Centre for Innovation
Mill Street
Oxford OX2 0JX
United Kingdom
http://www.capstone.co.uk

British Library cataloguing in publication data
A CIP catalogue record for this book is available from the British Library

ISBN 1-84112-080-4

Typeset in Garamond by
Sparks Computer Solutions Ltd, Oxford
http://www.sparks.co.uk
Printed and bound by
T.J. International Ltd, Padstow, Cornwall

This book is printed on acid-free paper

Substantial discounts on bulk quantities of Capstone books are available to corporations, professional associations and other organizations. For details telephone Capstone Publishing on (+44-1865-798623) or fax (+44-1865-240941).

Foreword

Despite the heated debate that has raged in recent years, shareholder value remains as topical an issue in Europe as it is controversial. Contributions to the ongoing dialogue regarding the successful procurement of (equity) capital cover the entire spectrum. The unions speak of 'sinking back into unbridled early capitalism', whilst European business administrators talk about 'old wine in new wineskins', and the analysts describe it as 'an absolute must'.

In our opinion, shareholder value is nothing more and nothing less than a sensible and, for many companies, necessary tool of strategic management to add to the ones they already use.

- Shareholder value aims to chart a value-based course toward growth by rigorously focusing on cash flow and applying a forward-looking, productive form of pressure on companies to be profitable (i.e. to generate market returns).
- Shareholder value lends objectivity to internal competition for resources and measures all businesses against the same standard (the cost of capital).
- Shareholder value links financial and operative indicators, thereby laying the foundation for a powerful and accurate system of management and controlling with clearly defined objectives and fields of responsibility (value drivers).

The crucial factor in all of this is the emphasis on growth through shareholder value. Applied correctly and responsibly, the concept of shareholder value – or, as we would put it, of value-based corporate management – leads to above-average company growth. Our European studies substantiate this claim: companies that are run along the lines of value-based management see their sales grow at around two times the average rate, while employee figures rise considerably faster (at 8.1% p.a., compared with 1.6%). The same companies also invest more and see their cash flow grow significantly faster. These are the findings of a five-year survey of 200 stock corporations in Europe.

Consequently, the doubts often aired about the social commitment of private ownership under the shareholder value philosophy can safely be set aside. Given proper implementation and a clear growth orientation, value-based corporate management will contribute to prosperity and economic growth. Growing companies can invest in new jobs, develop better products or superior services – if they did not, they would not grow – and purchase more from their suppliers. To put it another way: from an entrepreneurial vantage point, the concepts of shareholder and stakeholder management are by no means at loggerheads. On the contrary, the two exist in fruitful and mutually stimulating symbiosis. In the long run, it is impossible to maximise the value of a company – and hence the value of equity or shareholder capital – if the interests of the stakeholders are trampled underfoot. Value maximisation demands cooperation with these groups.

The reason why value management is such a powerful engine for growth is basically simple; implementing it, however, would appear to be less so. Sales growth drives entrepreneurial success (i.e. it creates value) faster than efforts to cut costs. Increases in cash flow generated by additional new sales are worth more in the long term than savings made by cutting costs. Cost-cutting alone does not provide a company with a lasting differentiator: measured in global terms, efficient companies will have the same cost advantages. What is more, cost-cutting alone is not sufficient to mobilise a company. The power to move ahead, to create value by means of new ideas and solutions, new products and market innovations, new forms of cooperation both inside and outside the company is either lacking or cannot be adequately harnessed in such approaches.

Viewed from this perspective, value management will always, perhaps primarily, be an exercise in transformation management: it is only the mobilisation of all a company's resources – employees, suppliers, customers – that can improve its market position, its customer orientation and its performance in terms of both speed and quality.

And this is exactly the point that our publishers and authors – all of them experienced consultants at Roland Berger & Partners – have focused on in this book. They have linked their extensive knowledge of value management with the results of our own studies and projects, and our extensive expertise in the field of corporate transformation, and presented their findings in a logical, intuitive order. The result is a book which provides a masterful outline of the practical outworking of value creation, with warnings against typical pitfalls to be avoided and, above all, useful guidance on the process of linking value creation programs with the changes and mobilisation that many companies so desperately need. At the same time, the bridge the authors build – between a growth orientation that actively involves the various stakeholder groups and an interactive approach to corporate transformation – provides a uniquely European blend of shareholder management – our response to the corporate realities of today.

Hamburg, June 1999

Dr Burkhard Schwenker
Member of the Executive Committee
Roland Berger & Partners
International Management Consultants

Summary of Contents

Contents

List of abbreviations

ACT	Advance Corporation Tax
bn	Billion
CAGR	Compound Annual Growth Rate
CDAX	Deutscher Aktienindex (German stock market index; broken down by sector)
CF	Cash flow
CFROI	Cash flow return on investment
CI	Corporation income tax
CIR	Cash investment ratio
CROCI	Cash return on capital invested
CVA	Cash Value Added
D	Germany
DAX	Deutscher Aktienindex (German stock market index; comprises 30 companies)
DCF	Discounted cash flow
D/E	Debt/equity ratio
DIRK	Deutscher Investor Relation Kreis (German Investor Relations Group)
DJ Euro Stoxx	Dow Jones Index for Companies in Euroland
DMG	Deutsche Morgan Grenfell
DP	Dividend proportion (before tax)
EBITD	Earnings before interest, taxes, depreciation
ECR	Efficient Consumer Response
EU	European Union
EVA	Economic Value Added
FCF	Free cash flow
FSR	Final shareholder value return
FTSE 100	Financial Times index for 100 companies
g	Rate of growth in perpetuity
GDP	Gross Domestic Product
HGB	Handelsgesetzbuch, German commercial code
i	Interest rate
ID	Interest-bearing debt (i.e. debt capital)
INV	Investments
IPO	Initial public offering
IRR	Internal rate of return
JIT	Just-in-time
m	Million
M&A	Mergers & acquisitions

MM	Modigliani/Miller
MVA	Market value added
NCV	Net capital value
NOA	Non-operating assets
NOPLAT	Net operating profit less adjusted taxes
OP	Operating profit
p.a.	Per annum
PD	Profit distribution (after tax)
R&D	Research and development
ROCE	Return on capital employed
ROE	Return on equity
ROI	Return on investment
SBU	Strategic business unit
S&P 500	Standard & Poor's index for 500 companies
t	Planning or forecast period in years
t_c	Rate of corporation income tax
t_t	(Rate of) trade earnings tax
τ	Correction factor for taxes on corporate income
TC(E)	Total capital (employed)
TCO	Total capital outstanding
VA	Value added
WACC	Weight average cost of capital

1 Managing Value – Responding to a Changing Corporate Environment

Value-oriented management concepts are being accepted and implemented more and more widely in Europe. Bayer, Cadbury Schweppes, DaimlerChrysler, General Electric, Hoechst, Mannesmann, Royal Dutch, SAP, Veba, etc. are among the leading proponents. There can be no question that, in line with the preferences of their shareholders, European companies need to adapt their management practices.

Value management concepts shape management principles, allocation procedures and, ultimately, the structure of portfolios with a view to long-term value creation. The shareholder value approach assesses the performance of companies or business areas based on the sum of their discounted future cash flows. The logic behind this approach is simple: expected market returns are the benchmarks for company performance. The fundamental principles on which these concepts are built are as follows:

- The cost of capital is the measure of value creation. The risk-adjusted cost of shareholder capital prescribes the expected yield. Differing levels of business risk are accounted for explicitly during calculation and evaluation. All lines of business are included in the expected market return calculation. Only those that earn more than the cost of capital actually add to the value of the company.
- Free cash flows are the basis for valuation. As a measure of performance, they are largely free of the distortions of accounting numbers. Alfred Rappaport, one of the fathers of the shareholder value philosophy, put it in a nutshell: 'Profit is an opinion. Cash is fact.' The concept of cash flow consistently looks toward the future; free cash flow is what drives the value of strategic projects.
- Cash values are applied uniformly as evaluation criteria. The cost of capital is discounted from free cash flows. In this way, the aspect of time is provided for explicitly in the calculation: money over time costs money.

Value-oriented corporate management produces a clear focus on a growth policy that creates value. Taking market returns as the measure of success automatically generates pressure to be profitable; this pressure, in turn, forces the development of forward-looking and hence creative projects or measures. No-one can afford to rest on the laurels of past successes: past profits are no guarantee of allocated funds for investment in the future.

The experience of the last few years has shown that European managers, especially in Germany, are increasingly grappling with the implementation of value-based management concepts. However, the European stock markets are different to those in the United States, in terms of both shareholder structure and the importance of stocks. In the USA, 48% of shareholders are private individuals and 37% are investment funds. In this situation, there is a clear consensus of interests: increasing the value of shareholders' wealth takes pride of place. The US stock market plays a considerably more important role in corporate financing than its European counterpart. As a result, market capitalisation as a proportion of GDP is far lower in European countries such as France (38%), Germany (28%) and Italy (22%) than it is in the USA (110%).[1]

Value management concepts are becoming more widespread on the back of a number of developments:

- greater competition for capital, driven above all by the globalisation of capital markets;
- the growing trend towards 'professional' shareholders and, in particular, the influence of institutional investors;
- the emergence of what is known as the market for 'corporate control' – i.e. the pressure arising from potential company acquisitions; and,
- the harmonisation of external accounting standards (the US GAAP regulations etc.), and statutory moves toward deregulation (Germany's 3rd Financial Market Development Act, the likelihood that pension funds will soon be granted licenses in Germany etc.).

Evidently, Europe has some catching up to do. Coopers & Lybrand substantiates this fact in an international study of the use of shareholder value methodologies at 300 companies in 13 countries. The results are unequivocal: 'Less than half of the companies surveyed in all countries – with the exception of Sweden and the Ukraine – indicated that shareholder value methods are applied on all three decision-making levels, i.e. for both routine and strategic corporate decisions as well as for communication with shareholders'.[2] In Germany, virtually all of the respondent companies claim to use the methods – especially in the area of investment appraisal. Nevertheless, only around a third apply shareholder value methodologies as their 'predominant' tools.[3]

---

[1] Deutsche Morgan Grenfell (1997c), p. 11.
[2] Coopers & Lybrand International (1997), p. 16.
[3] Coopers & Lybrand International (1997), p. 9.

1.1 Globalisation is driving competition for capital

The globalisation of markets that has taken shape in recent years has had a huge impact on capital markets. A glance at indicators for the international division of labour is enough to highlight the major trends in global economic development:

- The world's Gross Domestic Product has doubled in the last decade. Calculated on the basis of current market prices, the figure was US $14,364 billion in 1986 and US $29,700 billion in 1996.[4]
- World trade is growing faster than world production. For 1997, the IMF is forecasting growth rates of 7.3% for trade in goods and services, with 4.4% growth in real GDP.[5]
- Similarly, the value of exported goods has more than doubled in the last ten years, from US $2,035 billion in 1986 to US $5,249 billion in 1996.[6]
- Foreign direct investments (FDIs) more than quadrupled in the period between 1980 and 1990. After sluggish growth between 1990 and 1992, FDIs peaked in 1995 at just under US $300 billion worldwide.[7]

As globalisation has progressed and restrictions to foreign exchange and capital markets have been dismantled, global financial markets have emerged and capital has become increasingly mobile. Modern telecommunications allows profitable investment opportunities and efficient credit sources to be tracked down more quickly. Capital flows and goods flows are diverging. In terms of value, the volume of international financial transactions overtook the volume of world trade as far back as the beginning of the 1980s.

Globalisation is bringing change to all capital markets.[8] German FDI stocks, for instance, have more or less quadrupled, from just under US $60 billion in 1985 to US $235 billion in 1996. During the same period, foreign direct investors raised their commitments in Germany from around US $37 billion (1985) to around US $134 billion in 1994.[9]

The financial consequences of these developments are readily apparent:

- growing demand for funding amid substantially greater market transparency and faster decision paths; and,

---

[4] World Bank (1997).

[5] IMF (1997c), p. 5.

[6] IMF (1997a), p. 117.

[7] IMF (1996).

[8] See also Titzrath (1996), p. 92ff.

[9] UNCTAD (1996), pp. 239, 245.

- an increasing willingness among institutional and private investors to prefer foreign to domestic investments, with the result that more and more German stock corporations are having to compete with international companies in the battle for shareholders' funds.

Changes in the capital markets and their impact can be demonstrated using the German example as follows:

A survey of capital increases and new share issues shows that the German capital market absorbed US $18.6 billion (slightly less than DM 35 billion) in 1996. The volume of share issues in Germany doubled between 1993 and 1996, with annual growth rates of 26%. During the same period, the New York Stock Exchange grew by 6%; in the United Kingdom, the per-annum volume of capital increases and IPOs was around 5%.

More and more foreign companies are now using the German capital market as a source of funding. Of the 263 newcomers to the stock exchange between 1989 and 1992, some 30% were domestic (German) companies; in the four years that followed, this proportion fell to 7% (of 854 new flotations). Whereas 1989 saw one domestic share launch to every four foreign IPOs on the German stock market, by 1996 the ratio had shifted to 1:20.

Competition for capital on the German stock market is also intensified by the fact that shares are known to be unpopular as a private investment tool in Germany. German investors keep only around 6% of their high level and rising level financial assets in stocks – and this despite the fact that financial assets climbed from DM 3,187 billion in 1990 to DM 4,955 billion in 1996 (a growth rate in the region of 8% per annum).[10] The comparable quota in the USA is markedly higher. The fact that German institutional and private investors are increasingly placing their money abroad is evident from the trend in the FDI outflow from Germany: between 1984 and 1989, average annual FDI outflow came to US $9.6 billion. In 1995, the figure was US $35.3 billion.

The trend can thus be summarised as follows:

- In future, German – and probably all European – stock corporations will need to fight even harder to safeguard the sources that will fund their growth.
- Capital market-based assessments of company performance will have to be made more frequently than profit-oriented evaluations.
- Portfolios must be oriented consistently toward value creation. The returns that can be achieved in different lines of business have to be measured against the cost of capital.
- International standards of disclosure and reporting will need to be adopted.

---

[10] CAGR = Compound Annual Growth Rate. Deutsches Aktieninstitut (1997), 07-1-4.

1.2 The trend toward 'professional' shareholders

Only a relatively small – and slightly dwindling – proportion of the capital held in equity in Germany is in the hands of private investors (15%, compared with 48% in the USA). Despite 4% slippage over the past six years, companies still hold almost 38% of German stocks and therefore continue to play a significant role. In the past, many companies saw their share blocks as strategic investments and did not base them on rigorous yield/risk calculations. Yet this is now changing as companies find themselves exposed to growing pressure from investors. This pressure emanates primarily from institutional investors, whose influence has grown considerably stronger in recent years. Let us take a closer look at their role in Germany; the following figures attest to these facts:

- Around one-third of German shares are today held by institutional investors such as banks, insurance companies and investment funds.
- The power and the significance of this investor group are growing: their share of the market rose by around 7 percentage points between 1990 and 1996.

Table 1.1 traces the growth of institutional influence in terms of its proportion of the various sectors of German share assets.[11]

Percentage of shares held per sector	1990 (in %)	1996 (in %)	Change (in % points)
Private households	16.9	15.2	-1.7
Companies	41.6	37.6	-4.0
Public sector	3.6	3.0	-0.6
Banks	10.3	11.2	+0.9
Insurance companies	11.2	25.8	12.2	32.5	+1.0	+6.7
Investment funds	4.3	9.1	+4.8
Foreign	12.1	11.7	-.4

Table 1.1: Change in the shareholder structure in Germany.

---

[11] Deutsches Aktieninstitut (1997), 08-1-3.

Institutional investors apply their yield and shareholder value requirements consistently to their investments. Thus the wind blows colder for corporate helmsmen; shareholder meetings are increasingly emerging as a forum in which to voice critical questions and air controversial discussions. Investment fund managers demand a clear explanation of corporate strategies and objectives, press for quantifiable, value-based information, require company data to be lucid and broken down by line of business, expect systems of management compensation to be linked to share performance, and threaten to ditch their share blocks should companies fail to take their interests into consideration. The notion of investment funds intervening in the running of the company – already outlined by a number of sources – may still be way off in the future. The writing, however, is on the wall:

Institutional investors:

- are obliged to pass on the performance pressure placed on their own sales by their customers – they have very precise yield requirements;
- base their own decisions regarding the structure of their portfolios on future profit contributions, and thereby demand value-enhancing business plans – past successes are not simply projected automatically; and,
- insist on disclosure policies and investor relations that match their objectives – GAAP and IAS requirements are increasingly becoming the norm in Germany too.

The consequences are at once obvious and positive. A stronger focus is now brought to bear, on lines of business and projects that add to the value of a company. Companies are having to be more consistent in managing their commitments to hedge the financing of planned growth in order to attract investors. Most importantly, however, growth strategies – especially those involving high fixed-cost commitments, or diversification projects backed merely by the argument of 'company size' – must be subjected to quantitative evaluation of both risk and return.

Companies across Europe are increasingly sensing the need for value-based management concepts. They are going to have to base future portfolio decisions, controlling tools, compensation systems and the like, on a new set of international value management requirements. The trend has already begun.

1.3 The fictitious market for 'corporate control'

In the 1980s, company buyouts were a 'boom industry', especially in the United States. The growing number of mergers and acquisitions is now also seen to be having a substantial influence on the introduction of shareholder value-based management methods in Europe.

'Corporate raiders' and investment banks identify so-called 'value gaps' in hitherto ill-managed companies. These 'value gaps' are areas of potential for adding corporate value that appear to be feasible in the context of restructuring exercises, turn-arounds and strategic reorientation projects. The prospect of successfully tapping this potential holds out the promise of value enhancement. To this end, said 'raiders' and other companies acquire the rights to dispose of poorly managed companies and replace the existing top management level. This ability for third-parties to buy up blocks of shares and then exercise their rights as shareholders to bring about changes in top management and effectively take over the running of a company is a core component of the 'market' for corporate control. What is being traded here is not just the company itself, but also the power to decree how it is to be run – to appoint bodies, and determine corporate and business policy.

The line of argument behind this approach is simple. Competing management groups – such as the management currently in place in the company, and potential buyers for the company – get into a fight over corporate strategies that will allegedly increase earnings. One key question needs to be answered: who will allocate assets and human capital most efficiently in order to improve share performance and add value to the company?

The market for corporate control purportedly boosts managers' motivation to come up with value-enhancing concepts of their own that will diminish the raiders' prospective profits, thereby warding off a takeover that would, in most cases, put them out of a job.

As yet, there is still no solid empirical evidence to back up all these correlations.[12] Be that as it may, fear of a possible takeover does appear to be exerting a growing influence on Europe's managers, nudging them in the direction of innovative value-enhancement strategies in the process. Thyssen's attempt at a hostile takeover of Krupp in March 1997 contributed to this development, and showed that the German market for corporate control is also beginning to take shape. Olivetti's hostile takeover of Telecom Italia is a recent example. The various takeover risks inherent in this approach are outlined in Fig. 1.1. Nevertheless, the large proportion of voting rights held by banks at the shareholders' meetings of Germany's major stock corporations remains an obstacle to the further develop-

---

[12] For a detailed treatment of empirical studies on the subject of corporate control, refer to Günther (1997), pp. 33ff.

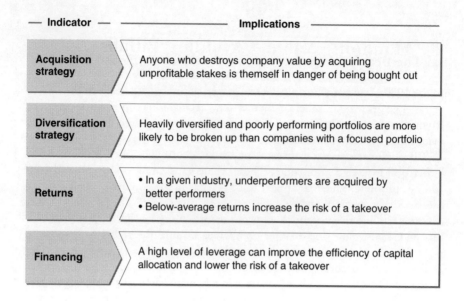

Figure 1.1: Takeover risks.

ment of the market for corporate control. In 1992, for example, the major banks had voting rights on shares held in custody accounts amounting to around 85% for Siemens, nearly 88% for Hoechst and about 90% for Mannesmann. Then there are the voting rights held by capital investment and mutual fund companies that themselves belong to the banks, which often amount to between 8% and 14%.[13] This concentration of voting rights in the hands of a few banks shows how difficult it is for external parties to gain control of a company – and proves that the market for corporate control in Germany and in other European countries cannot yet be liquid. Limiting the voting rights that can be held by the banks would change this situation.

This list of reasons why value-based management concepts are becoming increasingly widespread gives rise to the hope of a trend that will endure. Although it is still not possible to make empirical statements about increased usage, it would nevertheless appear to be the case that this concept – already applied on a broad front in the USA – will also take root and flourish in Europe.

Even so, our experience shows that the road to designing and implementing such concepts is beset with numerous pitfalls. Accordingly, it is to these pitfalls that we shall now turn our attention.

---

[13] Adams (1997), p. 22.

2 Managing Value – Avoiding Pitfalls

The management teams in many European companies are currently seeking to bring their corporate management and controlling practices into line with the goals and the philosophy of value management. Companies are beginning to use value metrics to measure the performance of their business areas. On the basis of these results portfolios are being restructured, by selling off corporate entities that destroy value and buying companies with potential for value creation. Operative value creation measures are also being initiated alongside these strategic decisions. Furthermore, while planning and controlling systems are being adjusted, performance-related and value-based compensation schemes for managers are meeting with wider acceptance.

Sadly, however, it must be said that, in many cases, value management concepts are not developed and implemented in line with the basic principles outlined at the start of Chapter 1. The same mistakes are being made time and time again:

- Precedence is given to a short-term rather than a long-term perspective.
- A generalised approach is applied in place of a company-specific one.
- Little or no attention is devoted to tax effects.
- Unsuitable target metrics are used in planning and controlling.
- Compensation and incentive schemes are ineffectual.
- Traditional dividend policies predominate.
- Not all interest groups are taken into account.
- The approach adopted involves too little dialogue.

If we reformulate these eight pitfalls of value management as positive statements, we obtain a number of essential conditions that must be fulfilled when a value management concept is introduced. Failure to observe these rules runs the risk of introducing a program whose methods are faulty and which does not exploit the main benefit, namely to provide for better corporate control. In extreme cases this can lead to misguided decisions. For example, profits on paper alone do not reflect a company's actual business development trend. The destruction of economic value and posted profits are not mutually exclusive. Cash flow can be negative even though results are positive. As a business ratio, paper profits therefore constitute an inadequate measure of whether the purpose of value management – to increase the value of shareholder capital – is in fact being achieved.

Members of the financial community, such as investment banks, do not take long to find out how serious managers are about really introducing value management. If an appropriate system of compensation is lacking, for instance, or if controlling continues to be based on traditional tools, then analysts' recommendations as to whether to buy, hold or sell a company's shares will tend to be negative. In such situations, not even professional investor relations activities can do much to help.

Let us take a closer look at these eight potential sources of error before moving on to an examination of the details of value management methodology.

2.1 The short term versus the long term

One accusation, frequently cited in the current debate surrounding shareholder value management, is that this concept of corporate management implies a mindset focused on short-term objectives. Value-driven companies are reduced to striving to improve annual or even mid-year performance, so the argument goes. Consequently, strategic planning and investment policy sacrifice future market and growth potential to the god of short-term share price rises. What justification is there for such fears?

Short-term perspectives lead to poor resource allocation

Experience in the USA – where many companies have been pursuing the philosophy of value management for some years – shows that managers are indeed often guided by the desire for fast profits. This focus on short-term objectives distracts them from long-term planning. Or worse still: it opens the door to risky deals pushed through in the hope of quickly being able to announce a positive set of figures. The cause of this kind of behaviour is usually rooted in the controlling mechanisms in place in such companies:

- Employment contracts often run for only two to three years and are extended only if the year's business performance is deemed sound.
- Management bonuses are linked to annual business performance; the need to invest in the future is ignored.
- The income of top managers is linked to share price increases. In many cases, however, the link is only to half-yearly or yearly increases.

And so we could go on. No magical arts are needed to push shareholders' income through the roof in the short term. Some of the payment systems used to remunerate top-level management in the USA are actually contingent on short-term improvements in share performance.

Let us take an example. If stock options make up part of the compensation package for a 60 year-old manager who is planning to go into retirement at 63, it should come as no surprise when the share price is inflated artificially. The manager will arrange for the company to repurchase its own shares while hiving off or liquidating parts of the business where performance is not up to scratch. Efforts to restructure the firm, which involve investing in projects that will only pay off in the 'dim and distant' future, will be neglected. This phenomenon has been observed in the USA for some time. In Europe, meanwhile, variable, performance-oriented salary systems are increasingly coming into vogue. Sadly, they are all too often linked to short-term conditions similar to many of the schemes operated in the USA.[1]

Even the practice of repurchasing one's own shares is often construed solely to induce short-term upward movement in the share price. In the USA, over US $170 billion was spent on share repurchases in 1996. These and similar activities – for example, the dismissal of 25% of the workforce in the 100 biggest American companies[2] – do nothing to add sustained value increases to a company in the long term. They can only serve to push up share prices in the short term – which in turn serves primarily to fatten the wallets of top managers and safeguard their jobs.

What, however, is being done to create value in the medium to long term? What should a company do when all its liquid funds have been spent to repurchase its shares, when it has pruned itself until it is 'lean and healthy', when all of its good, creative, innovative employees – the ones with the trail-blazing ideas – have long since left the company in abject frustration? What are the consequences of ignoring the fact that money has to be invested today and that, owing to the workings of depreciation, more modest results have to be reckoned with in order to safeguard the long-term profitability of the company? An investment strategy designed to maximise short-term profits in what are largely only image-boosting projects will not generate positive cash flows over the long term. This is not the way to lay a foundation for the possibility of profits in the future.

The consequences are many and varied, encompassing everything from impaired ability to innovate, sub-optimised productivity, loss of global competitiveness, shrinking market share, deteriorating capital equipment and the lay-off of employees, to outright bankruptcy. Attempts to maximise shareholder value are often seen to be associated with these problems; hence the accusation that the method is short-sighted. In the press, it is regularly bedevilled as lacking in social concern – a simplified expression of an excessively capitalist mindset. Is that really the case? Does the concept of shareholder value promote a short-term mode of thinking and acting? Does it truly result in the misplaced allocation of investment funding and the flawed exercise of corporate control?

Value management demands a long-term perspective

The questions we have just asked are clearly rhetorical; the answer, in each case, is negative. It is only misinterpretations of value management that lead down this road. A right understanding of value management requires a different way of thinking. Careful analysis of the approach necessarily leads one to the conclusion that value management actually demands a long-term perspective – a conclusion that can be drawn simply by examining the methods used to determine corporate value and evaluate planned investments.

---

[1] Cf. Chapter 2.6.

[2] Hamel (1997), p. 26.

Using valuation methods that are widely acknowledged and applied in practice today, shareholder value is calculated from the sum of discounted cash flows (hence the term 'discounted cash flow' method) that the company will generate in future. Borrowed capital, on which interest must be paid, is then deducted from the principal value determined in this way. A variety of company-specific risks are also accounted for in the discount factor.

A profitable company that invests in its own future may have negative cash flows in the short to medium term. The pay-off comes only in the long run. Under certain circumstances, the company may therefore not yield a nickel's worth of dividends today, nor for the next few years. Even so, it can still achieve a remarkable level of market capitalisation.

Conversely, an unprofitable company can generate positive cash flows in the short term if it is obliged to sell off part of its assets – in order, for example, to ensure sufficient liquidity to make repayments to its capital backers. A positive cash flow of this kind adds nothing to the value or market capitalisation of a company, however. Both the quantity and the quality of the cash flow are therefore important both to the value of the company and to the investor. Positive net cash flows in the near future are not an essential requirement.

In theory, the valuation of a company should include all cash flows until such time as its business activities have been completed. In practice, this is done by means of approximation. Clearly, the value of a company can only be increased if the cash flows in future years are dimensioned sufficiently to cover the cost of capital. Shareholder value management is, therefore, an approach to long-term, value-based corporate management.

This understanding leads us a step further. Value management in fact provides the only solid basis on which long-term planning data, even at the level of different lines or areas of business, can be calculated at all. Value management builds a bridge between what often tends to be the qualitative focus of strategic company management and the quantitative focus of modern financing and investment accounting. Areas of potential success for a company can be valued unambiguously on the basis of their earnings and risk profiles and then positioned within the overall corporate strategy as a function of their potential to add economic value.

Viewed from this standpoint, value management aims to bring about a systematic and sustained increase in value, in order to shore up the long-term success of the business. Only those companies that can generate new revenue flows on the market, tap new markets and face up to ever fiercer global competition by means of innovative products, forward-looking technologies and creative but realistic strategies, will be able to continue raising their value over the long haul.

Technological innovation means translating technical know-how into economic gain. Innovation is itself a long-term phenomenon or process. Knowledge and ideas have to be transformed into marketable products or services. This transformation takes time and cannot be done short-term. There is therefore a need for long-term planning, spending on research and development, and for the understanding of future trends. In many cases, these investments do not have to – and indeed cannot – pay for themselves in the immediate future.

A fine example of the pursuit of such long-term strategies is Amgen, an American biotechnology company. Close cooperation with universities and hospitals in the area of medical research, and ongoing investment in the company's own R&D activities, suggest that the future will bring forth further such successful products as those Amgen already makes for dialysis patients and for cancer sufferers adversely affected by chemotherapy. In recent years, the company has rewarded its investors with remarkable share appreciation, a development that is rooted in the long-term focus of its corporate policy.

Other companies, such as Synergen and Gensia, have succeeded in raising funding on the capital market to the tune of over a billion dollars without ever generating a dollar of revenue.[3] This can be seen as an indication that investors are prepared to reward planning and activities which have a long-term focus, and that the confidence of the capital market can be secured by a value-based approach to company management.

The logical conclusion would therefore be for European and German companies, when introducing the principles of value management, to learn from the mistakes that have been made in the USA. The bias toward maximising short-term profits and the use of management variables and compensation systems with an equally myopic focus must give way to strategies that evidence a more far-sighted perspective. Only long-term metrics and variables – such as shareholder value calculated using the 'discounted cash flow' method – can provide a reliable basis for corporate decision-making. In this context, investments are viewed within a suitably long-term framework and do not fall foul of pressure to maximise short-term earnings. This is the only way to ensure that a company acts in the best interests of its shareholders and increases the value of its shareholders' equity.

---

[3] Siegert/Böhme (1997), pp. 474 ff.

2.2 Generalised rather than company-specific approaches

One major mistake that can be made, in projects to introduce value management, is simply to adopt a 'one-size-fits-all' approach that does not distinguish between varying requirements. When drawing up and implementing value management strategies, it is important to make provision both for the peculiarities of the industry or industries in which the company operates and for factors that are specific to the individual company. The general-purpose shareholder value 'toolkit' must be adapted to fit each individual company. This is the only way to ensure the success of a value management project. If such adaptation does not take place, corporate management may end up charting the wrong course. This whole approach and the various aspects related to it are pictured in the chart below.

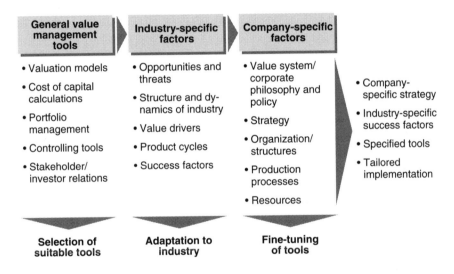

Figure 2.1: Company-specific approach to value management projects.

Choosing the appropriate value management tools

Over the past few years, both the theory and practice of value management have been the subject of intensive discussion. Many of the calculation methods used derive from theories of finance, investment and the capital market. The various approaches and methodologies used to gauge corporate value are accordingly multifarious and, in some cases, labyrinthine. Nor, in many cases, is it a straightforward exercise even to choose the most suitable management tools with which to periodically measure the increase in the value of a company.

It follows that selecting the right methods and tools is a crucial step in implementing a value management project. In the given context, 'right' means that the models used must have sufficient empirical validity.

In international M&A transactions, for example, the discounted cash flow method is the most commonly used way of putting a value on a company or parts of a company (see Fig. 2.2).[4] A number of empirical studies reveal a significant correlation between a company's cash flow trend and the development of the market value of its equity capital on the stock exchange. For this reason, modern approaches to value management use 'discounted cash flow' analyses.

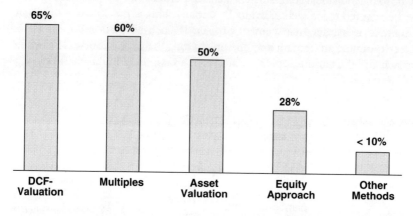

Figure 2.2: Methods used in international company valuations.[5]

In this context, one must also remain aware of the following pitfalls:

- The cost of equity capital and the cost of debt capital should be weighted and used as discount factors for cash flows in place of the cost of equity capital only.
- Not all liabilities are to be included in the cost of capital. Trade accounts payable, for instance, should be omitted as they will be 'reimbursed' in the course of the company's operative business activities.
- Distinctions must be made in the cost of capital obtained from different sources.
- Wherever possible, the figures used should not be based on book values.

Moreover, the tools used must lend themselves to practical application. A tool will only be used consistently if it can be used easily. The various methods used

---

[4] Cf. Blumberg/Helling (1996), p. 433.
[5] Cf. Blumberg/Helling (1996), p. 433. This study comprises an analysis of 258 international M&A transactions from 1991 to 1995.

to calculate the cost of equity capital for a company are a classic example. There are essentially two methods of determining this cost factor: the Capital Asset Pricing Model (CAPM) and the Arbitrage Pricing Theory (APT). Without going into the details at this point, the multi-dimensional structure of the APT method gives better results than CAPM in empirical capital market tests. CAPM nevertheless remains the method most widely used in practice. The reasons are simple: it is easier to apply with regard to the data resources it requires, the effort involved in calculation is less, and the factor used is unambiguous.[6]

Closely related to the issue of practicability is the need to be able to communicate and explain the methods and tools used. The fundamental way in which models work must be readily understandable to users and decision-makers alike. Models should be easy to explain, and plausible without requiring an in-depth understanding of all the details. In practice, a 'black box approach' – an approach in which key elements are not explained – is of no value.

Adapting tools to industry-specific conditions

Once suitable tools have been selected, they must be adapted to those conditions specific to the industry in which the company operates. The structure and dynamics of the industry will have a substantial impact on the success or otherwise of the company. Particular attention must be paid to identifying and assessing industry-specific value drivers, and to examining how the individual strengths and weaknesses of the company allow it to stand up to the demands of the industry compared with competitor companies. Value drivers – also called value generators – are generally understood to mean factors of influence or valuation parameters that underpin the calculation of shareholder value. According to Rappaport, the following measures number among these value generators, and must therefore be investigated as part of an industry-specific analysis:[7]

- sales growth rates
- operating profit margins
- income tax rate
- investments in working capital and fixed assets
- cost of capital.

These standard value drivers must nevertheless be broken down still further for the company and its business units. The aim must be to determine the key control variables for a focused program of value creation. Against the backdrop of these value drivers and industry-specific conditions, an individual forecast model must then be drawn up for the company's sales, turnover, costs and results development. The degree of accuracy needed for reliable decision-making can only

---

[6] A modified APT model suitable for practical application is presented in Chapter 3.1.
[7] See Fig. 3.17/Rappaport (1986), p. 50.

be achieved by putting together an exhaustive business plan in order to forecast cash flow, as explained in Chapter 3.1.

Company-specific adaptation

The last step in the honing of value management tools is company-specific adaptation. Here, considerations should centre on the issues of corporate philosophy and policy ('normative management'), strategic management, structures and organisation, and production processes and resources.

- The underlying principles of value management need to find their way into normative corporate philosophy, so that new ideas and existing principles can effectively cross-pollinate. A value orientation is needed to enrich the stock of ideas that guides a company. At the same time, however, the traditions of and the mission 'lived out' by the company must also be borne in mind. The value management philosophy, once adapted to fit the company, must then be integrated in corporate policy and strategic management. It is important to communicate these new principles both inside and outside the company.
- The next step is to adapt the tools of value management to the structures in place in the company. This is of particular importance for the existing management and controlling systems. Chapter 3.3 deals in greater depth with the procedures involved at this stage.
- On an operative level, individual production processes must be taken into account during the design and implementation of the value management concept. Value must be created for the customer on all levels of performance and production.

Tailoring value management tools to industry-specific and company-specific requirements is extremely important. In this way, the company's field or fields of activity can be used to identify potential for cash flow generation and the associated risks. Risks also derive from the financing structure. Companies that are highly indebted benefit from considerable 'leverage' effects – but also run a greater risk. Accordingly, it would, for example, be wrong to apply a uniform cost of capital rate throughout an entire enterprise including subsidiary companies or different lines of business. To do so would lead to a situation where low-risk units were effectively subsidising higher-risk units within the company. The cost of capital must be calculated and applied on a more clearly differentiated, i.e. risk-adjusted, basis. These factors, coupled with those referred to above, will have a significant influence on the future success of the company and must, therefore, be incorporated in the value management concept.

All of the above can be summarised by noting that any largely standardised program of value management will not match up with corporate reality and is therefore fundamentally unsuitable. It is imperative to work with the right tools; and even these need to be adapted to the peculiarities of a given industry and company. Individual value drivers and a 'customised' business plan, differentiated cost of capital assumptions and management variables are essential if a company is to be steered as accurately as possible toward the goal of value creation.

2.3 Ignoring tax effects

Companies seeking to apply the principles of value management use dynamic investment appraisals to evaluate prospective investment projects. These appraisals are designed to help quantify future success and thereby enable the calculations on which decisions are based to be expressed in monetary terms. Many companies fail to include taxes as a factor in their investment appraisals.

However, since tax has a significant impact on cash flow and the nominal cost of capital, it cannot simply be left out of the equation. What errors occur if only a pre-tax view is adopted? Is a protect calculation adequate to plot the effect that a planned investment will have on revenues? If not, what forms of taxation should be included in the calculation?

Pretax appraisals can lead to suboptimal investments

Investments trigger cash inflows and cash outflows. Taxes to be paid in relation to an investment constitute additional outflows. As such, they reduce the cash flow available to service shareholder equity and debt capital for a given period.

Where tax liabilities are omitted from the calculation, decisions to invest are often taken on an incomplete and therefore inaccurate basis. Under certain circumstances, this can lead to investment decisions that are decidedly less than optimal. This issue takes on particular significance when taxes cannot be paid out of residual cash flow and provisions for taxation have to be appropriated. Before payment is made, cash flow is positive; afterwards, it is negative.

The results projected by a before-tax appraisal can deviate considerably from those of an after-tax appraisal:

- An investment may be beneficial before tax but disadvantageous after tax – or vice versa.
- The sequence in which investment projects are to be realised may change.[8]

Let us take a somewhat more detailed look at the reasons for this situation.

Different cash flow and discount rates

The calculations produce different results because cash flow before tax is different to cash flow after tax, and because the tax rate itself modifies the discount factor and, hence, the net capital value of the investment (see Table 2.1 as an example for an investment case in the setting of the German tax system). Investment appraisals that bracket out the issue of taxation are therefore liable to two

---

[8] Schierenbeck (1993), p. 361; Schneeloch (1994), p. 146.

Table 2.1: Comparing the basis for an investment decision before and after tax – example for an investment case in the setting of the German tax system.

	0	1	2	3	4	5
(1) Gross cash flow of an investment case before tax	-160,000	+45,000	+45,000	+45,000	+40,000	0
Cash flow of outside funds						
(2) Debt	+100,000	(+80,000)	(+60,000)	(+40,000)	(+20,000)	(0)
(3) Interest payments		-6,000	-4,800	-3,600	-2,400	-1,200
(4) Repayment		-20,000	-20,000	-20,000	-20,000	0
Calculation of tax payments						
(5) Depreciation (linear 5 years)		(-32,000)	(-32,000)	(-32,000)	(-32,000)	(-32,000)
(6) Remaining book value		(+128,000)	(+96,000)	(+64,000)	(+32,000)	(0)
(7) Profit before tax = (1) - (3) - (5)		(+7,000)	(+8,200)	(+9,400)	(+10,600)	(-33,200)
(8) Trade earnings tax = -0.1667((7) + 0.5(3))[1]		-667	-967	-1,267	-1,567	0
(9) Corporation income tax = -0.30((7) + (8))		-1,900	-2,170	-2,440	-1,460	0
Total tax payment		-2,567	-3,137	-3,137	-2,193	0
Net cash flow before tax	-60,000	+19,000	+20,200	+21,400	+17,600	-1,200
Net cash flow after tax	-60,000	+16,433	+17,063	+17,693	+15,407	-1,200
NPV before tax	+1,201		Discount rates 2)	0.100		
NPV after tax	-2,774			0.058 3)		

1) Assumption: permanent debts   2) Assumption: alternative financial investment   3) $0.058=0.1(1-t_t)(1-t_c)$; with $t_t=0.1667$ and $t_c=0.30$

errors: (1) A cash flow that is put too high is discounted at (2) a nominal cost of capital that is also too high – given normal levels of mixed financing.

The 'drivers' behind the effect of taxation are the amount of taxable income and the tax rate:

- The fact that taxable income serves as the *basis for tax assessment* affects the after-tax value of capital, owing to the distribution of payment surpluses over time.

  Variations in business success rates over time cause fluctuations in the amount of tax to be paid as a result. After discounting, this gives rise to variations in the cash value of tax liabilities. The further taxable profits can be put off into the future and the sooner expenses can be charged, the lower this cash value will be. The earlier tax payments are made, the earlier will be the charge made against cash flow; the capital value of an investment diminishes accordingly. The more depreciation is able to lower the taxable base, the greater the tax break. High levels of depreciation reduce tax payments and therefore cause cash flow to rise. The earlier depreciation is realised, the sooner taxable income will fall and the higher, by consequence, will be the capital value of an investment.

- The absolute *tax rate* has two distinct effects on tax liabilities:

  (1) *The payment effect*
  As the tax rate rises, so too do tax payments. At the same time, this reduces current cash flow.

  (2) *The rate of interest effect*
  In this case, as the tax rate rises, the absolute amount gleaned from tax benefits increases owing to the existence of a proportion of borrowed funds (tax shield). Interest is booked as an expense and therefore attenuates the basis for tax assessment. Thus the absolute amount of tax to be paid is lessened.

The payment effect and the interest rate effect affect capital value in opposite ways. The more capital a company has borrowed from external sources, the greater is the rate of interest effect.

The crucial factor is the final net worth arrived at as a function of the mode of financing and the applicable tax rate. Since borrowed funds can cause final net worth to rise along with increasing tax rates (whereas this is not usually the case with finance derived from the company's own resources), it is advisable to include taxes in calculations in order to arrive at valid entrepreneurial decisions as regards the realisation of an investment project and how it is best to be funded.

Not all forms of tax need to be included

Since account must be taken of tax both in cash flow and in cost of capital calculations, one must first clarify which specific types of taxation are relevant. Chapter 3.1 contains a thorough treatment of the correct handling of taxes in the context of corporate valuation and investment appraisals.

Taxes can be accounted for in cash flow either explicitly or implicitly. For the sake of completeness, it would appear to make sense to provide explicitly for taxation in all its forms. However, to keep the structure of the investment appraisal as simple as possible, forms of tax that are easier to handle are dealt with implicitly in cash flow. This applies to taxes that can easily be calculated for an investment, such as sales tax (VAT) and general taxes on consumption. Explicit attention should be given to taxes that are liable to vary or be adjusted depending on the nature of funding, the terms of repayment and the method of depreciation. Taxes on income values fall into this category.

Taxes on income – trade tax, corporation income tax and income tax

Income tax

The cost of shareholder capital is the return an investor could achieve from an alternative capital market investment with an equivalent risk. Only income tax can be applied to the nominal cost of shareholder capital. In view of the large number of different investors subject to differing tax rates, this is, however, a difficult measure to pin down. Another argument against estimating income tax is that it will be the same, both for the object to be valued and for any alternative investment. For these reasons, income tax considerations have been discarded from the following considerations in general.

Trade tax

Depending on the country, trade earnings tax must be incorporated in the nominal cost of debt and/or in cash flow calculations. This tax exists for example in France, Germany, Italy and Spain.

In France, trade tax regulated by Art. 1447 and following paragraphs – CGI – is independent from earnings. Basis of taxation is the 'valeur locative' (rental value) of assets on the one hand and the sum total of wages and salaries paid on the other hand. The latter is taxed at a fixed rate of 18%. The amount of trade tax is calculated by multiplying the basis of taxation with a tax rate differing between communities. It can not exceed 4% of the annual value added. Trade tax is to be deducted from the basis of corporate income tax. It reduces the cash flow.

In Germany, Article 7 of the Trade Tax Law states that the taxable base consists of profits calculated in accordance with the regulations defined in the Income Tax Law plus additions and less deductions (Articles 8 and 9 of the

Trade Tax Law). Since half of interest paid is deductible from the basis of the trade income tax, the tax reduces not only the cash flow but also the company's nominal cost of debt. The tax rate differs between communities.

The 'imposta regionale sulle attività produttive' (IRAP) is Italy's regional trade tax. The tax rate is 4.25% and, from the year 2000, can be increased by up to 1% by the community. Tax basis is the value added. It is not deductible from any other corporate taxes. It reduces the cash flow.

Spain taxes its companies with a fixed amount of trade tax depending on the industry, location and size of the business. In addition to the fixed base of tax, the province can add 40% and the community may apply an additional municipal factor of up to 400%. The tax reduces the company's cash flow.

Corporate income tax

In addition to trade tax, incorporated firms are also subject to corporate income tax on both retained and distributed earnings. The corporation income tax reduces the cash flow. In four of the example countries – France, Italy, Spain and the UK – the tax rate is the same for retained earnings as well as for earnings paid out as dividends. This is not the case in Germany. A fact that makes the valuation calculus in this country somewhat more complicated.

In Germany, the rate of corporation income tax for distributed profits is currently 30%, compared with a 45% rate for retained earnings. Corporate income tax on distributed net income as shown in the balance sheet can be offset by the shareholders.[9] Companies tend to retain only parts of their earnings. The cost of debt should therefore be reduced after tax by a tax correction factor that takes account of the effects of both trade earnings tax and corporate income tax. This correction factor should be used to calculate the relative benefits that the use of debt will have on the amount of corporate income tax to be paid as a function of the level of retained earnings. A different tax correction factor has to be calculated for other countries.[10]

In essence, what this section is saying is that after-tax appraisals are the only method that facilitate well validated corporate and investment decisions. In accordance with the explanations detailed above, we would therefore urgently recommend that taxes always be taken into consideration. Table 2.2 provides a summary of which types of tax ultimately need to be provided for and where they should flow into the valuation model in selected European countries.

---

[9] Article 36, para. 2, subpara. 3 and Articles 36a–e, Income Tax Law; Article 49, para. 1, Corporation Income Tax Law.

[10] Cf. Chapter 3, excursion on taxes.

Table 2.2: Relevant types of tax in selected countries.

	France	Germany	Italy	Spain	U. K.
Trade tax					
• Basis of taxation	• Rental value of assets • Sum total of wages	• Profits - 0,5 x interest	• Value added	• Fixed amount depending on industry, location and size of business	/
• Tax rate	• Community specific 1) • 18%	• Community specific	• 4,25% (+ 1% depending on community)	/	/
• Deductability	• From corporate income tax basis	• From corporate income tax basis	• None	• None	/
• Reduces – cash flow	yes	yes	yes	yes	/
– cost of debt	no	yes	no	no	/
• **Corporation income tax** – Basis of taxation	• Earnings	a) Distributed profits b) Retained earnings	• Earnings	• Earnings	• Earnings
– Tax rate	• 33.33% plus temporary supplements	for a) 30% for b) 45%	• 37%	• 35%	• 31%
• Reduces – cash flow	yes	yes	yes	yes	yes
– cost of debt	no	no	no	no	no

1) ≤ 4% of annual value added

2.4 Unsuitable target figures for planning and controlling

Traditional planning, controlling and monitoring systems generally tend to be based on reference variables and ratios which, in turn, are based on external and internal accounting data. Such accounting figures are, however, simply not up to the task of guiding a company, and its various business areas, toward sustained value creation.

We identified two main sources of errors in the value-based management of a company:

- Attempts are made to manage the company using traditional controlling metrics, whose value orientation is insufficient.
- Errors are frequently made in the design and application of innovative, value-based metrics.

Traditional controlling measures are unsuitable

The extent to which a company's system of controlling depends on accounting data should be kept to an absolute minimum: this data is not suitable to ensure a form of management based on shareholder value. The correlation between the information in the annual financial statements and a company's performance on the capital market is too weak. It is perfectly feasible for profits to be posted and figures, such as the return on sales or the return on equity, to be eminently positive, whilst the economic value of the company has diminished.

Three criticisms can be levelled at the use of traditional indicators (see Fig. 2.3):

- The correlation with the goals of value management is too tenuous.
- The 'origin' burdens them with inherent deficits.
- They ignore too many financial considerations.

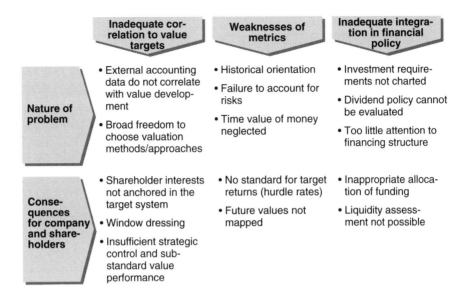

Inadequate correlation to value targets	Weaknesses of metrics	Inadequate integration in financial policy
Nature of problem • External accounting data do not correlate with value development • Broad freedom to choose valuation methods/approaches	• Historical orientation • Failure to account for risks • Time value of money neglected	• Investment requirements not charted • Dividend policy cannot be evaluated • Too little attention to financing structure
Consequences for company and shareholders • Shareholder interests not anchored in the target system • Window dressing • Insufficient strategic control and substandard value performance	• No standard for target returns (hurdle rates) • Future values not mapped	• Inappropriate allocation of funding • Liquidity assessment not possible

Figure 2.3: Problems with traditional indicators

Insufficient correlation with value goals

One of the central problems can be seen in particular in the choice and definition of appropriate management variables. This difficulty is effectively built into the equation by the relevant legislation in Continental Europe (especially Germany), insofar as statutory accounting and valuation rules seek to protect external sources of capital against loan losses. This differs from Anglo-American accounting practice in that comparatively little importance is given to the interests of the shareholder. The result is a misleading standard of measurement.

Various studies have proved that the traditional performance indicators used in accounting can lead to inaccurate assessments of company performance. As such, they represent an inappropriate basis for management decisions. For instance, the statistical correlation that exists between return on equity and company value performance – the correlation coefficient is R^2 of 0.3 to 0.4 – is very weak.[11] In some cases, the discrepancy between profit-based yield and economic, market value-based returns has been found to be very substantial. This can naturally result in poor strategic decisions and a misguided investment policy.

Moreover, the right to choose between alternative equations and valuation methods – such as an assortment of depreciation methods, inventory valuations based on a variety of consumption follow-up methods, and the option of putting certain expenditures on the balance sheet or not – leaves room for figures to be manipulated, a practice known as 'window dressing'. This, of course, makes it

---

[11] Deutsche Morgan Grenfell (1997a), p. 1.

impossible to manage a company along the lines of economic value indicators. Figure 2.4 illustrates the differences between the accounting perspective and the economic perspective. The exploitation of this room to manoeuvre can considerably influence the level of profit reported. Such distortions in the performance indicators used in accounting make comparisons of different companies within a given industry a hazardous business.

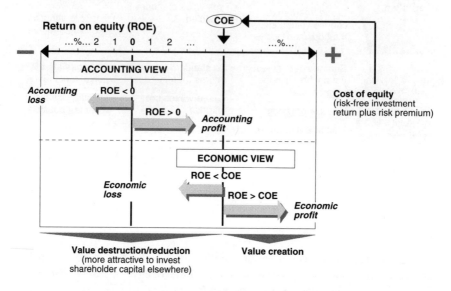

Figure 2.4: Economic profit and accounting profit[12]

The shortcomings of traditional indicators

Indicators such as return on investment, and measures of performance such as profit or operating results, look backward to the past. It is impossible to use them as benchmarks from which corporate management can derive target return values. How high should a company's profits be? Not even industry-specific comparisons, or comparisons over time, are suitable for prescribing hurdle rates for future investment decisions. There are two reasons why this is so. One is that these measures make no provision for the risks to which a company or business area is exposed. The other is that the time value of money is ignored. Both risk and the time value of cash flow represent categories of opportunity: a unit of money is worth more today than the same unit of money at some point in the future. Similarly, a 'safe' unit of money is worth more than one that is beset by significant risks. What does this mean for corporate management?

---

[12] Cf. Hax/Majluf (1984), p. 215.

Performance indicators such as profits or operating results, and the ratios derived from them, do not allow sufficient attention to be paid to the risks confronting different lines of business. Particularly in the context of a company's investment policy, risk is very important as a decision-making parameter. Neglecting specific risks can end in the ill-judged allocation of capital investment resources. This problem exists in cases where no specific risk premium is used to adjust target return values to cover the risk. The greater the risk in a given field of business, the higher should be the hurdle rate for investment decisions. These benchmarks cannot be derived from the figures presented by traditional accounting: they must instead focus on the opportunity cost to the investor. The shareholder value approach accounts for the risk premium in the discount factor.

In economic terms, the time value of money also represents an opportunity cost of investment. Investment decisions must, therefore, have recourse to dynamic, multi-period performance indicators.

Insufficient integration in financial policy

Another problem with traditional target metrics is that they are not sufficiently integrated in a company's overall financial policy. This applies especially to the charting of capital expenditure requirements, and to allowances for dividend policy.

Taking profit as a target figure does not say anything about funding needs, since the requisite capital expenditure on current and fixed assets is excluded from the income calculation. Initially, the implementation of investment projects has no effect on earnings. Investments only affect earnings through periodic write-downs. This form of 'accrual accounting' is often criticised because it does not clearly depict the impact of capital expenditure on liquidity. This kind of performance measure does not reflect the financing that will be needed to fund future growth.

Focusing on profit figures causes similar distortions by failing to take the company's dividend policy into account. Profit, or the goal of maximising profit, allows no clear statements to be made about the amount that is to be paid out in dividends (cf. also the 'dividend policy' pitfall).

Profits, and the ratios derived from them, are inadequate as measures to be used in value-based corporate management and controlling. Raising profit levels does not necessarily imply that the value of the company has increased.

Avoiding pitfalls with new, value-based target figures

The exercise of designing and implementing value-based target figures in line with the principles of shareholder value management can also be fraught with a number of problems which merit attention in practice.

Selecting a suitable measure of cash flow

Cash flow is one variable that avoids the difficulty of profit reporting caused by the choice of different valuation methods. Yet even here there is the problem of finding a suitable definition of cash flow. A number of definitions have been devised over the past few years, each of which varies according to its intended purpose. One cannot say that some approaches are wrong and others right *per se*, rather, the situation needs to be assessed with a view to the consistent application of individual measurement variables. Shades and nuances emerge, for example, in the attention devoted to tax credits and interest, the inclusion of capital expenditure in working capital, the way in which accruals are dealt with, and so on. These are discussed in Chapter 3.1.

Measuring periodic growth in value

One of the most important tasks is to produce consistent measures or indicators that can measure growth over a period of time. Much of what has already been written on the subject provides little in the way of a clear solution to this problem. The crux of the problem lies in linking the forward-looking approach of shareholder value calculations and backward-looking statements of income over a given period. The following example serves to clarify the point at issue: a company goes ahead with an investment which generates cash flows over a period of ten years (the planning horizon). Discounted at today's conditions, the investment project posts a positive risk-adjusted net present value. It is thus deemed to be beneficial, and the green light is given. Let us now assume that cash flows in the first three years are negative – as in the case of a new product, for instance. Positive cash flows are only achieved in the fourth year. Did this investment create or destroy value for the company during the first three years? Or, to generalise the question: what value-based milestones ought to be defined as periodic target values? And how can they be applied to the company as a whole?

Applying the opportunity cost principle consistently

In practice, consistently applying the notion of opportunity cost can be a very considerable headache. This becomes abundantly clear when attempting to nail down the cost of capital for a company. The weighted costs of equity and debt capital (to take a simple case) determine hurdle rates to the implementation of capital spending projects. In the case of debt capital, for example, it is not historical costs but rather the opportunity cost that should be included in the calculation, i.e. the yield that the investor could earn from an alternative investment with equivalent risk. At first sight, this is not necessarily an intuitive approach. As controlling is re-engineered, acceptance for such principles will first have to be established.

What becomes apparent is that it is imperative for a value management approach to be applied using the right target and management variables if the benefits of this superior form of corporate controlling are to be realised. The implications of this can be summarised as follows:

- Market value figures and cash flows should be used instead of accounting figures.
- Cash flows should be included in addition to profits and the traditional returns upon which they are based.
- Dynamic, forward-looking ratios should be used in place of static, historical ratios.
- Discount rates should be based on opportunity cost rather than the minimum rate of return as defined by internal accounting.

2.5 Ineffectual compensation and incentive schemes

Working for a company has to be worthwhile. To meet this requirement, it is important to come up with incentives for managers which, firstly, reward every-day performance and which, secondly, reward the right kind of performance. The first aspect primarily concerns the structure of compensation, i.e. the relative weighting of fixed and performance-related components in the overall salary package. It is necessary for the performance-related share of pay to be sufficiently high and genuinely variable if one is to wean people off an 'administrative' mentality and nurture a value-creating corporate culture. The second aspect concerns finding the right link between performance incentives and reference variables that will lead to the desired success. From the shareholders' point of view, this success is reflected in increases in the value of the company and in the dividends paid out to them. The system of incentives and compensation should therefore be tied to criteria based on shareholder value.

Current systems of compensation are inadequate

The current structures of compensation for managers in most European countries are inadequate on a number of counts. The key problem areas can be summed up as follows:
- The fixed component, i.e. the performance-*in*dependent component, is far too high in international comparison.
- In many cases, the so-called 'variable' component is not really variable at all – and is often paid out whether managers perform or not.
- Furthermore, bonuses generally tend to be based on assessment bases which take account neither of the interests of the shareholders nor of the economic situation of the company.

Lack of performance-linked incentives

According to an international study conducted in 1997, the variable portion of executive compensation varies between 20% and 38% in main European countries. For example, the variable proportion in Germany accounts for only 20%, in France for 26% of total payments to business managers. Only in Japan is the variable part lower. These figures, compared to compensation schemes in the U.S.A. and Canada, are shown in Fig. 2.5.

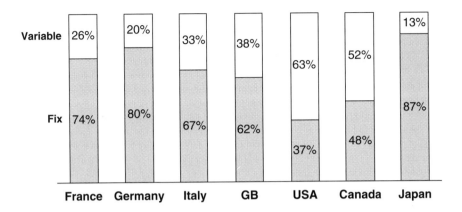

Figure 2.5: Structure of management compensation[13]

Such structures offer little incentive to perform. Top performers receive insufficient financial rewards. Compared with the USA, the salaries of European managers can only be categorised as modest. The consequence is a high rate of executive turnover: the best people leave the company. Bonus payments in the USA amount to around 60% of the total compensation received on average by top managers. The 'uncertain, earnings-linked entrepreneurial element' is anything but commonplace in Europe. To a large extent, performance and success oriented thinking and actions are left to the individual's own intrinsic motivation. This, however, is a source of motivation that defies any attempt at controlling or monitoring by the company or its shareholders. Moreover, it appears that variable compensation is in many cases linked neither to individual nor to corporate performance. In the past, dwindling market share, alarming losses or regressive share performance have evidently been no obstacle to the disbursement of management bonuses in many companies. A bonus that is, in effect, a constant is hardly likely to foster an entrepreneurial outlook.

Compensation is based on unsuitable reference variables

What makes matters worse is that variable components are linked to measures of performance that do not necessarily reflect the interests of the shareholders who own the company. Variations on the theme of profit ratios form the basis on which performance is measured in 73% of the companies surveyed, followed by turnover in 9% of cases. Value-based figures are ignored more or less completely. These statistics are collated in Fig.2.6. As stated in the previous section, there is no guarantee that paper profits will not be accompanied by a loss of

---

[13] Egon Zehnder International (1998), p. 1. Board members of international corporations with more than 1 billion US$ sales.

economic value to the shareholders. This is the point at which proponents of shareholder value begin to voice their scepticism, demanding that variable compensation be based on reference variables which genuinely reflect the economic value created by the company.

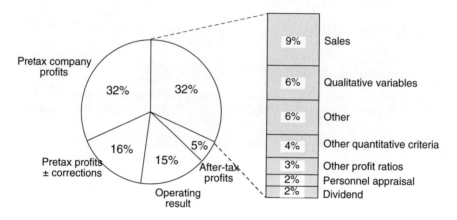

Figure 2.6: Reference variables for variable compensation[14]

Creating effectual compensation and incentive schemes

To enable value management to be applied in the context of corporate strategy, management compensation should be linked to value-based metrics. It is important to design the entire system of incentives and compensation in such a way that employees are motivated to increase the value of the company or, at least, of their division. This is an area where European companies have a lot of ground to make up.

Remunerating managerial staff in major stock corporations in which the functions of ownership and control are not embodied in one and the same person is, from a theoretical viewpoint, the classical 'principal agent' problem. How should incentives be created for the employed agents – the management – such that they will represent principal – shareholders' – interests to the best of their ability despite maintaining their own personal goals and attitudes to risk? At stake here is the need to optimise the structure of contractual relationships on behalf of the owners. If one assumes that the interests of the owners lie in increasing the benefit they gain from the company, i.e. in increasing the value of their stock, then the need is to maximise the symmetry that exists between this objective and the objectives of management.

---

[14] Kienbaum Personalberatung (1996), p. 4; example Germany.

Objectives of value-based compensation

The objective of value-based compensation is to map the earnings-risk profile of the shareholders onto the management, as outlined in Fig. 2.7. This form of 'duplication' can be achieved by placing part of the business risk on the shoulders of the managers. To begin with, this means reducing the basic salary so that the bonus constitutes a weightier element of the total potential remuneration package. Secondly, value added to the company or a series of suitable indicators must be used to determine the basis for the variable component. In this way, linking the incentive and compensation scheme to the results of actions taken by management effectively transfers some of the entrepreneurial risk onto the managers themselves. This should apply across all management levels. An earnings-risk profile on a par with that borne by the shareholders is a sure way of ensuring that, gradually, an 'administrative' culture is replaced by an 'entrepreneurial' culture.

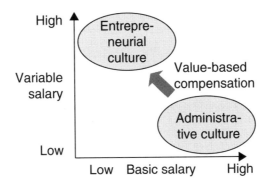

- Managers should be motivated to increase the value of the company
- Compensation should be structured in a way that reflects the risks/opportunities facing shareholders

Figure 2.7: How value-based compensation systems work.

Heed must be given here to the following pitfall, however: investors who place their money via the stock exchange generally only bear what can be deemed a 'systematic' risk (market risk), since they can build up portfolios in order to diversify any unsystematic, company-specific risks. Second or third-level managers and executives do not have this diversification facility available to them. As a result, they carry a greater risk from the company's business activities than do the shareholders. This asymmetric risk structure can make management organs unwilling to take risks and can thus lead to underinvestment.

On a practical level, the problem can be alleviated by continuing to provide an appropriate basic salary to managers within a system of value-based compensation. This gives them a secure remunerative component that is independent of the development of the business. By contrast, the residual claim of the shareholders is based solely on the company's business performance. The basic salary also fulfils the function of compensating for what material on the subject often refers to as a greater aversion to risk on the part of the agent than the principal.

The structure of compensation should be such that poor performance brings in less than is earned today, whereas very good performance yields considerably greater rewards. Accordingly, the fixed salary component would merely ensure an adequate basic living. Those who perform well must also be rewarded for doing so in the form of a higher variable salary. A value-based mindset must be communicated to middle management levels and, subsequently, to the lower levels of the corporate hierarchy by means of suitable bonuses and incentives. Moreover, it is essential for value to be instilled as the long-term basis for orientation. Together, these objectives stake out a series of requirements that are placed on value-based compensation systems.

Requirements on value-based compensation systems

Compensation and incentive schemes that are performance-linked and reflect shareholders' interests must satisfy a number of requirements if they are to effectively map out the contractual relationship that exists between the managers and the owners of a company. As far as behaviour and results are concerned, the creation of value for the company has to move centre-stage.

From a management perspective, systems of compensation must meet the following requirements:

- fair, objective and comparable assessment;
- unambiguous points of reference that clearly show where value has been created or destroyed and influence compensation accordingly;
- high degree of transparency; simple and easy methods;
- distinctions between individual and collective performance aspects;
- motivation born of a favourable working environment;
- ability for managers to influence the reference metrics to be measured; and,
- use of up-to-date data and figures.

At the same time, the following criteria are important from the point of view of the shareholders:

- compliance with shareholders' interests by means of value management-linked incentive and compensation tools;
- stipulation of clear scales of returns to index value creation;
- implementation of strategic/long-term and operative goals; and,
- systems that are easy to manage, explain and communicate.

Developing and introducing shareholder value-based systems of compensation, and incentives which satisfy these requirements, is an essential ingredient in any comprehensive value management project. An entire chapter of this book (Chapter 3.4) is devoted to approaches, methods and structures for the successful implementation of value-based compensation and incentive schemes.

2.6 Traditional dividend policy

At the present time, practices vary concerning how dividend pay-outs are to be handled. Some companies seek to maintain constant dividend pay-outs over the years; others link dividend pay-outs to financing and investment decisions. Within the framework of value-based company management, this would appear to be a somewhat dubious procedure.

Traditional dividend policy is not compatible with the concept of value management

The goals pursued by traditional dividend pay-out policies are many and varied. Examples include the following:

- Dividend pay-outs are kept to the strict legal minimum in order to feed 'war chests' for planned, strategic market launches, expansionary moves and similar activities.
- Companies whose strategy is to maintain as much external debt as possible tend to distribute profits in the form of dividends and borrow the capital they need to spend on investment projects.
- In good years, high profits are not paid out in full so that reserves can be accrued. This practice allows management to continue to pay out customary dividends in lean years, too – while also allowing the company to obscure its real position at least to some extent. The aim is to make investors believe the company is on a sound financial footing with robust earnings, thereby propping up a stable share price that is shielded against excessive volatility resulting from possible speculation about the dividend amount.

Nevertheless, constant dividend payments – indeed, dividend payments in any shape or form – are not suitable as an indicator of a company's economic situation. The amount paid out as a dividend today says little about how the company will develop in the future, since no correlation can be established between the outflow of funds today and a putative outflow of funds tomorrow.

Take Germany for example: only between 20% and 40% of distributable profits are actually passed back to shareholders on average – compared with 45% to 60% in the USA.[15] Although Article 58 of the German Stock Corporation Law prescribes a minimum dividend pay-out of 50%, the board of management can resolve to retain higher proportions subject to approval at the annual general meeting.

---

[15] Amihud/Murgia (1997).

'Agency costs' – still a problem in some European countries

The reason for the extremely low level of dividend pay-out, stated in the example of Germany, can be attributed to the very high 'agency costs'.[16] Small investors often transfer their voting rights to banks because they themselves do not wish to attend shareholders' meetings. The result is that banks often hold a majority of voting rights at shareholders' meetings for companies toward whom they also act as creditors.

To maximise the security of the loans they have granted, banks may have an interest in limiting the dividend pay-out and encouraging the build-up of reserves – acting rather in their own interests (as a source of external debt) than in the interests of their clients (the shareholders). Legal stipulations mean that most countries in Europe do not have this 'German' problem.

Yet the agency problem sheds light on another hotly debated issue in relation to dividend policy in Europe. Literature on the subject often attributes a signal effect to dividend pay-outs. Increases in the dividend, so the argument goes, are tantamount to improved earnings potential in the long run; hence, managers simply choose dividend pay-outs as a channel to announce this happy circumstance to their investors.[17] At the same time, however, it is also noted that management does not necessarily act in the best interests of the shareholders – a contradiction which casts doubt on the real signal effect of dividend policy.

In our view, management can send wrong signals by raising the dividend pay-out, thereby pretending to show the capital market evidence of positive business trends, while, in reality, everything may be far from rosy in the corporate garden. One reason for such a course of action may be a desire to attract the attention of potential equity holders in order, for example, to raise urgently needed extra capital stock.

This example alone is sufficient to show that the capital market must look long and hard at any such management 'signals' and should never simply take them at face value. The upshot is, however, that serious doubt is cast on the signal effect of dividend policy *per se*.

Value management argues for the pay-out of residual dividends

If the prevalent dividend policy merely serves the purpose of ensuring a regular annual outflow of funds to shareholders, yet – as explained above – without allowing those shareholders to draw any valid conclusions about business trends or the general state of the company, one is forced to question whether this kind of dividend represents the optimal way of handling shareholders' invested capital.

---

[16] 'Agency costs' are understood to mean that, owing to diverging objectives, managers do not always act in the interests of their shareholders.

[17] Cf. Perridon/Steiner (1995), p. 482.

What would dividend policy look like if it were based on the principles of value management?

Strictly speaking, management should not be paying out any kind of dividend in the first place. Investors are, after all, putting money into the company in the hope that the business activities engaged in by its managers will create added value, which will in turn be reflected in a higher share price. In other words, the investors make funds available for specific business activities, expecting that the management will find profitable projects to increase the value of the company.

If, instead, the management starts distributing funds generated by these activities, what it is in effect saying is that it is unable to find and implement any other strategically beneficial projects. In an expanding company with a strategic mindset, one would expect to see a rise in demand for additional capital rather than the availability of funds for distribution.

The contention that investors expect constant injections of liquidity does not hold true. If investors need liquidity, they can get all the liquidity they need by selling their shares – which, hopefully, will have increased in value.

Management is therefore acting in the interests of the investors when it finds investment projects that cover the cost of capital, not when it returns liquidity to the said investors. In many cases, investors never ask for such dividends and now have to reinvest them, with the result that added costs are incurred in brokers' fees.

Should the management be genuinely unable to unearth any advantageous investment objects, however, then available funds should indeed be paid out. Why? Because, if the management keeps funds in the company that could be put to better use elsewhere by the shareholders themselves, it is destroying shareholder value.

For this reason, value management requires the pay-out of residual dividends. All financial resources that cannot be reinvested in such a way as at least to cover their own cost of capital should be distributed to the shareholders. The residual cash flow, i.e. the cash flow left over after realisation of all investment projects that are beneficial from a value management perspective, is paid out as a dividend. Consequently, decisions about dividend amounts are more or less a by-product of optimised investment and financing decisions. The decision as to how profits are to be appropriated should therefore only ever be taken once investment and financing has been clarified.

It follows that the dividend to be paid out may vary from year to year. As we see today, the absolute amount distributed says nothing either about how the company's business is developing or the quality of management. What it can do, however, is ensure that the capital invested by the shareholders is put to the best possible use.

Today, disbursing the residual dividend can be a competitive advantage when wooing potential shareholders on European and other international equity markets. Within the framework of a value management philosophy, it is the responsibility of corporate management to communicate this dividend policy and explain it clearly in the context of a professional investor relations strategy.

2.7 Failure to take account of all interest groups

European companies' growing preoccupation with value-based management concepts has sparked off an intense debate among broad swathes of the public at large, most of which revolves around the issue of the goals and purposes that a company should pursue. To whom does management owe its allegiance? To whom must it answer for its decisions and actions? This issue is the confluence of two apparently contrary streams of thought:

- The Anglo-American shareholder value approach, which posits the pursuit of the interests of the shareholders as the sole objective of corporate management, is the one view. According to this view, the task of management is to raise the company's share price and the dividends paid out to shareholders. Everything else is of subordinate importance. This classical approach to shareholder value often goes hand in glove with comprehensive restructuring exercises, relocations of production facilities abroad, downsizing and mass dismissals – to the good of the shareholders and the detriment of the employees.
- The other view corresponds rather to the Continental European philosophy of corporate management. According to the stakeholder approach, a number of different interest groups have a right to place legitimate claims on a company and to be involved to a certain extent in the making of important decisions.

Mediating between shareholders and other stakeholders

We postulate the thesis that the two views can not only be harmonised but are in many respects mutually dependent. In today's world of global competition, no company can afford to earn meagre returns for its owners. Investors would waste no time in withdrawing their funding from such a company and channelling them instead into more profitable undertakings. Consequently, corporate management must, as its overriding goal, pursue the creation of value for its shareholders. On the other hand, the immense influence that today's companies exert on people's economic and social conditions places a burden of a social responsibility upon them. Should a company neglect this responsibility, this can lead to negative consequences – including the company's business success.[18] A mutual dependency thus exists between a company's financial and social performance. To put it bluntly: failure to take due account of the different groups who have a stake in the company can have extremely negative repercussions for business

---

[18] For example as a result of consumer boycotts, or the damage done to corporate image by negative press coverage.

success. A comprehensive value-based approach must, from the moment of its inception, make suitable provision both for the shareholders' viewpoint and for the viewpoints of the other interest groups – the other 'stakeholders'. Figure 2.8 provides an overview of the most important stakeholders in a company and their respective interests.

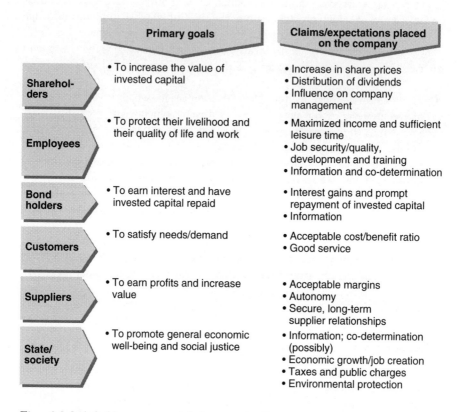

Figure 2.8: Stakeholder groups and their respective interests.

Why stakeholder management?

Aspects of the theoretical foundation of the stakeholder approach can be traced back to the institutional-economic design of the organisation. On this basis, the company and its relationships to its environment can be viewed as a network of explicit and implicit contracts; the entire organisation and its connections to the environment can be disaggregated into separate contractual relationships between individual entities.

Numerous categories of specific contractual relationships can be mapped out in the stakeholder approach. And these relationships in turn can be used to derive the claims of the individual stakeholders.

Shareholders are associated with the company on the basis of an 'ownership' agreement. The principle of ownership is a fundamental and constituent building block of the market economic order. This is the principle on which the various proprietors' rights to act are based, especially the formal right to exercise control over and manage the company, as well as the right to dispose of earnings. For this reason, it is the primary task of management to pursue a corporate policy in line with the interests of the shareholders. The shareholder value approach thus constitutes a heavy focus of integrated value management and should take high priority.

The interests of other interest groups can also be derived from contractual relationships, however. Employees, customers, suppliers, creditors and, to a certain extent, even competitors are all stakeholders whose claims are primarily the result of economic contracts. These contracts initially regulate the exchange of services and goods, but also directly imply all pre-contractual, post-contractual and subsidiary rights and duties that the company must take into consideration. The assertion of specific claims is therefore based primarily on market mechanisms, i.e. demand and supply. In some cases – for example toward employees – companies entertain more extensive obligations on account of special dependency relationships. We will return to this issue later on.

The third group of stakeholders derives its claims on the company from a higher level of social contracts, which usually constitute implicit contractual relationships. These include the government or state – which, via the agency of legislation, nevertheless exercises a very direct influence over the company – the public, the unions, churches, associations and other groups. The grounds for their claims and the possibilities for asserting them vary greatly but are all perfectly legitimate. Peter Ulrich, an economist from the university of St. Gallen, Switzerland, thus describes the 'large corporation as a quasi-public institution'[19] which, in view of its profound influence even on the private sector of economic units (e.g. the problem of negative external effects) bears essential social responsibility. This problem is highlighted particularly acutely in relation to environmental protection.

Yet what does this plurality of interests mean to value-based company management? How can the stakeholder approach be applied?

The invisible hand of the market

In many cases, it can be observed that focusing on financial performance, i.e. a primary orientation toward the interests of the owners, automatically causes a company to perform in social terms as well. The interests of the remaining stakeholders, too, are best served by a company that is continually creating and sustaining value. Even so, in a fiercely competitive environment, profits must first be earned before they can be used to benefit other stakeholders. Via the

---

[19] Ulrich (1977), p. 1.

agency of Adam Smith's famous 'invisible hand of the market', an orientation toward shareholder value contributes to the well-being of all parties. The examples that follow serve to clarify how value-based companies generate not only shareholder value but also stakeholder value:

- Companies with high sales and earnings growth both safeguard and create jobs. They are in a position to remunerate their employees in line with what they produce, often above the level of their competitors. Attractive development and career opportunities instil a high degree of motivation. Many value-based companies have introduced participation models allowing employees to participate in the value growth of the company. The software company SAP is a leading example of the successful implementation of this kind of equity interest scheme. Hennes & Mauritz and the financial service provider MLP are further outstanding examples of companies which generate high returns for their shareholders and manage to create new jobs on a large scale into the bargain (see Fig. 2.9).
- Customers and suppliers alike stand to benefit from companies that create significant amounts of value. Successful businesses can offer their customers low-cost, high-quality, innovative products and services backed by rigorous customer orientation. Suppliers benefit, for example, from improved cooperation and greater planning stability.
- The government receives higher amounts of taxes and levies from companies that create value, which thus contribute to overall economic prosperity.

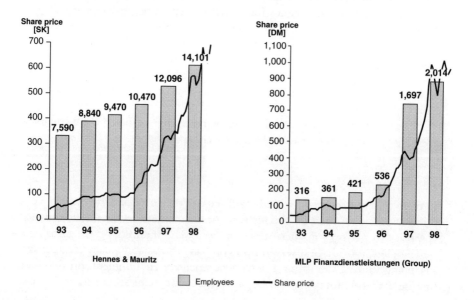

Figure 2.9: The parallel orientation of shareholder and stakeholder value.

To summarise, it can be stated that increasing shareholder value intrinsically creates the conditions for optimising stakeholder value. Josef Ackermann, board member of Deutsche Bank, sums up the whole argument very succinctly: 'The self-interest of the company harmonises largely with the general economic good'.[20]

Preconditions for successful value-based corporate management

As explained above, maximising shareholder value often goes hand in hand with the satisfaction of stakeholder interests. However, this is not always possible. One should not be blind to the fact that there is also potential for conflicts of interest and goals between the individual groups of stakeholders. Optimising the economic performance of a company – a consistent shareholder value-based management approach – is a necessary precondition to the success of any value management venture. But it is not the only condition. An element of social responsibility must be added in the context of active stakeholder management.

All in all, the only value management programs that hold out the promise of success in Europe, are those that actively take account of the interests of the various stakeholders. This reflects the European tradition whereby social responsibility is incumbent upon private ownership. Any company that fails to tread this path runs the risk of fielding heavy internal criticism from the workforce and equally heavy public criticism from the media and politics, to the extent that implementation of the program gets bogged down or delayed or, in extreme cases, is thwarted altogether. Growth strategies must be the key means by which shareholders and the other stakeholders are satisfied. For this reason, an entire chapter of this book (Chapter 4) is devoted to the subject of growth.

---

[20] Ackermann (1996), p. 10.

2.8 Insufficient dialogue

One criticism frequently levelled within companies – particularly from the ranks of the line organisation – is that the shareholder value concept is pure theory, a crazy notion concocted by top management, in cahoots with a few off-the-wall management consultants. Its value in practice, the claim goes, is as close to zero as makes no difference. In any case, the activities and demands of day-to-day business move to the beat of a different drum. It is not the shareholder but the customer who must be the focal point if turnover is to be raised and growth achieved.

In all too many cases, the idea of value management never seems to make it out of the boardroom. What mistakes are made when trying to apply value management within a company? What do managers need to watch out for when attempting to breathe life into the philosophy within their own company?

In practice, two main errors crop up again and again in the design and implementation of value management projects. They are in large measure responsible for the failure of the concept in the organisations concerned:

- failure to involve the company's own line organisation and subsidiaries in the analysis and design stages of a value management project; and,
- failure to embed the project in a process of change management process/transformation.

Failure to involve line organisation and subsidiaries in value management design

When a value management concept has just been introduced, the first complaints are usually heard from the direction of the line organisation, which can often be found puzzling over how the management's sophisticated new concept might possibly be worked out in real, everyday life. Cost of capital rates has been decreed; and line managers have no clue as to how they might ever succeed in earning them in their respective lines of business.

Often it is not even clear to the line managers how the said costs of capital were arrived at. Was top management simply gazing into space when the figure suddenly occurred to them in a blinding flash – a figure which may in fact be way too high and have little or nothing to do with the harsh realities of daily business? 'Unit *xy* might be able to do something with figures like these, but not us. Those guys upstairs are always having some bright idea or other … and we are the ones who have to carry the can'. These are the kinds of sentiments so often voiced by unit managers and departmental heads who are suffering from a virulent attack of value management.

Middle management is crucial to the success of the value management approach in any company. Yet, rather than involving its representatives in the conceptual phase and benefiting from their understanding of day-to-day business, it is often the case that no dialogue is sought with this group during the initial phase. This leaves the company, and in particular those responsible for implementing the project, with a complex array of problems to confront:

- How do you win the commitment of the people who have to work with the concept day in, day out, if their personal success has to be measured against a standard with which they are not in agreement, which they have had no part in defining and which they simply do not believe to be the right measure?
- How do you restore the motivation of employees who have the feeling that they have been left out of important company decision-making processes, and who now believe that the company questions their ability because they were not asked to share their knowledge or opinions at the decisive moment?
- How do you motivate managerial staff to get to grips with a new concept and use it as the plumb-line for their management systems if they still have serious misgivings about it but have never had the opportunity to air their grievances to the management?

To avoid having to face up to these and similar questions in the first place, it is important to communicate with everyone affected by a value management project from the word go – by getting the people involved in workshops, for instance. It is not enough for the management idea to catch on in the boardroom, and for the board alone to get a handle on it. This corporate management toolkit stands or falls by practical implementation, not by the ideas behind it.

Within the framework of value management, it is of supreme importance to get together and talk about the definition of the cost of capital and to plan cash flows for the coming years. A discussion of the risk position of a given business unit is inconceivable without involving the unit managers or departmental heads. These are the people who know their business best and who will therefore be most likely to be able to make valid statements about beta factor estimates, about the development of future cash flows, about the identification of value drivers and about business economics estimates.

By proceeding thus, one is also cementing the commitment of these managers who, later on, will be largely responsible for implementing the concept successfully. Reservations about the concept itself can be talked through before value management ever sees the light of day. Knowledge gaps can be eliminated. Drafting the concept and drawing up a plan of action together helps ensure that all those concerned will be willing and active participants.

A positive attitude on the part of managerial staff toward the new concept of corporate control will spill over to all the other employees down the line. This way, a company can make sure that everyone pulls together. The same applies for subsidiary companies. If the parent company merely sends them a breakdown of the cost of capital that they now have to earn without involving them in the process of determining the appropriate rates, then subsidiaries, too, can be expected to exhibit the same reservations and resistance as described above.

Ambitious goals are easier to both set and achieve if everyone concerned views them as worth working toward. Subsidiary companies must also adhere to the same, clear corporate vision as their parent organisations. The goals and the mode of operation of value management must be clear and readily understandable to all.

Failure to dovetail the project with change management

Like any other project that is initiated from the top down, the implementation of a value management concept can easily go awry if the entire project is not integrated in a process of change management. The following points must be borne in mind in this kind of transformation process:

- If interdisciplinary teams and workgroups are not set up, there is the danger that value management will be ill-coordinated and will not elicit the same degree of commitment across all business areas.
- If the finalised concept is complicated and difficult to communicate, it will never be fully accepted by all employees nor be applied in everyday practice.
- Since change has to take place in the minds of all employees, and since this usually involves learning processes which take time, an unrealistic schedule for the process of change can cause frustration and misunderstandings among the workforce.
- The process of change should be supported by employee training in workshops and information sessions. The future will be different to the past and therefore requires different procedures.

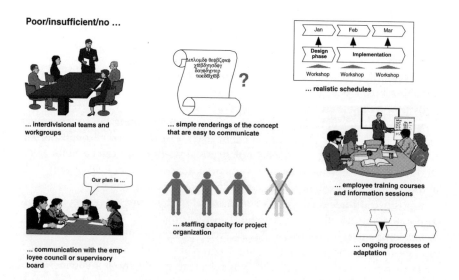

Figure 2.10: Mistakes frequently made in the change management process.

- If the employee council and the supervisory board are not informed and actively involved in the planned changes from an early stage, one runs the risk of encountering resistance that can erode the success of the concept at least during the initial phases.
- Sufficient staffing capacity must be assigned to project organisation to prevent doubts about feasibility from surfacing during the design phase. A core project team dedicated exclusively to this work for the duration of the project should be under the control of a steering committee. Besides handling design, the project team is responsible for implementing all interdisciplinary activities. It communicates with line organisation, provides training, ensures that results are achieved and prepares for implementation in cooperation with the lines. The lines themselves will later incorporate the results of project work in their day-to-day business. Line employees, too, should be given sufficient time to take part in developing the value management toolkit if the project is to lead to the desired success. A company can only be assured of the subsequent commitment of everyone concerned if they are all actively involved in the project.
- When dealing with value management, it is important that the system be adjusted to reflect changes in the business environment. It may, for example, be necessary to modify the cost of capital in the next fiscal or a subsequent exercise in line with interest rate changes on the capital markets.

The concept as such is to be understood merely as an aid, a set of tools. The use of these tools in everyday business should be focused on actions rather than figures. Planned values, for instance, will often be overshot or not reached. Not all events can be foreseen and included in planning. Hence dialogue before and during the introductory phase must be accompanied by a healthy dose of pragmatism.

The bottom line is that the 'human factor' must never be neglected when introducing the principles of value management. The approach outlined above – 'interactive' project work with the line organisation and a comprehensive program of change management – are important keys to successful implementation.

2.9 Summary: three groups of pitfalls

The eight pitfalls dealt with in this section outline practical experience culled from Anglo-American and European corporate reality. They provide an initial insight into what companies need to remember when designing and applying value management programs. The pitfalls can be split into three groups. The first group consists of errors of methodology and comprises the following pitfalls:

• a short-term rather than a long-term perspective;
• a generalised approach rather than a company-specific one;
• a failure to account for tax effects; and,
• the use of unsuitable target metrics in planning and control.

All these methodological errors lead to inaccuracies and can have such a serious impact that the overriding goal of value management – to improve corporate control – is scarcely reached.

The second group of pitfalls centre around the neglect of value management 'subsets' when developing and introducing the concept:

• ineffectual compensation and incentive schemes; and,
• a traditional dividend policy.

The former point involves upholding the received and mostly rigid system of compensation; the latter involves upholding the dividend policy that has been customary to date. In other words, value management is introduced only half-heartedly, with the result that the leverage with which the value of equity capital can be raised is not exploited to the full.

Finally, the third group of pitfalls describes mistakes that occur during the introduction and implementation of value management concepts:

• failure to take account of all interest groups; and,
• insufficient dialogue.

The first of these two points seeks to apply value management with no consideration for any stakeholders other than the shareholders. The second involves a one-sided or 'top-heavy' approach to introduction in which top management fails to work together with the line organisation to draw up the essentials of the plan. Either pitfall will cause value management to meet with more resistance and delays than are necessary.

In the interests of optimised corporate control, the full use of all available levers and the smooth implementation of value management concepts, it is thus imperative that all eight pitfalls be avoided. Chapters 3 through 5 examine in detail how this can be done, referring back to the actions recommended in this section as and when appropriate.

3 Focus On Methods – Developing Value Creation Programs

Having described the numerous pitfalls in some detail, the reader may well, by this time, be asking what a value management program ought to look like in concrete terms if a company is to adapt successfully to this new framework of conditions and actually create value for both its shareholders and the other interest groups. It is our understanding that a comprehensive value management approach must comprise five key components.

The first step is to determine the value of the company and its constituent business areas or units. Identifying the value drivers, i.e. the most important levers for value creation, is also part of this initial component. Strategic and operative value creation programs are then worked out (component 2) on the basis of these results. The next component centres around the need to supplement the management and controlling systems already in place to cater to the requirements of value management. Yet another element of this comprehensive

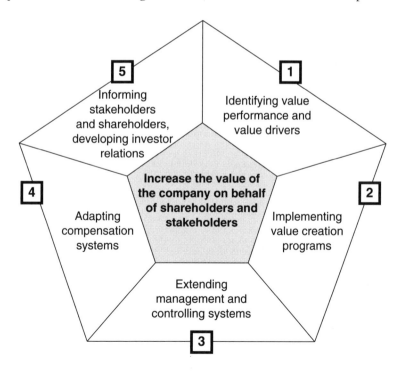

Figure 3.1: Key components of value management.

approach is the design and introduction of value-based compensation systems. And the whole undertaking is rounded off by an improved flow of information to stakeholders and shareholders (investor relations). These five steps will give a clear value orientation to major aspects of corporate management. In addition, 'culture change' must be wrought within the company.

The focus of each of the methods used in these five key components of value management is explained in more detail below. The structure of the present chapter – the contents and sequence of the sections it contains – revolves around the pentagon shown in Fig. 3.1. As a rule, this is also the chronological order in which a value management project will work through these issues. Some key components (nos. 3, 4 and 5) can be performed in parallel. More information on the sequence of events and on project management and culture change are provided in Chapter 5.

3.1 Identifying value performance and value drivers

The logic of the value management approach

According to the principles of value management, a company must generate adequate returns for its owners, in line with the relative opportunity cost of investment, i.e. the returns that shareholders could achieve from alternative investments with similar levels of risk. A company whose returns exceed the opportunity cost to its owners creates corporate value and, hence, shareholder value. This means that an analysis of the value performance of a company or one of its business units centres around two main indicators: shareholder value and returns. Before looking at the individual steps involved in determining value performance and identifying value drivers, let us first shed some light on the logic behind the calculation of these two measures.

(Absolute) shareholder value

As explained in the chapter on pitfalls, of the various approaches to corporate valuation (such as net asset value or capitalised value methods), the modern philosophy of shareholder value recognises only one, namely the 'discounted cash flow' (or DCF) method. This method sees the value of a company as being the sum of the discounted cash flows that it will earn in future. Based on this understanding, the purchaser of a company acquires the right to future cash flows.[1] Most of the asset value of the company, which the purchaser buys along with the acquisition, is needed to generate this cash flow. Besides this necessary operating capital, companies are often also in possession of assets that are not essential to their business operations, such as financial assets. These non-operating assets are added to the sum of discounted cash flows.

Given that a broad selection of definitions are used for cash flow, some attention must be devoted to the issue of which one to use. Cash flow is defined as the difference between payments made to the company and payments made by the company. For the purposes of company valuation, a measure known as 'free cash flow' is used. Free cash flow is the cash flow before interest, after tax and after spending on current and fixed assets. Free cash flow thus defines the amount that is available for distribution to shareholders and/or to make debt or interest repayments to external capital backers. The sum of these discounted future payments constitutes the value of equity and debt, hence the value of the company as a whole (excluding non operating assets).

---

[1] We have consciously refrained from explaining the theoretical basis at this point; cf. Drukarczyk (1996), pp. 3.ff., 102 ff.

Future cash flows are discounted in order to factor in the time value of money. Since it is possible to invest money on capital markets, one Euro is naturally worth more today than it will be in a year. The amount used for the discounting factor is the opportunity cost to the investor and therefore represents the cost of capital to the company. Since free cash flows service both equity and debt, the weighted average cost of capital (WACC) method is applied.[2]

Since cash flows discounted in this way reflect the value of the company as a whole, interest-bearing debt must also be subtracted to obtain the value of equity capital (shareholder value). Accordingly, the calculation of shareholder value can be represented by the following formula:

$$SHV = \sum_{t=1}^{T} FCF_t / (1 + WACC)^t + CV/(1 + WACC)^T - ID + NOA$$

where:

SHV   is shareholder value (value of equity capital)
FCF_t is free cash flow in the year t
CV   is the continuing value
ID   is interest-bearing debt
WACC is the weighted average cost of capital
NOA are non-operating assets
t   is the year
T   is the last year of the forecast period.

All future cash flows are included in the summation formula. For operational purposes, a distinction is drawn between cash flows that can be planned in hard figures for a specific forecast period (e.g. 5–10 years) and what is known as the continuing or residual value, i.e. the value of the company after the forecast horizon.

Shareholder value, when calculated thus, is a key measurement and control variable in value management. It indicates whether a company or its business units have any positive corporate value at all. Its development can be monitored over time and compared with the company's share price on the stock exchange (cf. Chapter 3.3).

Alongside this method of calculation, which is also called the 'total capital/ WACC method', there is also what is known as the 'adjusted present value' method. The latter initially uses DCF and assumes full equity financing to determine the value of the company. Cash flows are discounted merely by a factor for the cost of equity. To account for the effect of any external debt, the sum of any tax shields arising therefrom is then added.[3] The advantage of this approach is that it is more exact than the total capital method in cases where the capital structure

---

[2] Brealey/Myers (1996), pp. 457 ff.
[3] For a more detailed explanation, see Drukarczyk (1996), pp. 156 ff.

is subject to extreme fluctuations (e.g. leveraged buyouts). Notwithstanding, it is less well suited to the valuation of business units, since these often do not have a capital structure of their own. For this reason we generally recommend that the total capital/WACC method be used. In any case, the weighted average cost of capital provides a much more appropriate hurdle rate for a company or business area, e.g. for the assessment of investment projects that are not under-pinned by any specific financing structure.

Shareholder value should be calculated with the aid of a PC-based computational model which indicates the value drivers as well as the calculation components outlined above. Figure 3.2 illustrates the structure of a computational model we often use for the total capital method. The section entitled 'Essential steps', which immediately follows these preliminary remarks on the logic of the approach, adheres to the same structure.

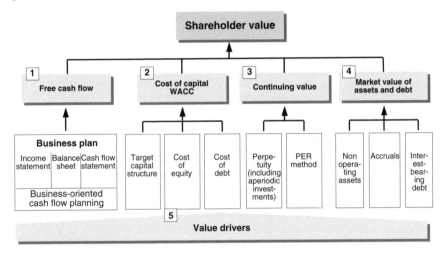

Figure 3.2: Elements in the calculation of shareholder value.

Determining the value of business areas/corporate groups

In the context of value management, statements must be made about developments in the value of individual business units and of the entire corporate group. Determining the value of an individual business unit is no problem, provided that two conditions are met:

- The business units must be clearly delimited. Before engaging in a value management exercise, it is therefore important to examine the existing organisational structure to determine whether each business unit constitutes a homogeneous entity and can be distinguished clearly from all the others. This is of particular importance in relation to the business unit's risk profile, since different cost of capital rates must be applied to each unit to reflect their respective risk levels.

- All the elements depicted in figure 3.2 must be calculated for each business unit: cash flow forecast, cost of capital, continuing value, non-operating assets (where applicable; this is often attached to group headquarters), external debt, total capital employed, and value drivers.

The shareholder value of a group can be calculated from the sum of the values of its business units plus non-operating assets and less group overheads, taxes and debt from sources outside the group (see Fig. 3.3). The logic matches up fully with that of the approach described above.

The item 'group overheads' covers corporate functions (e.g. accounting, controlling, legal department, and so on) that cannot be assigned directly to individual business units by means of internal orders, and which are therefore not recorded as outflows in the cash flow calculation.[4] Cash outflows from these corporate functions are compared with the benefit they bring, insofar as this can be expressed in terms of a monetary value, e.g. synergies achieved by joint marketing. Cash flows for the corporate departments are planned and discounted as for the business units.

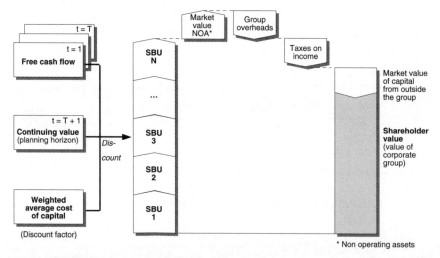

Figure 3.3: Calculating shareholder value for corporate groups.

At corporate level, tax on income is the difference between the sum of taxes on income paid by all the business units individually and the tax liability of the group as a whole. Owing to tax breaks resulting from international tax optimisation or the carryover of tax losses, this can actually be a positive amount. If the individual business units calculate their cash flows before tax, a net tax outflow will show up at corporate level. Although a number of European corporations

---

[4] Copeland/Koller/Murrin (1990), pp. 257 ff.

only ever calculate the cash flows of their business units before tax (because tax policy itself is seen as a corporate function), we recommend that after-tax views be used across the board in order to enable valid investment decisions to be taken at the level of individual business units (cf. the section on 'Taking account of tax effects' below).

Debt from sources outside the group is made up of borrowed funds that cannot be assigned to individual business units. Such debt should, wherever possible, be assessed at face value, e.g. in the case of loans. For companies with a high credit rating, calculations based on book values provide a sufficiently accurate approximation.

Value return as a measure of value creation

As an absolute measure, shareholder value is difficult to interpret and communicate. For example, is a value of DM 1.5 billion acceptable for business unit A? Comparisons over periods of time and target/actual comparisons allow useful conclusions to be drawn. For the purposes of corporate control, however, a further, more readily comprehensible answer to the question is needed: when does a company or one of its business units create value?

The question is answered by comparing the return on investment (ROI) with the cost of capital. A company or its business units create value when they generate a return on investment that is higher than the cost of capital. We also refer to this ROI as the shareholder value return. It is calculated as the internal rate of return on total capital employed (TCE) at the present time and on future free cash flows. The shareholder value return is thus a dynamic return on total capital employed and can, as such, be compared directly with the weighted average cost of capital (WACC).

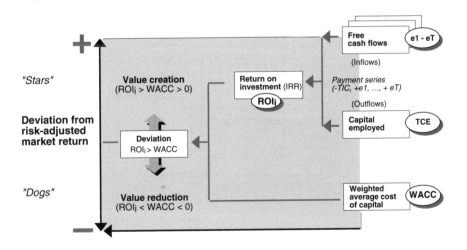

Figure 3.4: Difference between value creation and value reduction.

This gives us a simple rule with which to distinguish between value creators and value destroyers. Total capital employed is added as a new calculation component to the equation. This figure is easy to derive for the entire corporation from the face value of equity and debt. For individual business units, it is estimated on the basis of asset values (cf. step [4] in the section that follows).

Essential steps

(1) Forecasting free cash flows

We explained the logic behind free cash flow at the start of this chapter. There are two ways of calculating it: the indirect and the direct method. In this context, it becomes very important to draw up a business plan.

Indirect calculation of free cash flow

The indirect method of calculation determines cash flow from the net income for the year plus expenditure that does not affect cash outflows (e.g. depreciation) less earnings that do not affect liquidity (e.g. sales that lead to an increase in accounts receivable). The calculation is thus based on the income statement and the balance sheet for a company or business unit. Minor modifications to the income statement enable free cash flow to be determined as given in Table 3.1.

	Year 1	**Year 2 ...**
Sales revenues + Other operating revenues		
= Total revenues		
− Materials expenditure − Personnel expenditure − Other operating expenditures − Property taxes		
= Earnings before interest, taxes and depreciation (EBITD)		
+ Cash flow from changes in net working capital − Investments in property, plant and equipment and intangible assets + Extraordinary payment surplus + Increased accruals		
Free cash flow before taxes on income		
Taxes on income		
Free cash flow (before interest/depreciation)		

Table 3.1: Indirect calculation of free cash flow.

To begin with, this calculation is used to identify operative earnings before interest, taxes and depreciation (EBITD). Taxes from income and property are treated like other expenditures and have already been accounted for here. Cash flow from changes in net working capital is added to EBITD.

	Year 1	Year 2
Increases in trade accounts payable + Increase in downpayments received − Increase in trade accounts receivable − Increase in downpayments made − Increase in inventories (RMS, purchased goods)		
= **Cash flow from changes in net working capital**		

Table 3.2: Cash flow from changes in net working capital.

Capital spending on property, plant and equipment and intangible assets is then subtracted and the payment surplus from extraordinary items is added. If accruals are treated as an external fund, any increase in accrued reserves will be subtracted from free cash flow.[5] Taxes on income are then deducted from the pre-tax free cash flow calculated in this way.

Direct calculation of free cash flow

The direct calculation method determines cash flow from the difference between earnings and expenditures which affect liquidity. Consequently, the cash inflows and outflows of a company/business unit are investigated as part of a cash flow projection. Hence the calculation in Table 3.1 only includes those sales revenues and other business earnings that affect liquidity. Similarly, the various types of expenditures are estimated in relation to their effect on liquidity. Cash flow resulting from changes in net working capital is omitted from the direct calculation method.

Compared with the indirect method, this method has the drawback that free cash flow cannot be calculated from the income statement and the balance sheet. In other words, all earnings and expenditures must be examined to see how far they affect liquidity. Direct calculation is thus by far the more laborious method, since it requires a separate inflow/outflow statement. On the other hand, the advantage of this method is that it forces companies to examine in detail the assumptions on which plans for the effect of earnings and expenditures on

---

[5] See step (4) in this chapter for a treatment of accruals.

liquidity are based. Moreover, this method is largely free of the room to manoeuvre that can exist in balance sheets and income statements. We therefore advise people, at least for the first year, to calculate free cash flow using both methods. Doing so effectively subjects planning assumptions to a plausibility check, since both the indirect and the direct calculations must arrive at the same result.

Drawing up the business plan

A business plan is the bedrock of calculations of future free cash flow. The business plan encompasses a target income statement, a target balance sheet result (including investment planning) and a cash flow statement, although the latter will differ for the two calculation methods. A number of important rules apply concerning the procedure to be adopted:

- Firstly, the forecast horizon must be defined, i.e. the duration of the period for which cash flow must be calculated. The minimum period should be five years; ten years would be ideal. Either way, the forecast horizon must cover one entire business cycle. The value of the company or business unit at the end of this period is determined separately as the continuing value.
- Analysing internal and external year-end reports from the past five to ten years will supply important background information for planning. This exercise enables figures to be calculated which, on the one hand, can be used directly for planning purposes and, on the other hand, can help check the plausibility of planning data.
- When drawing up the business plan, it is important to do things in the right order. The point of departure should be sales, which must be planned on the basis of market analyses and forecasts. The next step is to identify individual operating expenditures and changes in net working capital. We then recommend that capital spending and a statement of asset additions and disposals (including write-downs) be planned. Having drawn up as exhaustive a balance sheet as possible, interest-bearing debt, interest, taxes, net profits, dividends and cash flow should be calculated in an iterative process in order to complete the business plan.

(2) Calculating the cost of capital

The cost of capital is a pivotal computational factor in the value management approach. As a discount factor for free cash flow it has a considerable impact on the value of the company. At the same time it represents the hurdle rate, i.e. the standard by which investment decisions are accepted or rejected.

As we briefly mentioned earlier on, the cost of capital is calculated as the weighted average cost of capital (WACC), covering both equity and debt capital. The cost of equity is weighted according to the proportion of the company's capital made up by equity and then added to the cost of debt (multiplied by the proportion of capital accounted for by borrowed funds). Figure 3.5 serves to illustrate the calculation.

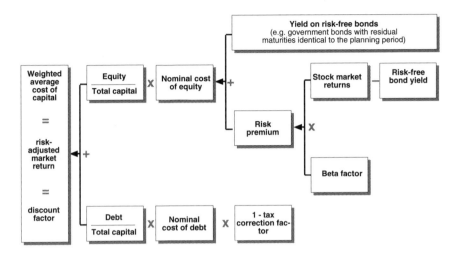

Figure 3.5: Calculating the weighted average cost of capital (WACC).

The cost of equity is calculated from the returns on risk-free bonds plus what is known as the market risk premium. The return on risk-free bonds is the interest that investors could expect from investing their funds in low-risk fixed-interest securities (e.g. government bonds). The risk premium is the premium which, according to the theory of finance, shareholders will expect over and above what they could have earned from investing in government bonds.[6] This premium is calculated from the general risk premium valid for the stock market – i.e. the difference between stock market returns and the returns on risk-free bonds – and the company-specific level of risk measured by the 'beta factor'.

The section that follows offers a practical guide as to how to identify these individual values.

Stock market returns, yield on risk-free bonds

Since these returns flow into the discount factor for future cash flows, it is expedient to assume the returns that would be expected by the investor. Identifying these returns is no easy task, however. It is therefore necessary to examine historical returns by way of approximation.

As evidenced in Table 3.3, numerous studies have been conducted to calculate and compare stock returns and risk-free bond yields over various periods. As a pragmatic solution, our advice to companies is to use the mean values of

---

[6] Bodie/Kane/Marcus (1989), pp. 228 ff.

Table 3.3: Studies to determine the risk premium.

Authors	Country	Period	Base	Stock market returns	Risk-free investment	Risk premium
Scientific studies						
• Sinquefield/ Ibbotson	U.S.	1926–1986	• S&P500 • Long-Term Government Bonds	12.1%	4.7%	7.4%
• Stehle/Hartmond (1991)	Germany	1954–1988	• All shares traded in Frankfurt • Fixed-interest securities	12.1%	7.5%	4.6%
• Bimberg (1991)	Germany	1954–1988	• SBA share index plus dividend yields • Government bonds	11.9%	6.6%	5.3%
• Morawietz (1994)	Germany	1870–1992	• SBA share index plus dividend yields • Fixed-interest securities	8.9%	5.8%	3.1%
Pragmatic approaches						
• American investment banks	Various countries	Methodology unknown		around 12%	6–8%	4–7%
• Roland Berger & Partner's calculations	Germany	1969–1997	• MSCI Germany • REX-P 10 years	10.1%	7.5%	2.6%
Recommended reference variables (mean values)				11.5%	7%	4.5%

the various studies as the basis on which to calculate the cost of shareholder capital. Companies wishing to calculate their own risk premium would do well to bear the following points in mind:

- The share index used for reference purposes should be as broadly based as possible (e.g. the S&P 500, FTSE 100 or the DJ Euro Stoxx) – rather than the Dow Jones Industrial Average or the DJ Euro Stoxx 50, for example, which list only 30 and 50 companies respectively.
- Share performance should be observed over an extended period to prevent excessive fluctuations from distorting the overall picture.
- The government bonds to be analysed should have similar maturities to the periods for which share performance was monitored. It is therefore preferable to use a long-term bond index (such as the REX P10 in Germany).
- If a performance index which assumes that dividends will be reinvested is taken as the reference share index, the same should apply to the bond index selected.

The beta factor

According to the capital asset pricing model (CAPM), the risk premium for a share corresponds to the market risk premium multiplied by the beta (ß) factor. The beta factor acts as an indicator of the individual level of risk to which a company is exposed. It is defined as the covariance of the share performance (including dividend payouts) of companies and a share index divided by the variance of the performance of the index.

The beta factor thereby measures the degree to which a given share and the stock market as a whole develop in parallel.[7] The beta factor for a company can be interpreted as follows:

$ß = 1$: Fluctuations in share values correlate fully with those of the share index. The risk factor for the share and the index is identical.

$ß > 1$: The value of the share is subject to more pronounced fluctuations than the share index. The risk factor for the share is greater than that for the index (in cyclical industries such as the computer industry).

$ß < 1$: The value of the share is subject to less fluctuation and is exposed to less risk than the share index. This generally applies to stable industries such as the power utility sector.

There is no difficulty determining the beta factor for companies listed on the stock exchange. The beta factors for DAX companies are published in the business daily 'Handelsblatt', for example. Other sources we would recommend include publications by investment banks (so-called 'beta books') and stock market

---

[7] Bodie/Kane/Marcus (1989), pp. 236 ff.

Table 3.4: Beta factors for Dow Jones EuroStoxx companies.[8]

Company	Beta	Company	Beta	Company	Beta
ABN AMRO HOLDING	1,38	ENDESA	0,83	PORTUGAL TELECOM	1,24
AEGON	1,12	ENI	0,78	REPSOL	0,82
AHOLD KON.	0,89	FIAT	1,10	RHONE POULENC 'A'	1,18
AIR LIQUIDE	0,67	FORTIS B	1,18	ROYAL DUTCH PTL.	0,77
AKZO NOBEL	1,36	GENERALI	0,86	RWE	0,75
ALCATEL	1,36	ING GROEP CERTS.	1,43	SAINT GOBAIN	0,98
ALLIANZ	1,15	KPN (KON)	1,06	SCHNEIDER	1,33
ALLD.IRISH BANKS	1,13	L'OREAL	1,24	SIEMENS	1,07
AXA	1,20	LUFTHANSA	1,08	SOCIETE GENERALE	1,42
BNC.BILBAO VIZCAYA	1,46	LVMH	1,29	TELECOM ITALIA	1,07
BAYER	1,00	MANNESMANN	1,29	TELEFONICA	1,18
CARREFOUR	0,68	NOKIA	1,38	UNICREDITO ITALIANO	1,39
DEUTSCHE BANK	1,23	PARIBAS (EX-BQ.PAR.)	1,47	UNILEVER CERTS.	1,07
ELECTRABEL	0,55	PETROFINA	0,71	VEBA	0,79
ELF AQUITAINE	0,66	PHILIPS ELTN.(KON)	1,47	VIVENDI	1,01
ELSEVIER	0,58				

information services, such as Bloomberg and Datastream. Since shares may be subject to short-term fluctuations, a longer period – perhaps two years – should be taken as the basis for calculation.

In the context of value management, beta factors also need to be identified for business units and for unlisted companies. Two calculation methods are appropriate in such cases:

1   observation of reference companies; and
2   estimates of risk drivers.

In the first of these procedures, the management of the business unit identifies listed companies which pursue the same activities and have a similar risk profile. Beta factors are determined for these companies. Since the beta factor also encompasses financial risk, e.g. on account of a high level of indebtedness, the beta factors for the reference companies will need to be adjusted to account for differences in the capital structure in the business unit concerned. This is a procedure known as 'unlevering' and 'relevering'. Unlevering converts the beta factor for the degree of debt/equity ratio of the reference company to the beta factor of a company with no debt. The resultant value is referred to as the 'asset beta'. Relevering then converts the asset beta to match the degree of debt/equity ratio of the company (or business unit) for which the cost of capital is to be calculated.[9]

---

[8] 2-year betas for DJ Eurostoxx corporations that have been listed for 2.5 years or longer; source: Datastream (27 April 1999).

[9] Brealey/Myers (1996), pp. 213 ff.

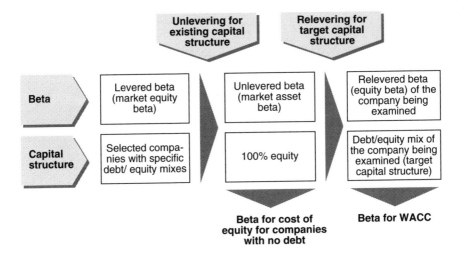

Figure 3.6: The logic behind unlevering and relevering.

The calculations are performed using the following formulas:

Unlevering: $\beta_u = \beta_l / (1 + (1 - \tau) \times D/E)$

Relevering: $\beta_l = \beta_u \times (1 + (1 - \tau) \times D/E)$

where:

β_u is the beta factor excluding debt ('unlevered', 'asset beta')
β_l is the beta factor including debt ('levered')
τ is a correction factor to account for the tax shield resulting from debt[10]
D/E is the debt/equity ratio.

The beta factors calculated in this way can be averaged to provide an approximation of the beta value for the business unit.

In the second of the two procedures, the beta factor is estimated by the business unit management. To do so, the individual risk drivers are discussed on the basis of a grid and the variants that apply to the business unit are identified. Comparative values from other companies or business units should be referred to in order to simplify the discussion.

The theoretical background to this estimate of the beta factor is the 'arbitrage pricing theory'. This theory explains a company's level of risk by using a factor (beta), but also by using a number of variables (e.g. economic cycles, interest rate

---

[10] τ is not the tax rate itself but merely a correction factor; cf. the section on 'Taking account of tax effects' below.

fluctuations etc.).[11] Since calculating the empirical risk factor for a share using this theory is a decidedly laborious task, we have developed the following pragmatic and interactive approach to estimating risk drivers. The approach has already been applied successfully in a number of contexts.

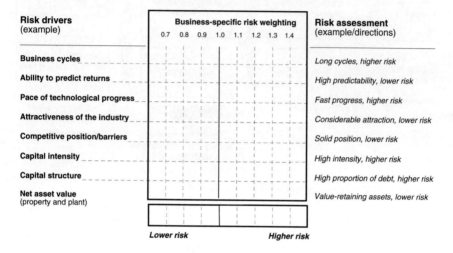

Figure 3.7: Grid for estimating the beta factor.

Either method has advantages and disadvantages. For this reason we recommend that the two be combined. The strengths of the reference company approach lie in the objectivity of the beta factor identified and the method's broad acceptance among analysts and investors. The reference companies are, however, selected on a subjective basis; nor is it always possible to transfer beta factors one-to-one from companies abroad. Estimating risk drivers has the advantage that it can be applied to any line of business or any business unit and is normally accepted subsequent to discussions with management. Its main drawback, however, is that the resultant risk estimate is ultimately subjective.

Nominal cost of debt

The nominal cost of debt is the average rate of interest that the company pays on interest-bearing debt. As a rule it is not difficult to calculate. An overview of interest-bearing capital from external sources (bonds, bank loans etc.) and a weighted average of the interest rates must be drawn up.

The use of borrowed funds affords companies a tax break (or a 'tax shield'), because interest repayments reduce the amount of tax to be paid. This effect is built into calculations of the weighted cost of capital by the tax correction fac-

---

[11] Bodie/Kane/Marcus (1989), pp. 293 ff.

tor. This factor reduces the cost of debt and, hence, the overall cost of capital, thereby producing a higher value than in the case of pure equity financing.

If long-term accruals – in particular company pension reserves – are a major item on the balance sheet, a cost of capital will need to be estimated here too. A variety of empirical studies have been published on the subject; most have come up with an average cost of capital of between 7 and 9%.[12] The calculation is made by comparing the face value of accruals for taxes with the face value of pension payments.

Capital structure

Another key element of the calculation is the company's target capital structure. Someone has to define what the relative proportions of equity and debt are to be in future. Equity is estimated at its market value. Where minor variations in capital structure occur over the years, a mean value can be taken. However, should the relative proportions of debt and equity be more volatile, it is better to use the adjusted present value method outlined above to determine the value of the company.

Real-world examples

As part of its 'Win' value creation program, Siemens put its cost of capital at 10% at year-end 1997.[13] This figure was calculated from the following main components:

* cost of shareholder capital of 11% after tax;
* cost of debt of 4.3% after tax; and
* shareholder capital as a proportion of total capital: 85%.

This cost of capital figure applies for the Siemens Group as a whole. The divisions that make up the group have different costs of capital in line with their respective business risks.

DaimlerChrysler[14] defined the following cost of capital after the merger:

* at group level: 9.2% after taxes;
* in the industrial divisions/business units: 15.5% before taxes; and
* for financial services: 20.0% before taxes.

The first two hurdle rates are applied to the ratio Return on Net Assets, whereas the relevant ratio for the third is Return on Equity. Thus, DaimlerChrysler uses

---

[12] Günther (1996), pp. 191 ff.
[13] Schmitz (1997), p. 14.
[14] Gentz (1999), pp. 9 ff.

the WACC-methodology except for financial services. The hurdle rate of 9.2% for the group level is calculated as follows:

- 70% equity at 11.6% (risk free rate: 4.7%, beta: 1.1, market risk premium: 6.25%)
- 10% financial liabilities at 2.9% (5% interest with a tax shield of 42%)
- 20% accrued liabilities at 3.9% (6.8% discount rate according to US GAAP with a tax shield of 42%).

Taking account of tax effects

In Chapter 2.3 and at the start of this chapter, we pointed out that the after-tax view as the basis for value determination and management/controlling is still something of a rarity in the corporate world. Business units, in particular, seem particularly prone to using pre-tax calculations, since tax policy or tax optimisation is felt to be the job of central corporate units. We would agree with this point, but nevertheless maintain that after-tax observations are also useful at the level of business units. Every unit or line of business should be valued from the investor's point of view, as though it were an autonomous operation. Offsetting the losses made by one unit against the profits made by another seems to us to be nothing more than a 'back-door' internal tax subsidy. Such tax advantages are achieved by the corporate unit responsible and should be included in the value calculation at corporate level rather than for individual business units. We therefore recommend that after-tax valuations be used across the board.

Consistent after-tax valuation allows you to work with a free cash flow after taxes and a weighted cost of capital after taxes. The issue of identifying the tax correction factor for the cost of debt remains open (cf. step 2).

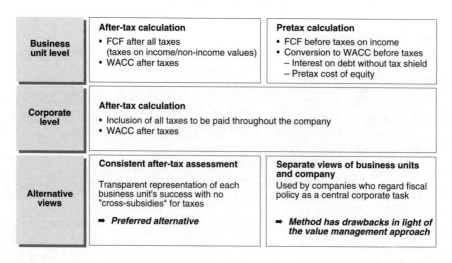

Figure 3.8: Different options for pretax calculations.

The correction factor is used to calculate the tax shield offered by borrowed funds. In general, all interest-bearing debt reduces earnings before taxes, and thus taxes. In the WACC method, this tax shield is incorporated by reducing the cost of debt by means of the tax correction factor (cf. Fig. 3.5).

In the US the tax correction factor is equal to corporate income tax.[15] In Europe however, the correction factor is more complex. Firstly, there are trade taxes in several countries that are based on earnings. Thus, there is a tax shield on trade tax in these countries as well. Secondly, in a few European countries private investors can deduct at least part of the corporate taxes paid by the company on distributed earnings from their personal income tax:[16]

- *France*. The shareholder obtains a tax credit (*avoir fiscal*) of 50% of the cash dividend. This *avoir fiscal* is added to his taxable income. At the general level of the corporate tax rate (33.3%), the scheme leads to the full compensation of the corporate income tax to the investor. At the current level of 40% corporate tax (two temporary 10% supplements to 33.3%), the compensation is only partial.
- *Germany*. The shareholder obtains a full tax credit for the net income paid out as dividends. Therefore, dividends are only taxed at the personal tax rate of the investor. The corporate income tax rate for dividends is significantly lower than that for retained earnings (30% versus 45%).
- *Italy*. The shareholder obtains a tax credit of 58.73% of the cash dividend. Given the corporate tax rate of 37%, this tax credit is usually equal to the taxes paid by the company.
- *Spain*. Private shareholders obtain a tax reduction of 10% for dividends from national corporations.
- *United Kingdom*. Corporations pay an advance corporation tax (ACT). The shareholder's taxable income consists of the cash dividend and the ACT. The personal investor obtains a tax deduction of the amount of ACT. For private investors who pay the lower tax rate of 20%, this scheme leads to a full compensation of corporate taxes.

Consequently, private investors get at least a partial tax deduction for profits paid out as dividends. In all countries with a full tax credit on dividends, an increased indebtedness and higher interest payments do not create a tax shield for investors. For earnings that are not paid out as dividends but retained, the investors do not obtain a tax credit. In the selected European countries, debt financing thus creates a tax shield over the net income retained and partially over dividends (i.e. in France, Spain and the UK where the tax deduction is only partial). In addition, debt financing creates a tax shield for trade tax in those

---

[15] Brealey/Myers (1996), pp. 457 ff.
[16] Domann (1995), pp. 33ff; Lobis (1998), pp. 34 ff; Müssener (1997), pp. 41 ff; Tillmanns (1998), pp. 54 ff; o. V. (1994), pp. 24 ff.

countries where there is a trade tax and where it is based on an income figure after interest. Therefore we calculate the tax correction factor as follows:

$$\tau = t_t + t_c \times (1 - DP) \times (1 - t_t) + (\Delta t_{cr-c} \times DP)$$

where:

τ is the tax correction factor

t_t is the trade earnings tax rate (only applicable for countries with trade tax that is based on earnings, e.g. Germany)

t_c is the rate of corporate income tax

DP   is the dividend proportion (that part of pretax profits that is appropriated for dividend payouts plus corporate income tax)

$1 - t_t$ reduces taxable income for corporate income tax by trade earnings tax to be paid

Δt_{cr-c} is the difference between tax credit on dividends for private investors and corporate income tax rate (zero for Germany and Italy).

The formula looks complicated but has the advantage that it can be adapted to various countries. The part $(1 - DP)$ only applies to countries where the investor obtains a tax deduction on corporate taxes paid on dividends, $(1 - t)$ only applies if there is a trade earnings tax that is deductible from corporate income tax (e.g. in Germany), and the part Δt_{cr-c} is only relevant if there is partial tax deduction on dividends for private investors. So, under the US tax system, the formula is quite simple: $\tau = t_c$. In France all parts of the formula currently need to be applied.

As the tax correction factor depends on the company's dividend policy in most countries, and corporate taxation is subject to continuous change, we prefer not to state a calculation of the tax correction factor for different countries. In general, with a dividend policy that pays out about 50% of the net income, the tax correction factor lies between 0.2 and 0.3 in the five European countries mentioned above. If profits are retained completely, τ lies between 0.3 and 0.5. If a company's dividend policy changes over time we recommend calculating an average tax correction factor for several years.

(3) Calculating the continuing value

Depending on how long the forecast period is, the continuing value can account for a significant part of the company's value. It must therefore be calculated very accurately. We recommend the use of two methods: the perpetuity method; and a valuation based on multiples.

Perpetuity

The perpetuity formula calculates the value of a never-ending cash flow which is either constant or increases at a given growth rate (g). We recommend a version of the perpetuity method that is extended to include the effects of aperiodic investments.[17] This extension is necessary because, in some industries (such as the paper industry), major capital investments can falsify any calculation of the value of the company if they are realised shortly after the forecast horizon. For such investments, outflows and additional cash flow generated by the investment must be taken into consideration (ΔFCF). Figure 3.9 provides an overview of the procedure adopted and the formula used to calculate the continuing value.

When applying the perpetuity method, a number of important points must be borne in mind:

- As stated above, the forecast period should be at least five years and should reflect a complete business cycle.
- Since cash flow in the last year of the forecast period is what forms the basis for the perpetuity calculation, it is important to ensure that this cash flow is not distorted by extraordinary effects.
- The growth rate g should not be too high. Growth rates in excess of 2% imply real growth, which, for mature industries, must often be deemed an overly positive assessment.

Valuation based on multiples

The continuing value can also be determined by the use of earnings or cash flow multiples, i.e. ratios between the market value of equity and profits or a company's cash flow. The result is a fictitious value that would be attached to the company were it to be sold off at the end of the forecast period.

Multiples from comparable companies should be identified first as the basis for calculation. It makes sense to combine this with the analysis of reference companies to determine the beta factors. Investment banks frequently work with the price-earnings (P/E) ratio, which can also be found in a number of publications. However, this ratio contains the problem of profit as an accounting number and is therefore less useful than a cash flow multiple.

The comment about the length of the forecast period for the perpetuity method also applies here. In addition, the last year's profit/cash flow must not be distorted by extraordinary effects but should represent a sustained value.

---

[17] Aperiodic investments are understood here to mean investments that are made at prolonged and, in some cases, irregular intervals, with the result that they do not fall entirely within the forecast period.

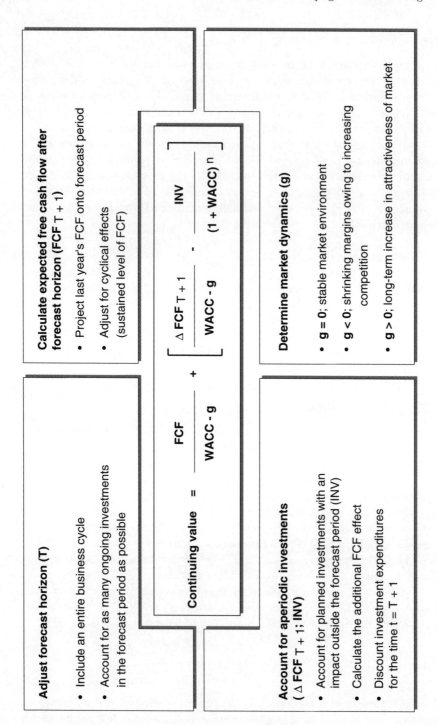

Figure 3.9: Calculating the continuing value in perpetuity.

(4) Calculating the market value of assets and debts

As explained at the beginning, shareholder value is calculated by adding non-operating assets to the sum of discounted cash flows and then subtracting debt, including accruals. It is also necessary to determine total capital employed in order to calculate the shareholder value return.

Non-operating assets

Non-operating assets (NOA) generally represent excess liquidity that is not required for operative business. Examples can include securities held as financial investments, funds in bank accounts, or even works of art. It is important for the purposes of value determination that NOA be calculated at market prices. This is usually no problem for financial investments. For works of art and all other assets for which market prices are not regularly published, experts will need to be called in.

Debt capital

Only interest-bearing debt needs to be considered here. Short-term liabilities such as down payments received or trade accounts payable, as part of working capital, must not be subtracted.

As far as possible, debt should be valued at market prices. This is easy to do for listed bonds. In the case of other instruments of finance, the following points can assist with the valuation process:

* *Fixed-interest bank loans.* The value of a loan fluctuates in line with the current market rate. The market value of substantial loans can be estimated by referring to bonds and loans with similar cash flows and risks. In the case of minor balance sheet items, we recommend that the book value be taken as the market value by way of approximation.
* *Variable-interest loans/floating Euronote programs.* The value depends on the spread achieved over and above the variable interest rate. The amount (book value) of the loan should be used here. The spread should be considered only if it brings with it considerable benefits.
* *Swaps.* In the case of debt-for-equity swaps, the cash flows for the company after the swap (net) should be calculated and the liability value estimated by referring to bonds and loans with similar cash flows.

Accruals

Accruals are accumulated to cover potential company liabilities that may at some time lead to outflows. Prime examples include company pension reserves, provisions for taxes and goodwill accruals. Such accruals can also take on the quality of reserves if they are higher than the face value of the payments that will likely have to be made.

We would propose two alternative calculation methods to deal with accruals: either a payment-oriented method or a method which treats them as external funds.

The payment-oriented method incorporates only those accrual-related transactions that result in cash flows. In accordance with the definition of cash flows given above, increases in accruals are not included in the calculation. Nevertheless, obligations to make payments at a later date must be taken into account. To this end, the face value of all future obligations to make payments must be calculated. This figure must also include outflows for which increases in accruals would only be effected in the years to come. In consequence, the face value of these commitments will be greater than their balance sheet value, provided that existing accruals have not taken on the nature of major reserves.

In the second method, accruals are treated as external funds similar to the way that pension funds are handled in English-speaking countries. Increases in accruals are seen as outflows that reduce free cash flow and transfer future payment obligations to external funds. For this reason there is no need to subtract the face value of all payment obligations: all that needs to be subtracted is the current nominal value, less any undisclosed reserves. For the purposes of this method, interest on accruals is seen as income that is effectively paid into the company from the external fund.

If applied carefully, both methods will produce similar results. Since the amount of work involved is also comparable, we do not give precedence to one method over the other.

Total capital employed

When calculating the shareholder value return (the internal rate of return), capital employed is deemed to be an outflow at the starting point. Capital employed should not be made up exclusively of balance sheet figures but should also, as far as possible, include the opportunity cost of investment for the company or line of business. We propose the following calculation:

Working capital
– short-term, non interest-bearing liabilities
= net working capital
+ financial assets (excluding NOA)
+ property, plant and equipment (replacement value/cost of production)
+ capitalised leasing expenditures (where applicable)
+ intangible assets (where applicable)
= **total capital employed.**

Non interest-bearing liabilities, such as down payments received or trade accounts payable, are not included in working capital since they do not constitute tied shareholder capital. Financial assets, which are part of the company's business capital, are then added to the net working capital value arrived at in this way. Property, plant and equipment is taken at its replacement value or, if it is manufactured in-house, at cost. It will usually be necessary to work with assumptions in this context. Even so, this calculation is more accurate than one that uses book values.

Two items are to be included only in certain cases. Companies that have leased a large proportion of their assets should capitalise their leasing expenditures and include them in total capital employed. In some industries (pharmaceuticals, chemicals and advertising, for instance), even intangible assets generated by the company can also be a part of capital employed. Intangibles should therefore be given a value by capitalising and depreciating the relevant expenditures, e.g. research and development costs.[18]

(5) Identifying value drivers

As mentioned briefly above, we understand value drivers to be the key control variables with which the value of a company or business unit can be increased. Such drivers can be price levels, certain types of expenditures, or changes in net working capital.

A company that knows its business will also often have a knowledge of the key value drivers. These drivers can only be evaluated precisely, however, by changing the core assumptions on which cash flow planning is based and by observing the impact of these changes on shareholder value. In view of the vast number of forecast assumptions involved, this kind of 'sensitivity analysis' is best conducted using an integrated PC tool that uses macros to automatically change a given assumption by a certain percentage, and then indicates the resultant change in shareholder value.

Figure 3.10[19] displays an excerpt of such a tool for a paper manufacturer. The 'value tree' shows the free cash flow on the left hand side, and then step by step drills down to various value drivers such as standard rate (price) of graphic paper or productivity of direct labour. In the lower level of each box, the average %-change assumed in the original business plan is displayed on the left hand side. The number to the right serves to type in changes in the assumptions. With these changes, a new shareholder value is then calculated.

Our approach therefore draws clearer distinctions between value drivers, drilling down to a finer level of detail than Rappaport's five standard value drivers.[20] We consciously identify individual value drivers because we want each company to discover what its particular value-oriented control variables are. This approach

---

[18] For details, see Lewis (1994), pp. 57 ff.
[19] The tool itself comprises far more control variables.
[20] Cf. Chapter 2.2, especially Fig. 3.17.

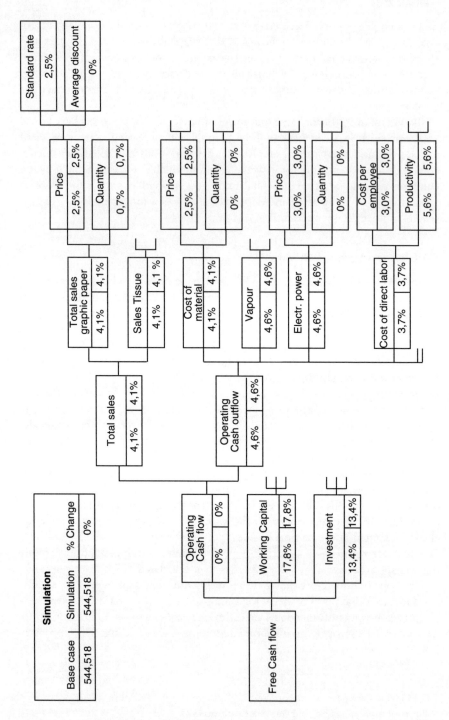

Figure 3.10: Value-driver sensitivity analysis conducted with a PC tool (excerpt).

facilitates a focus on the most powerful value creation levers, which will be different in every company, and should be defined in as operational a way as possible.

Results: value performance and value drivers

What, then, are the results of the first component in the value management concept? The company and its business units have successfully been able to assess their 'value performance'. In other words, they have used shareholder value, and the shareholder value return, as metrics to verify whether they are actually creating value for their owners. At the same time, they have identified those elements that drive value.

Model, Inc.

Shareholder value		Base:	1.7.98
Business plan			**After taxes**
+ Sum of discounted free cash flows			
Short-term component to 2000/01			3,779,200
Short-term component as of 2001/02			60,339,047
Discount rate:		8.88%	64,118,247
+ Continuing value			
Long-term component			140,040,646
Rate of growth:		1.00%	
Method:		perpetuity	
= Value of company			204,158,893
- (Long-term) nominal debt			21,046,405
(excluding interest-free loans)			
- Accruals			(3,465,299)
Discount rate:		nominal	
+ Free liquidity/non-essential operating capital			41,765,304
Shareholder value			221,412,493

Figure 3.11: Screen dump of a shareholder value calculation made with a PC tool.

Based on careful business planning, each business unit can obtain clear information about shareholder value. The result of a calculation made with the same PC-based tool that we use might, for example, look something like Fig. 3.11.

The individual components that went into the calculation are clearly indicated. The sum of discounted free cash flows is further broken down into two components which reveal that Model AG, a rapidly growing young company, will in total generate no positive cash flows worthy of the name in its first three years to 30 June 2002.

The comparison of the sum of discounted cash flows in the forecast period with the continuing value of the company allows conclusions to be drawn about the level of risk contained in the business plan. This is illustrated in the next figure.

Figure 3.12 shows the very slightly modified result of a valuation that we performed for a client on the basis of their cash flow forecast for several business units in a current growth industry. The business units not only differ extremely in terms of the absolute contribution made to the value of the company, they also differ in terms of their percentage of continuing value. Business units A and C have far too large a share of continuing value. In other words, almost the entire value of these two units will be generated only after the forecast horizon (in this case, at the end of ten years). The forecast data needs to be examined very carefully here, as one might suspect what is known as the 'hockey stick' effect. This is a term used to refer to plans that become unrealistically positive the further one looks into the future. Such cases can have a free cash flow in the last year of the forecast period that is unrealistically high and which results in an overrated continuing value. Alternatively, the assumptions on which the continuing value is calculated – especially the rate of growth – may themselves be unrealistic. Either excess can be avoided, however, by carefully following the procedures for cash flow planning and continuing value calculation described in steps 1 and 2 in this chapter.

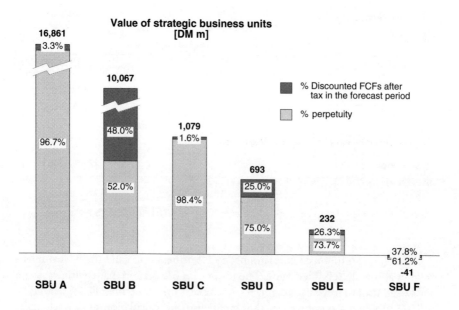

Figure 3.12: Comparison of value and proportion of continuing value.

Our view of shareholder value has so far failed to take any notice of capital employed. This is done by the shareholder value return, i.e. the internal rate of return on capital employed and the cash flows. All of the business units shown in Fig. 3.13 can boast attractive returns, since their cost of capital lies between ten and twelve percent. The unrealistically high returns for business units D and E suggest the need to re-examine cash flow forecasts in both cases.

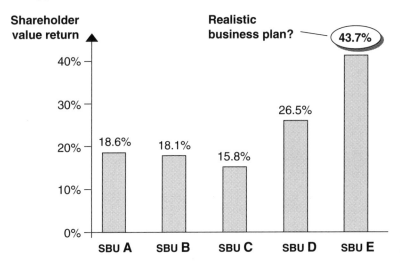

Figure 3.13: Shareholder value returns from the business units.

Another very important result of this first component of the value management concept is transparency about the value drivers. The exercise has identified the key points on which value creation programs should concentrate, as will be explained in the next chapter. Figure 3.14 provides an example of value drivers in the telecommunications industry.

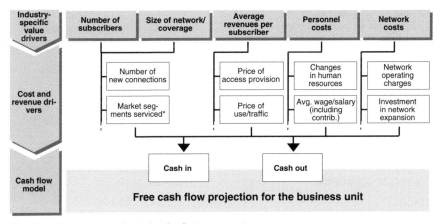

* E.g. electronic payment transactions, telematics, fleet management

Figure 3.14: Example of value drivers in the telecommunications industry.

3.2 Implementing value creation programs

Now that we have used the methodological and arithmetic definition of a calculation model to lay the foundation for value-based management – i.e. now that we have defined free cash flows and the cost of capital, worked out shareholder value returns and company value figures and, above all, used the business model to translate business-specific value drivers into decision models – the obvious question still begs to be asked: so what? Many a controller has lost both sweat and sleep over concepts whose methodology is nothing if not 'clean'. Business unit managers have identified and quantified their value drivers. Strategists have done their bit to assess threats, opportunities, strengths and weaknesses in the group's various business units. Now, however, is the time to steer away from the backwaters of conceptual aspects and plunge into the mainstream of implementational issues. Value creation programs must be implemented in order to:

- tap potential for strategic value creation by means of portfolio decisions;
- improve running business by means of operative activities; and,
- optimise financial value drivers on the basis of a financial engineering exercise.

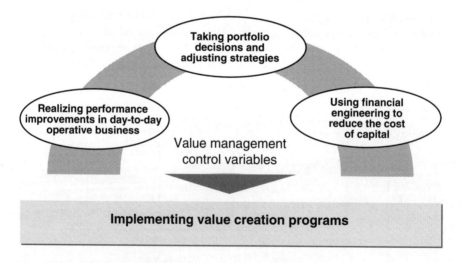

Figure 3.15: Three dimensions of value creation programs.

Portfolio decisions and strategy adjustments

The value-based assessment of businesses aims to develop or expand a portfolio of value-creating business units. Strategic and portfolio-related value creation concepts should be based on a value portfolio. The data from the business plan calculations in the model shown and strategic analysis data both flow into this portfolio. Every strategic business unit is positioned within this portfolio, whose two axes reflect:

- deviation from risk-adjusted market returns; and
- strategic 'fit' with the corporate vision.

This value portfolio, devised by Roland Berger & Partners, ensures that the two criteria along the x and y axes are independent of each other. The danger of findings that lead to distortions on the grounds of significant correlation is thus largely precluded. The portfolio distinguishes between 'stars' and 'dogs', recommending:

- further growth or holding patterns with no strategic investment for the 'stars'; and
- optimisation or discontinuation/hiving off of the 'dogs'.

This portfolio serves to represent the results of analyses; yet at the same time it throws up a number of critical questions, possible courses of action and 'standard strategies'. In this context, two questions need to be answered:

1   On the basis of the calculations performed using the arithmetic explained in Chapter 3.1, how is a strategic business unit to be positioned within the value portfolio?
2   What conclusions are to be drawn? In other words: how does one define what actions will increase the value of the portfolio?

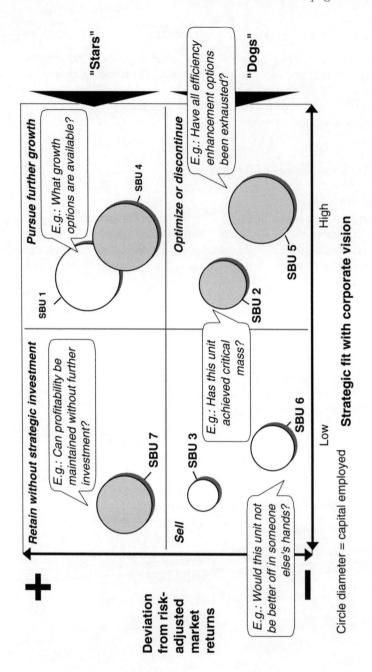

Figure 3.16: Value portfolio.

Position of the SBU in the value portfolio

The portfolio is derived from the summarised positions of individual business units along the two axes mentioned above, namely strategic fit with the vision of the company (x axis) and deviation from risk-adjusted market returns (y axis). The logic of value creation and value reduction is explained in Fig. 3.4; the concept behind positioning is therefore simple:

- forecast free cash flows
- calculation of capital employed
- discounting and calculation of the internal rate of interest
- comparison with the rate determined for the total cost of capital and, hence, the definition of value creation and value destruction.

The 'stars' in the value portfolio are thus those business fields that create value in the sense understood by the shareholder value philosophy. They do this by means of:

- sustained cash flow growth, achieved by engaging in activities in attractive industries, for example, and/or by attaining to an outstanding competitive position;
- optimised management of investments (intangible assets, financial assets, property, plant and machinery, and working capital) and how they are financed (cost of capital); and
- consistent risk management, e.g. by applying hedging strategies in currency management, drawing efficient distinctions in the area of customer numbers, 'anticipating' risks in planning wherever possible, and so on.

The 'dogs' do exactly the opposite.

Rappaport puts together a system for improving corporate value in the shareholder value network. This illustrates the importance of the link between the company's objectives in wanting to create value and the fundamental valuation factors and value drivers used – incremental sales growth, operating profit margin, rate of tax on profits, investments in working and fixed capital, cost of capital, and the period over which value is created.[1] Figure 3.17 below depicts the interrelationships postulated by Rappaport and thus represents a key element in value management programs.

The quantitative positioning of a strategic business unit (SBU) along the y axis derives from a comparison of the return on investment with the total cost of capital. Value is created only if the return on investment is greater than the total cost of capital. The relevant point of arithmetic reference is determined individually for each corporation and each of its business units.

---

[1] Rappaport (1986), p. 56.

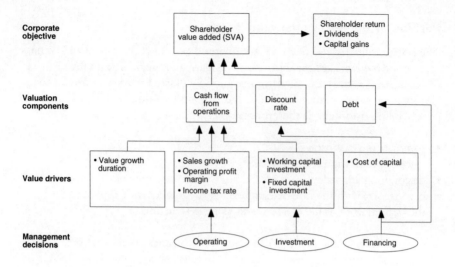

Figure 3.17: Rappaport's shareholder value network.[2]

Problems arise in the positioning of business units where certain areas are cross-subsidised by internal transfer prices, allocations and similar practices. To avoid distorting the picture, these factors should be eliminated before a position in the value portfolio is defined. Alternatively, their influence on the position of an SBU should be indicated explicitly.

Various criteria can be applied to identify a line of business as a value creating unit from a strategic point of view. Based on the system used by Porter, we recommend adoption of a strategic perspective of the relevant markets/industry, customers/recipients, products/technologies, competitors, and the distribution system. Related qualitative aspects (value drivers) are summarised in the figure below, although it should be noted that the list is naturally offered by way of example only and cannot possibly be exhaustive.

The strategic fit relative to the company's vision – the position on the *x* axis – can be pinpointed by two essentially trivial questions of corporate management: Does the company want to get involved in a given business? And does it master the business? The following questions are examples of those that need to be asked when it comes to operationalisation:

- Does the line of business in question fit in with any putative focus or core business strategy within the portfolio, or is the SBU a value creating element as part of a policy of diversification?[3]

---

[2] Rappaport (1986), p. 56.
[3] See also Prahalad/Hamel (1997), for example.

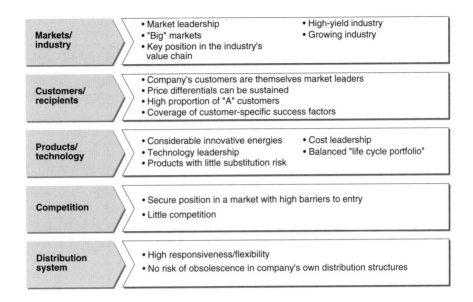

Figure 3.18: Strategic requirements for value creation.

- Can the SBU fully satisfy the necessary factors of success?[4]
- Does the SBU combine the requirements such as critical mass, yield, growth rates, risks and corporate culture defined in corporate goals?[5]
- Do potential synergies justify committing the company to the strategic line of business concerned?[6]

The strategic fit with the vision of the company is translated into operational terms by a pragmatic scoring method. How the criteria shown here by way of example are quantified, must be decided for each company individually; at this point we would expressly distance ourselves from any 'one-size-fits-all' recipe. Figure 3.19 illustrates the logic behind portfolio decisions based on value creation and strategic fit.

In many cases, this process will result in portfolio adjustments. Table 3.5 lists examples of actual divestitures made on the grounds that units did not fit in with corporate vision.

---

[4] See also Krüger/Schwarz (1997), for example.
[5] See also Hax/Majluf (1984), pp. 52 ff, for example.
[6] See also Rappaport (1995), pp. 126 ff.

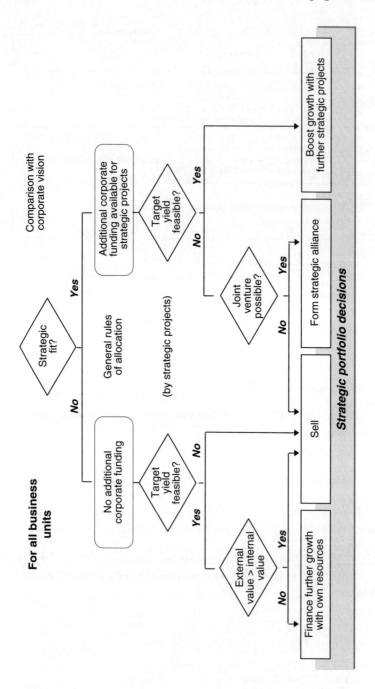

Figure 3.19: Decision tree to define the company's target portfolio.

Group	Companies sold (examples)	Reason for divestiture
Daimler-Benz	• AEG Hausgeräte AG and AEG Lichttechnik GmbH (1994) • Fokker N.V. (1996) • Dornier Luftfahrt GmbH (1996)	• Group reorientation (return to a focus on vehicles) • Abandonment of the goal of an integrated technology group • Elimination of all loss-makers
Hoechst	• Jade Cosmetics GmbH (1995) • Marbert GmbH (1995) • Riedel-de Haen AG (1995) • Hoechst CeramTech AG (1996) • Hans Schwarzkopf GmbH (1996) • SGL Carbon/Börse (1996)	• Concentration on core business with strong value orientation
Mannes-mann	• Hartmann & Braun AG (1995) • TI Group plc (1995) • Mannesmann Fahrzeugteile (1995) • Fahrradgeschäft Hercules (1995) • Mannesmann Tally GmbH (1996)	• Withdrawal from electronics and IT industries • Structural improvements
Preussag	• Hagenuk GmbH (1995)	• Withdrawal from telecommunications
Thyssen	• Wehrtechnik Thyssen Henschel (1996) • Baustahlgewerbe GmbH (1997) • Berkenhoff und Drebes GmbH (1997) • Thyssen Magnettechnik (1997) • Rheinische Kalksteinwerke GmbH (1997) • E-Plus (1997)	• Removal of activities whose results or strategy did not fit in with the group's portfolio
Veba	• Sale of stake in Hapag-Lloyd (1997) • Polyolefine oper. Vestolen GmbH (1997) • Raab Karcher Ambiente (planned 1998) • Raab Karcher Tankstellentechnik (1998)	• Restructuring • Deregulation of the electricity market necessitated portfolio adjustments • Strategy of concentration
Viag	• PWA Waldhof-Aschaffenburg AG (1995) • Didier-Werke AG (1995/96)	• Concentration on core business • Withdrawal from fire-resistant segment

Table 3.5: Divestitures in the absence of a suitable strategic fit.

Analyse the value portfolio – adapt the strategy

Combining value-based portfolio analysis with the evaluation and selection of strategies is important because strategic management is the bedrock on which value can be created:

- Strategic (re)orientation must be determined in such a way that only those SBUs which yield a shareholder value return higher than the cost of capital are retained in the portfolio.
- 'Dogs' are to remain in the portfolio only until such time as they can either be transformed into value-creating stars or sold off to 'more suitable proprietors'.
- Consistency is of the essence! The portfolio must be adjusted: there is no room for strategies based on back-scratching, megalomania etc. Strategic management has to rely on the 'hard figures' produced by value management.

Group, company and individual SBU strategies must all be examined in this light, although the focus will be different in each case:

- Corporate and group strategies build on investments made in individual business units in order to create a portfolio structure that creates value throughout the enterprise. 'If the current portfolio cannot generate the target level of shareholder value creation, corporate strategy may be directed toward restructuring the company's business mix via acquisitions, strategic alliances, divestitures, internally developed new business ventures, or changing the mix of capital allocated to the company's existing businesses'.[7]
- SBU strategies focus on the issues of positioning, market leadership, benefit to customers, business system design and so on.

This is not the place to get involved in a discussion of strategic planning processes or the tools, analysis models and strategic concepts they use; it can be assumed that most companies will have their own corporate functions with sufficient relevant expertise. Chapter 3.3, however, does look in some depth at the need to adapt strategic planning and controlling as value management concepts are introduced.

Rather than engage in a discussion of the 'strategic toolbox', this book restricts itself to:

- a table summarising the business strategies listed in the book 'Wertmanagement' by Peter Gomez. This table provides a useful outline of possible business strategies and their key thrusts (Table 3.6); it is here translated into English;
- an overview of a few basic strategic concepts taken from the book by Rolf Eschenbach and Hermann Kunesch (Table 3.7); and
- an outline of strategic imperatives and measures for the value portfolio described above. In other words, our aim is to present alternatives for each of the items in the value portfolio.

'Stars' that fit the corporate vision

These are the strategic business units which create value by earning shareholder value returns over and above the cost of capital, and which evidently fit in with corporate strategy. In the context of portfolio theory, these are the 'classical stars' and, hence, the cash producers and value drivers. The goal of corporate strategy must always be to position its own core businesses in this quadrant.

The further growth of these SBUs should be promoted, and this will necessitate strategic growth concepts. Funding will therefore have to be allocated in order:

---

[7] Rappaport (1986), p. 78.

Table 3.6: Alternative business strategies and their underlying thrusts.[8]

Normative portfolio strategy	• Divestiture strategy	Sell off parts of the company to free up resources for more promising units
	• Deterrence strategy	Maintain current position and generate high cash flows for as long as possible without investing additional capital
	• Investment strategy	Expand market position through a deliberate investment policy
	• Segmentation strategy	Concentrate energies and investments on attractive markets in order to build up a competitive position
Competitive strategies	• Cost leadership	Gain an edge over competitors in terms of production and overhead costs; increase market share by means of low prices
	• Differentiation (performance leadership)	Systematically differentiate products and services from those of competitors by means of innovation and service
	• Concentration on niche markets	Focus consistently on certain (sub)markets, customer groups, technologies, sales markets, regions
	• New rules on the market	Define new 'rules of the game' which consciously shake up and redesign the existing market/industry order
Product/ market strategies	• Market penetration	Intensify market coverage, cut costs/prices and adopt similar measures to get a stronger grip on the market
	• Market development	Tap new customer groups, formulate new applications, services, delivery channels and problem/system solutions
	• Product development	Develop new products/product lines
	• Diversification	Penetrate new markets with new products, either by building up a presence or by means of acquisitions
Synergy strategies	• Technological orientation	Concentration on products and services that are based on the same product technology or can be manufactured using the same production technology
	• Customer orientation	Offer a full line of products to satisfy a particular set of needs for a given customer group (e.g. all accessories and equipment for skiing enthusiasts)
	• Functional orientation	Make available a wide range of products to fulfill a certain function (e.g. lighting)
Integration strategies	• Downstream integration	Open up direct market access, e.g. by developing a company-owned sales organization or merging different levels of commerce and retail
	• Upstream integration	Consolidate the company's position by protecting procurement sources and achieving cost benefits be integrating upstream stages

---

[8] Gomez (1993), p. 173.

Table 3.7: Overview of strategic concepts.[9]

Author	Contents	Core concept/ statement	Strengths	Weaknesses
Ansoff	Organised detection of weak signals and measures to improve responsiveness	Weak signals	Promotes flexibility	Management must be open and receptive
Drucker	Discussion of most important strategic issues a company will have to confront	Engender an understanding of strategic tasks	Easy to grasp	Lack of tools and instruments, especially for strategy selection
Gälweiler	Basic system of strategic management linked to operative control variables	Strategic pretax metrics	Integration of a complete model	Metrics used to provide orientation are controversial
Ghemawat	Strategy selection (clinging to strategic decisions or flexibility) explained by referring to the past and to earlier strategic points-setting exercises	Commitment	Company history is taken into account	Theoretical, scientific; difficult to implement
Hahn	Planning and control system for strategic management that is linked to operative management	Integrated planning and control system	Link between operations and strategy	Technocratic
Hamel, Prahalad	Redefinition of strategic constraints against the background of future strategic competitive advantages	Core competences, strategic intent	Motivation to face strategic challenges	Normative
Hax/Majluf	12-stage concept for developing strategies using familiar strategic tools such as scenario techniques, portfolios etc.	Traces the process of strategy planning	Easy to understand; covers all corporate levels	Bureaucratic
Hinterhuber	Structure and sequential process for strategic management, paying special attention to vision and corporate culture	Sequential process for strategic management	Clearly structured; detailed treatment of implementation	Delimitation of separate components unclear in places
Itami	Presentation of intangible assets as the basis for competitive advantages; treatment of coherence between internal and external strategy	Intangible assets	Focus on human aspects	Only Japanese examples, hence limited practical validity

[9] Eschenbach/Kunesch (1994), pp. 21 ff.

Table 3.7 (continued)

Author	Contents	Key concept/ statement	Strengths	Weaknesses
Malik	Ways of coming to terms with complexity in an organic system and steering the company within a metasystem	Problem-solving behaviour; ability of systems to live and grow	Interdisciplinary approach	Very abstract
Mann	Strategic controlling tools; vision and potential for success lay the foundation	Strategic tools; finding your vision	Tool-based support; clear visual impact; practical	Normative
Mintzberg	Outline of various forms of strategy determination and how they interrelate with the organisational structure	Weak signals	Empirical, practical analysis	No coherent concept that can be applied directly
Porter	Development of competitive strategies at the level of the business unit; systematic approach to explaining and shaping competitive advantages	Industry analysis; value creation chain	Clear visual impact	Data acquisition and operational application often cause problems
Probst/ Gomez	Self-contained, systematic management process	Network; paper computer	Readily understandable and cogent methodology	Danger of oversimplifi- cation
Pümpin	Structure and further development of strategically successful items and corporate dynamics in order to surmount complexity issues	Strategically successful items; corporate dynamics	Plenty of attention given to practical examples of implementation	Too little attention given to surrounding context
Turnheim	Appeal for new thinking and new management methods based on the chaos theory	Chaos management; mock-up corporate games; restructuring strategies	Hands-on assistance for practical application	Limited to large companies
Ulrich	Presentation of a system- oriented management model	Founder of the St. Gallen-based systemic management school	Interdisciplinary approach	Difficult to apply; no practical assistance

- to achieve or consolidate market leadership;
- to maintain or establish barriers to entry;
- to achieve or consolidate cost leadership; and
- to achieve or consolidate a leading position with regard to product and technology innovation.

Packages of strategic measures represent the consistent further development of, and investment in, these business units; where possible they should be based on a clear innovation strategy. The company must capitalise on its areas of core competence – which it has evidenced by virtue of being positioned in this quadrant of the value portfolio. At the same time, attention must be given to defining a growth strategy. Only growing companies can remain successful in the long term (thanks to research and development, staff development etc.). In order to do business on a large scale, in particular, rapid growth is naturally required. Chapter 4 more closely examines the motivation for growth strategies and the tools that can be used: acquisitions, alliances, internal growth by means of capacity and personnel reductions etc. The third strategic measure for SBUs which fit in well with the corporate vision is the possibility of committing to new lines of business. Existing core competencies and skills must be developed and carried over to additional businesses to ensure that value creation is sustained.

'Stars' that do not fit the corporate vision

This designation can be given to strategic business units which, although they fully satisfy the requirement for shareholder value returns (i.e. although they create value), nevertheless do not clearly match up with the strategic objectives mapped out by the corporate vision. These lines may be 'non-core businesses', niche businesses, or whatever; either way, they are in all cases value-creating business units.

From a strategic point of view, these SBUs should be retained, but without further strategic investment. Careful attention must be given to how this is done, however: a careful eye should be kept on the risks arising from the poor fit. Alternative opportunities should be analysed in the light of the question whether it would not be more efficient to divest such units, and invest instead in the 'stars' that fit the corporate vision – thereby reallocating resources to growing business lines that harmonise with the corporate vision. For the purposes of strategic controlling, these lines are extremely important. No strategic investments should be made in these areas; funds should only be allocated in order to maintain their ability to generate adequate returns.

It is not possible to define strategic activities for these SBUs in terms that have any general validity. It would, however, be conceivable to adapt or modify corporate strategy as and when opportunities arise. In the case of business units whose value-driving prowess is significant enough to warrant changing corporate strategy in the interests of remaining attractive to the market, a growth strategy can and should be considered. The same applies for the expansion of niche suppliers.

If the decision is taken to stay with the existing corporate strategy, the company will benefit from positive value contributions for as long as possible and, should the cost of capital no longer be recouped, should then investigate withdrawal from this line. Financial commitments should be limited to investing in replacement.

'Dogs' that fit the corporate vision

These business units destroy value because:

- their free cash flows are inadequate for reasons such as too thin margins (price pressure, competition, costs), too little sales growth (products, technology etc.) or the fact that cash flows are not sustained;
- investment has been inappropriate or excessive (surplus plant capacity, inventories etc.); and
- their cost of capital is too high.

The strategic recommendation reads: optimise or run down. Since the line in question fits in well with the company's strategic orientation, the question of who is the 'best owner' can be ignored for the time being. For now, the company must effect a strategic reorientation and/or restructure operations in an attempt to cover the cost of capital and ensure that value can once again be created and sustained.

A strategic reorientation at the level of the SBU can be implemented by means of new product/marketing strategies (targeting market leadership), by repositioning business units, possibly by developing growth strategies (where there are reasonable prospects for a positive contribution to the value of the company), or by actions designed to achieve critical mass. Money is to be invested in these business units only if such investment will yield returns that are above the cost of capital and which can therefore transform entire lines into value creators. If none of these measures work, preparations should be made for selective withdrawal.

Operative value creation concepts that can be applied for such lines are dealt with in the following chapter.

'Dogs' that do not fit the corporate vision

The fact that an SBU is positioned in this quadrant of the value portfolio indicates that it neither aligns with the strategy of the company, nor does it contribute to the creation of value. In other words, these businesses do not fit in with the portfolio and are actually destroying value. In such cases, the principles of value management must take effect: resources are only to be invested in those commitments that produce a positive shareholder value return. In the interests of the core business strategy, such commitments are to be divested.[10] The strategic imperative here is thus abundantly clear. Selling them is merely an acknowledgment of the realisation that some other owner can and will be able to create more value out of such business lines than the existing owner.

Priorities need to be defined for the strategic options outlined above for the various units. It is not possible to define a generic order. Nevertheless, it is a matter of urgent importance always to begin by adjusting/restructuring the portfolio such that value destroyers which do not fit in with corporate strategy are sold off. Apart from the obvious benefit of eliminating value-destroying business units, the sale of these units will ultimately also be necessary to lay a solid financial foundation for successful growth strategies. Strategic restructuring can then be followed by the expansion of core businesses on the basis of growth concepts and the establishment of new commitments.

Implementing operative value creation programs

Operative value creation programs should focus particularly on improving the 'dogs' in the value portfolio, but should not neglect those SBUs in which greater value could be created by increasing efficiency. As far as those 'dogs' that harmonise with corporate strategy are concerned, it is only natural and reasonable to consider the likely payback from a restructuring program: does the added value that is likely to be created by performance improvements justify the investment that will be necessary to achieve these improvements? Rappaport's shareholder value network (see above) illustrates the relationships between value drivers and their influence on shareholder value (see Fig. 3.17 earlier in this chapter).

Whereas portfolio issues require strategic structural decisions for the SBUs, the need to increase value on an operative level tends rather to centre around the tools to be deployed in day-to-day business. Three questions are crucial to the efficient design and implementation of operative value creation programs:

- What should an operative value creation program do?
- How should it be done?
- What factors of success must be considered when performing these activities?

Let us start by answering the first question. Essentially, the answer to the 'what' question is simple: get cash flow up and the cost of capital down! Since there is any number of operative action catalogues, and since the problems faced by a given company can be very involved, we advise people to take a pragmatic approach when selecting and defining alternative operative concepts. Figure 3.20 summarises these alternatives, citing examples.

---

[10] For details of the core business strategies applied as part of a strategic reorientation and calculations for the 'best owner' method, see Bühner (1990), pp. 96 ff.

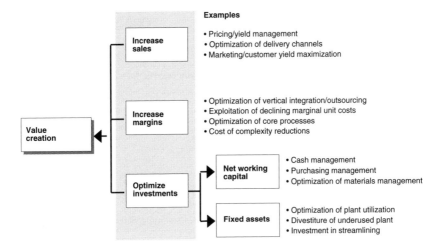

Figure 3.20: Approaches to operative value creation.

Increase revenues

While restructuring and downsizing programs mostly home in on the cost lever, the aim of systematic sales and marketing activation is to generate new sales revenues, in order:

- to raise and sustain the cash flow basis;
- to increase market share by means of higher volumes;
- to achieve economies of scale in the form of degressive fixed cost ratios and, on the procurement side, the ability to exploit new potential.

When seeking to increase operative revenues, the primary issue is to take the assortments, products, technologies and services defined by strategic decisions and position them on the market in such a way that ambitious sales, results and cash flow targets are met.

Sales activation is a topic for which each company has to draw up its own concrete plans of action. A selection of some of the tools and methods that can be applied is listed in Fig. 3.21.

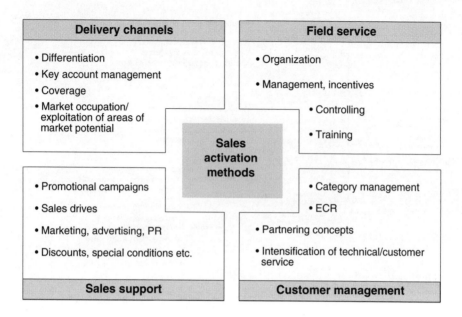

Figure 3.21: Methods of sales activation.

Increase margins

Operative value creation programs to improve margins aim to identify and realise sustained improvements in efficiency that allow potential reserves of value to be tapped. In our experience, four key issues determine which method is to be adopted:

- How does the business system fit in with the existing value creation chain and division of labour? The interfaces between individual function areas must be analysed and overhead cost drivers identified.
- Do functions or core processes exist whose deployment of resources/performance ratios is unsatisfactory? Cost benefits should be achieved by defining the scope of performance without detracting from the benefit to the customer or diminishing convenience (beware the cost of complexity!).
- Can efficiency be enhanced by modifying the procedural organisation? Core processes need to be (re)oriented consistently (in terms of time, costs, interfaces etc.) and coordination functions distributed more efficiently.
- Does the existing structural organisation represent a competitive way of handling core processes? Hierarchies are to be made 'leaner' by the consistent delegation of responsibility, while the division of labour between centralised and distributed functions is to be optimised.

Merely conducting a function-specific analysis of overhead costs is not enough. What is needed is a more discriminating methodological approach which taps process-related cost-cutting potential by means of re-engineering and uses function- and task-specific procedures to streamline the function side. Whether or not effectiveness and efficiency can be sustainably improved hinges on the need to simultaneously optimise the procedural and structural organisations in place across the whole of the company. Figure 3.22 suggests one suitable approach.

To quantify the effects of value creation programs, we would refer readers to the works of Porter and Rappaport. Porter uses the corporate value chain to present the margin targeted by the operative improvement.[11] Building on this approach, Rappaport then establishes a link between the operative value drivers in the elements of this value chain and both the corresponding cost types and the change in net working and fixed capital. To take an example of operative activities:[12]

- Operating costs derive from manufacture, assembly, testing and packaging.
- The increase in net working capital derives from changes in creditors and semimanufacture inventories.
- The increase in fixed capital derives from changes to production facility equipment.

These are the mechanisms that operative measures seek to fine-tune. And this activity must be accompanied by measures to optimise the value creation depth with a view to suitably realigning the business system in the wake of a rigorous task/performance analysis. The euphoria that initially greeted the advent of outsourcing activities has subsided somewhat. To arrive at the right conclusions in a 'make or buy' decision scenario, a catalogue of questions must be worked through to define the required program of performance. Figure 3.23 submits a proposal for this 'make or buy' analysis.

---

[11] Porter (1989), pp. 62 ff.

[12] Rappaport (1986), p. 67.

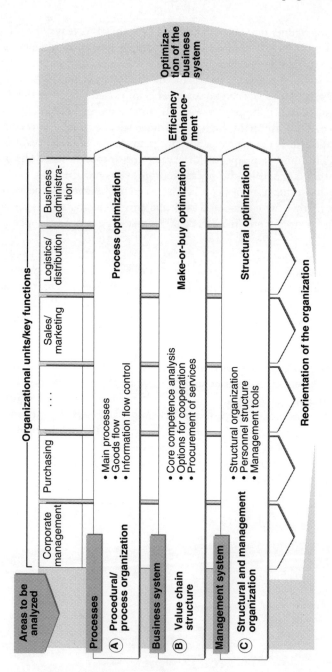

Figure 3.22: Operative efficiency enhancement based on an integrative approach.

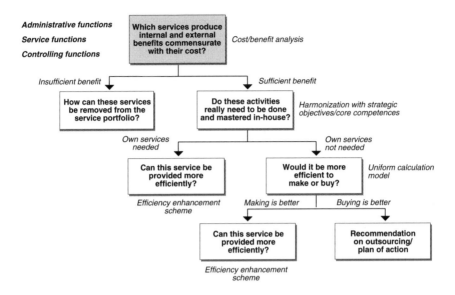

Figure 3.23: Decision tree for performance assessment.

In addition to this across-the-board approach to improving margins, there are any number of individual operative activities to be dealt with in efforts to better margins and implement restructuring. A few possible points of departure are listed below:

- reducing the cost of complexity by adjusting assortments and/or customer portfolios;
- running down inventories, receivables, payables etc. to bring about financial restructuring; and
- reducing materials, personnel, logistics and other costs to improve earnings.

Optimise investments

The aim here is to optimise cash flow by means of a carefully orchestrated asset management program. Investment must be steered in such a way:

- that it adds value – i.e. it generates cash – and is not left fallow;
- that the resultant plant dimensions do not cause excess capacity leading to ruinous price wars;
- that investments in goods inventories are planned and implemented in a way that avoids cash outflows for surplus inventories; and
- that liquid funds as a proportion of working capital (cash, receivables etc.) are kept to a minimum thanks to efficient treasury management.

Fixed and net working capital – plant, technical facilities, operating and business equipment, logistical facilities, unfinished, half-finished and finished goods, spare parts, receivables, cash etc. – are thus the 'knobs' that need to be tweaked by operative value creation measures (cf. Fig. 3.24).

Packages of operative measures can have either a proactive or a reactive focus. In a prophylactic context the tools of value-based investment controlling come into play. Purchasing and materials management are optimised and a cash/treasury management unit is set up. To optimise the 'dogs' in the value portfolio, it is necessary to examine and apply the reactive options, since the damage has already been done.

	"Reactive measures"	"Proactive measures"
Property, plant and equipment	• Sale and lease back • Investment moratorium • Divestment of non-essential assets	Value-based investment planning and decisions
Financial investments	• Sale • Holding reduction	
Inventory/ stocks	• Special sales and stock depletion • Returns to suppliers • Changes to scheduling parameters • Changes to supplier relationships (JIT, consignment warehouses etc.)	Purchasing/materials management
Receivables/ cash	• Factoring • Reduction of overdue receivables • More intensive dunning • Changes to payment terms	Cash/treasury management

Figure 3.24: Optimising investments.

Shifting investment planning and decision-making procedures onto a value management basis ensures that investments are approved only if they satisfy the stipulated yield requirements. DCF arithmetic is used to 'vet' them; and clearly defined rules make up the approval process. Furthermore, investments must also be subject to stringent *ex post* controls. The introduction of value-based management concepts must lead to a change in investment procedures – a subject we examine in greater depth in Chapter 3.3.

Operative measures in the area of purchasing and materials management begin with the key value drivers for numerous industries. In the paper industry, for example, the funds tied up in operating assets account for around 50% of total assets. The comparable figure in mechanical engineering and textiles is around 40%, and in the automotive industry around 30%. As far as purchasing management is concerned, the starting points from which investments can be optimised, and thus make a contribution to value creation, can be issues such as price negotiations, pooling, global sourcing, supplier integration and so on. Materials management requires close scrutiny of just-in-time inventories, efficient planning and controlling procedures and precise directives for target materials management metrics. Figure 3.25 gives an example of what concrete measures might be taken in the area of inventory management.

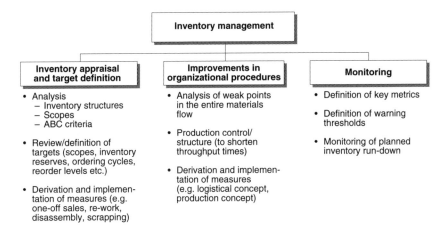

Figure 3.25: Example of concrete measures for inventory management.

Within the framework of liquidity and profitability controlling, cash management systems help to cushion interest and exchange rate risks and optimise near-money investments:

- Receivables and payables at corporate level are offset; internal cash flows are reduced so that the ensuing transaction costs no longer exist.
- Interest charges are lowered by transactions to and from company-internal bank accounts.
- Financial surpluses can be invested and financing requirements covered in such a way as to optimise interest levels, thanks to transparency about the financial position of the company.

Factors of success for design and implementation

When it comes to the design and implementation of operative value creation measures, the question of the factors of success that govern such activities still remains:

- Priority is to be given to the most powerful value drivers.
- Analyses are to be conducted with the necessary pragmatism.
- Ambitious goals are to be set early on.
- Work is to be done in teams.
- Measures taken are to be monitored and successes communicated.

Gaining the right focus is essential to operative value creation programs. If all operative levers are to be worked at once, one can very quickly become over-stretched. On the basis of the individual value drivers identified for the company, operative projects can instead be varied using exactly the right levers.

Analyses which stand up under close scrutiny lay a foundation on which operative value creation measures can be drafted and moulded. However, it is important to proceed pragmatically at this stage and not to get mired in too much detail. The objectives must be clear: to focus on innovation and, above all, to work in a way that can be measured and quantified.

To produce positive results fast, targets for improvement should also be formulated at an early stage. The classical three-stage procedure – draw up measures, quantify effects, implement measures – should be compressed into two steps: agree objectives, identify and implement measures. Doing so commits everyone involved to common goals right from the outset and prevents them from running aground in the sands of detailed analyses of what impact which measures will have on the realisation of defined goals.

Work should be leveraged by teams. Wherever possible, teamwork should be carried over into corporate divisions. And it is of paramount importance to have the right mix of skills, entrepreneurial qualities, promoters and responsibilities represented on each team.

Also of crucial significance is that all activities should converge in a single measures management tool. This is necessary to maintain transparency and a systematic approach across such a multi-faceted project. At the same time, such a tool will enable value creation to be measured and the results communicated accordingly. Figure 3.26 provides an outline of what a measures management tool contains.

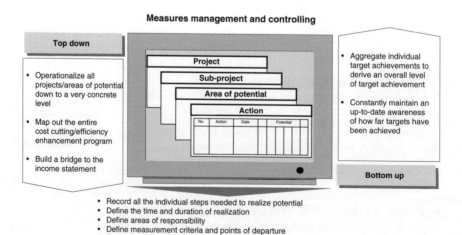

Figure 3.26: Measures management and controlling.

Financial engineering

We understand financial engineering as the set of activities and variables used by a company to control its sources of finance in order:

- to keep a cap on the cost of capital;
- to be able to finance growth; and
- to limit risks or ensure that they remain in a balanced relationship to earnings.

Having concentrated predominantly on measures relating to assets in the context of operative value creation, let us now shift our focus to the potential that derives from liabilities management. Since there is already no lack of reference works on the subject of financing, we will restrict ourselves here essentially to a few key aspects. Figure 3.27 sums up the various forms of financing that can influence the structure and cost of capital. Equity and debt financing measures can be used to influence the cost of shareholder capital and borrowed capital respectively. The ratio of external to internal funding is what determines the capital structure.

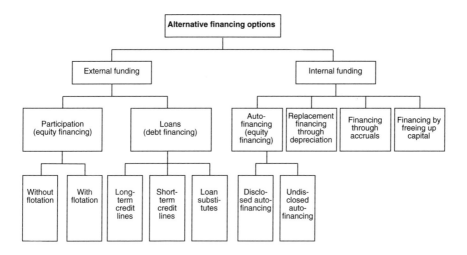

Figure 3.27: Types of financing.[13]

Minimise the cost of capital

This section deals with three points which correspond to the three key factors influencing the weighted average cost of capital (WACC) calculation:

---

[13] Perridon/Steiner (1995), p. 322.

- To what extent can optimising the capital structure keep the cost of capital down to a minimum?
- How can the cost of shareholder capital be reduced independently of the capital structure?
- How can the cost of borrowed capital be reduced independently of the capital structure?

Altering the capital structure

To begin with, we need to ask whether it is at all possible to influence the cost of capital by means of changes to the capital structure. In their basic model, which excludes taxes and other market imperfections (transaction costs, barriers to information etc.), Nobel prize-winners Modigliani and Miller (hereafter abbreviated to 'MM') refute the claim outright.[14] Their model proves that the average cost of capital and the value of the company depend on the company's degree of indebtedness. The returns demanded by shareholders grow in linear correlation to the degree of indebtedness, with the result that the weighted cost of capital remains a constant.

Needless to say, our financial markets do not match the criteria used in MM's basic model. Notwithstanding, we still believe this to be the best model currently available for evaluating the influence of the capital structure on the cost of capital and on company value. Two additions suffice to provide sufficient realism: provision for tax breaks on the use of debt capital; and the 'cost of financial distress' where debt becomes excessive.[15]

Figure 3.28 shows that the tax breaks on debt capital produce a higher value than when a company is financed entirely by equity capital. The 'cost of financial distress', i.e. the cost arising from the risk of insolvency, has the opposite effect to the tax breaks: higher interest is charged on borrowed funds, for example, while the company's credit rating is worse. Based on this logic, it is indeed possible to come up with an ideal capital structure for a company – a structure which, given certain cash flows, will maximise company value and minimise the average cost of capital.

The ideal capital structure can be pinpointed precisely by means of a spreadsheeting exercise: the weighted average cost of capital is calculated using the formula described in Chapter 3.1, and is then recalculated for different levels of debt until the optimised level is located. During this exercise, the following points should be borne in mind:

- The beta factor rises as debt increases, owing to the greater financial risk/risk of insolvency.

---

[14] Brealey/Myers (1996), pp. 449 ff.
[15] Brealey/Myers (1996), pp. 474 ff.

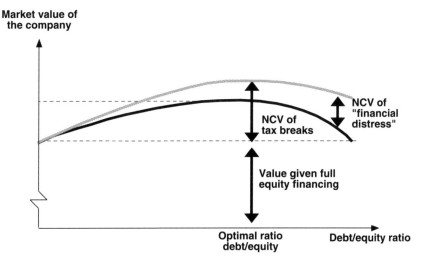

Figure 3.28: Optimised degree of indebtedness.[16]

- The tax breaks afforded by borrowed funds are quantified using the tax correction factor.[17]
- The 'cost of financial distress' must be expressed in the form of higher interest on debt as more and more debt is incurred.

Reducing the cost of equity capital

A look at the calculation components for the cost of equity capital in Chapter 3.1 reveals that the only 'knob' the company can tweak here is the beta factor. Since the beta factor measures share price fluctuations relative to a share index, the company can only exercise an indirect influence on this factor by seeking to keep business risk within limits through a consistent policy of risk management. Risk management could, for instance, involve engagements in futures or currency futures contracts, foreign exchange options, currency swaps etc. to hedge currency risks, or limit the risk of changes in interest rates by means of forward trade agreements, interest rate options, futures or swaps, interest limitation agreements or the use of similar instruments.

Portfolio decisions whose sole ambition is to reduce the beta factor are to be advised against, since even lines of business with high beta factors can still contribute value to the company. Microsoft Corporation is a fine example: despite a high beta factor of around 1.5, the Redmond-based software company has unquestionably created substantial value in recent years.

---

[16] Brealey/Myers (1996), p. 485.
[17] See 'Taking account of tax effects' in Chapter 3.1.

All in all, the purpose of all the value management measures outlined in this book is to cause share prices to rise. Especially in times when stock prices and share indexes are falling, they can significantly reduce the beta factor. Successful value management increases shareholder satisfaction and improves the view taken by analysts and banks, thereby making it easier to obtain share capital. Choosing the right timing and the right conditions is a decisive factor in capital increases, since these factors will together determine how much funding flows into the company per share issued.

Reducing the cost of debt capital

Given a suitable mix of the various forms of borrowed funding, the cost of debt capital can also have an impact on the company. Essentially, distinctions can be drawn between four categories of debt:[18]

*   *Long-term credit lines* such as debentures, loans against borrower's notes, long-term bank loans, shareholder loans, participation certificates;
*   *Short-term credit lines* such as business loans, borrowing on current account, discount credit, loans against securities or commodities, commercial papers and medium-term notes;
*   *Innovative bond forms* such as zero bonds, floating rate notes, dual currency bonds, bonds linked to swaps;
*   *Loan substitutes* such as factoring, asset-backed securities, leasing.

From all these different forms of credit, a company will have to work out the precise mix that will minimise the average cost of debt. In this context, it is important to choose not only the right instrument, but also the right place, currency and time. For example, a Eurobond denominated in Australian dollars and linked to an interest rate/currency swap might provide a very attractive set of conditions for the issuer.

Dividend policy

Since dividend policy is also a means of influencing the capital structure, it is worthwhile briefly referring back to the subject at this point. Chapter 2.4 exhaustively stated the case that a company is acting in the interests of its shareholders if it distributes the residual dividend, i.e. surplus funds that are not required to finance value-creating projects. The amount available for distribution is, however, restricted by the amount that can be appropriated from net income under German law. The dividend may not exceed the surplus of earnings for a reporting period divided by expenditures for the same period, less any losses carried

---

[18] Perridon/Steiner (1995), pp. 352 ff.

forward that need to be amortised and allocations to statutory reserves (where appropriate).[19]

The option of using the dividend to influence the capital structure to a limited extent is consistent with the residual dividend approach. The company should distribute that part of net income that is left over after financing has been secured for value-creating projects and the optimised capital structure has been preserved. If, for example, a company is planning sizeable investments that will lead to additional borrowed funding and increase the degree of indebtedness, it would be better to retain profits in order to preserve the ideal capital structure. The extent to which dividend policy can influence the structure of capital is, of course, limited. Where capital requirements are high and the proportion of profits available for distribution is relatively low, it will be necessary to subscribe additional share capital.

Current corporate practice in Europe still largely favours dividend continuity. Given this tradition, calls for a residual dividend policy will initially meet with scepticism and resistance – despite the fact that other 'practitioners' have in the meantime added their voice to the cause.[20] In light of this, we would recommend that the new dividend policy be introduced in gradual stages. The first step is to use the investor relations channel to inform people of the advantages of the new policy. Once the key analysts have been convinced, dividend policy can be adjusted. At the same time, more open communication about results and value development within the framework of investor relations effectively blunts the arguments brandished by adherents of the signal effect of dividends. Open information is a better means of communication than the dividend amount.

---

[19] For more details, see Drukarczyk (1993), pp. 421 ff.

[20] e.g. a partner of Stern Stewart & Co.; cf. Stewart (1990a), pp. 16 ff.

3. 3 Extending management and controlling systems

As explained in Chapter 2.4, a large number of companies are managed on the basis of the wrong metrics. This section is intended as a guideline to show how existing management and controlling systems can be redesigned and/or extended to cater to value management requirements.

If this is to be done, a uniform system of planning and measuring business success, which makes the creation and destruction of value transparent, must first be established throughout the company. It is essential that this system apply the innovative principles of value management:

- a forward-looking approach based on future cash flows;
- a focus on cash flows rather than numbers in the income statement;
- a dynamic view which takes account of the time value of money; and
- risk-adjusted cost of capital rates which make provision for the varying levels of risk faced by different business units.

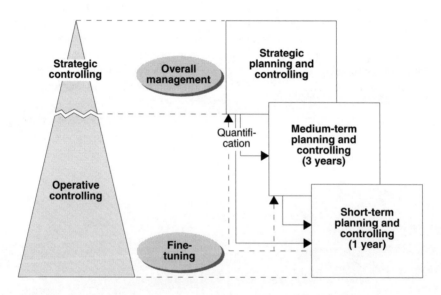

Figure 3.29: Outline of a management and controlling system.

In addition, the management and controlling processes (the contents, process steps, people responsible, time frames, and system support) must be defined unambiguously. The contents should consist of clearly defined management variables that can serve as the basis for a value-based compensation system. Reporting should, after all, be recipient-oriented: the data reported – including the value metrics – should tell the addressees what they need to know.

Figure 3.29 offers an insight into a traditional 'total system' for the planning, management and controlling of company activities. The system comprises the key elements of strategic and operative management and controlling. The corporate vision and strategic corporate objectives are defined on the strategic level; different but related strategies are defined for the business units and for the company as a whole. On the operative level, short- and medium-term targets, plans of action, and budgets for operative business are drawn up. Despite the use of different management parameters, strategic and operative planning must be closely interwoven. The controlling function should regularly monitor target compliance on all levels. The form the overall system takes will depend largely on the goals of corporate management. Where a group has a strategic holding company which manages affiliated companies and participations, operative control will be less intense than in cases where operative management is anchored at business unit level. For our purposes here, let us assume a system in which all components are fully represented.

Within the framework of value management, one aspect of the contents of the management and controlling system is of crucial significance: investment planning and controlling. It is here where resource allocation is decided and, hence, where value creation is determined. We have therefore felt it expedient to split this chapter into three separate sections: one on strategic planning and controlling; one on operative planning and controlling; and one on investment planning and controlling.

Strategic planning and controlling

Value management demands a fundamental reorientation of strategic planning. As explained in Chapter 2.4, European companies tend to base their strategic planning on the traditional metrics of market share, competitive position, sales growth and results. In a value management context, increasing the value of the company and its business units becomes the single most important metric. The other traditional indicators are demoted to second rank. They are only used as goals if achieving them contributes to value creation. This is best explained by taking sales growth as an example. According to the value management philosophy, sales growth of, say, 10% p.a. is not suitable as a primary strategic goal:

- either because corporate value could still be destroyed despite this high figure, i.e. the investment needed to fuel this growth would not bring in sufficient returns to cover the cost of capital
- or because 10% p.a. may be too little if value creation based on a higher, alternative sales target appears realistic.

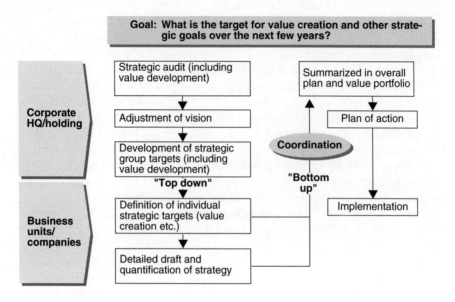

Figure 3.30: Strategic planning process.

In multi-business companies, the strategic planning process is generally a mixture of 'top-down' directives from central management and 'bottom-up' independent plans submitted by the decentralised units and then coordinated at corporate headquarters. In this process, value management leads to four major new developments, each of which is explained below.

1   At the corporate level, value development during the previous reporting period is analysed in a strategic audit.
2   Targets for value development are formulated by corporate headquarters and stipulated for the business units.
3   Once the details have been fleshed out, each strategy is quantified by the business units and the likelihood of targets being met is examined with respect to corporate value.
4   While it is coordinating the individual strategic plans, corporate headquarters also defines a new value portfolio.

Analysing value development

The following metrics should be included in the audit:

•   the development in market value (assuming the company is listed on the stock exchange) and in market value as a proportion of the industry's market capitalisation;

- the shareholder value added that the company and its business units earned in the previous reporting period; and
- the shareholder value return, i.e. the internal rate of return (IRR) on capital employed and free cash flows.

It is usually not difficult for stock corporations to determine the first figure. If parts of the share block are not being publicly traded, it will be necessary to work with approximations. For example, unlisted ordinary shares can be assigned a value based on the value of preferred stock and the customary market premium of around 20%. For companies whose activities are concentrated largely in a single industry, it can be very interesting to determine the company's market value, or market capitalisation, as a proportion of the market capitalisation of the industry as a whole. This figure is calculated by dividing the company's own market capitalisation by that of, say, the ten biggest companies in the industry. A comparison extending over several years will then reveal whether the company has created more value for its shareholders than other players in the industry.

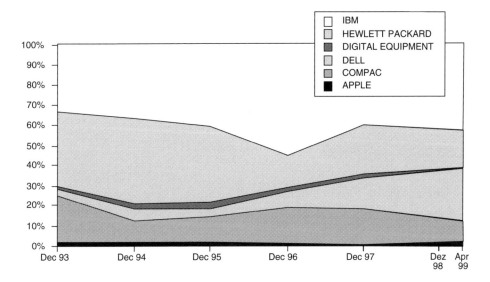

Figure 3.31: Market capitalisation as a proportion of industry market capitalisation – example.

Shareholder value added is calculated by the *ex post* insertion of actual values into cash flow planning for the previous forecast period. At the end of a year, planned cash flow for year 1 of the original planning exercise is thus replaced by the cash flow actually realised. At the same time, changes in the capital structure and the cost of capital must also be examined. Based on these new figures, realised shareholder value is calculated for the first year after the last planning exercise. The difference between this value and the value calculated originally is what we call shareholder value added. The figure that results answers the question: by how much did shareholder value change over the past year? It takes no account of changes in value arising from alterations made to planning in subsequent years, and there are two reasons for that. One is that this would necessitate a completely new planning cycle which, for the audit, would involve too much work and need only be done later. The other is that certain business units would probably try to compensate for value losses in the year just ended by submitting more ambitious plans for the year ahead, in order to avoid being 'found out' as value destroyers. New insights for subsequent years are thus only incorporated in new plans.

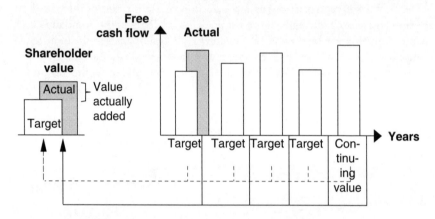

Figure 3.32: Model for calculating shareholder value added.

The calculation for the internal rate of return is related to that for shareholder value added. Here again, the cash flow realised in year 1 and the actual amount of capital deployed are included *ex post* in the calculation. The other cash flows remain unchanged for the reasons cited above.

These three figures enable the strategic planning process to identify what needs to be done based on the company's value development record. A comparison of market capitalisation and calculated shareholder value for the entire company (including value added) can be used to assess whether the company is currently undervalued or overvalued on the market. In addition, shareholder value added and the internal rate of return for each business unit can furnish information on the degree to which plans were realised and how realistic planning targets actually are.

Formulating value development targets

Based on the insights gained from the strategic audit, corporate management can then formulate its strategic goals. As explained above, the focus here is on value targets, whose orientation should be derived from the share price, calculated shareholder value and the shareholder value return.

Sweeping statements along the lines of 'We will increase our market value by 15%' are rather pointless, given that share prices are susceptible to pronounced fluctuations. For this reason, it is advisable to link targets to share indexes. In the case of diversified corporations, the DJ Euro Stoxx or their national index (FTSE 100, DAX, CAC40, etc.) should be defined as the standard of measurement. Hence the following statement might reasonably be made: 'Our share price should increase by 2% more than the DJ Euro Stoxx'. Stock corporations with a single core business area are recommended to measure themselves against a sector-specific index. A retail company, for instance, could formulate the following target: 'Our share price should increase by 1% more than the DJ Stoxx Retail index'. Above all, the increase targeted should be based on the ratio of market capitalisation to calculated shareholder value. Companies that are undervalued should therefore set higher targets.

Targets that relate to calculated shareholder value are based on increases compared to the value calculated for the last planning cycle. Since this latter value will, as a rule, already have been based on ambitious goals for future cash flow improvements, care should be taken to avoid setting value creation targets that are too high. Demands for double-digit growth lead only to unrealistic planning data. Moreover, targets should be allowed to vary for the different business units, giving due consideration to the respective situation and outlook for each one.

Targets for shareholder value returns, i.e. for the internal rate of return (IRR) on future free cash flows and capital deployed, should be based on the weighted average cost of capital. In accordance with what we said in Chapter 3.1, the minimum target for the company and for each business unit or line of business should be an IRR that exceeds the weighted average cost of capital. Given that shareholder value calculated on the basis of the discounted cash flow approach by and large comprises the same calculation components (cash flows, cost of capital), the mathematics of the IRR targets must be consonant with shareholder value targets.

Quantifying a strategy

Based on the targets prescribed by corporate management, the individual business units draw up their own strategic plans following the procedure illustrated in Fig. 3.33. The procedure shown here differs from the planning process traditionally used at this level in three key points:

- Value creation remains of central importance to the individual strategic goals, too. The business unit managers use the results of the audit to calculate the extent to which the target value can be met; they then define second-level targets that are based on the individual value drivers for the industry. Examples could include a 3% price hike given a constant sales volume, or a 1% reduction in materials purchasing costs.

- The strategy is quantified in detail, i.e. it is underpinned by cash flow planning. This is the only way to verify whether value creation targets have actually been met. In this way, it is also possible to compare alternative strategy options and select the best of the bunch.
- The portfolio analysis involves not only the classical market attractiveness/competitive position portfolio but also the value portfolio. Numerous variants are discussed in the section below.

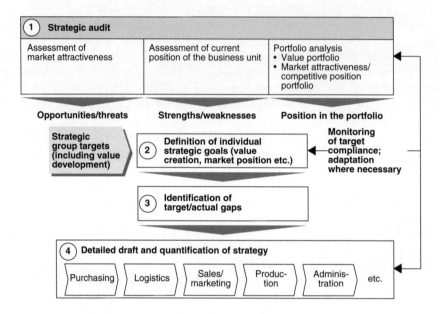

Figure 3.33: Strategic planning at business unit level.

Defining the value portfolio

In the strategic planning process, each business unit determines its own position in the value portfolio. When its turn comes to harmonise the individual strategies, corporate headquarters then gains an overview of the overall value portfolio for the company. Consequences are then drawn with regard to investment in the individual units. The portfolio we recommend using for this exercise is explained in detail in Chapter 3.2. The vertical axis provides information about whether value is being created or destroyed; the horizontal axis indicates whether a unit fits in with corporate vision. As a result, management should have a clear idea of which units to invest in, and which to restructure or possibly even sell off.

A number of other models that can also be used within the framework of portfolio analysis are discussed briefly below.

The Marakon profitability matrix[1]

The vertical axis of this matrix indicates what is referred to as the 'equity spread'. This is the difference between the return on equity (ROE) and the cost of the company's or business unit's equity. The horizontal axis reflects sales growth relative to market growth. The diagonal line is the cash investment ratio (CIR = 1)[2] at which returns from the business to the shareholders are equivalent to the investment needed for growth. The underlying logic can be explained by assuming a constant capital structure in which growth can be achieved only by investing proportionally more equity, i.e. by reducing free cash flow.

The matrix allows conclusions to be drawn concerning the individual business units. All business units to the left of the diagonal line are earning positive free cash flows; those above the cost of equity capital are creating value for the company. Business unit X is positioned here and is growing at a rate faster than that of the market. This is, therefore, the ideal position to be in. Current growth and return on equity in this business unit should be maintained. Units positioned to the left of business unit X – i.e. units that are growing more slowly than the market – are similarly very attractive from the point of view of earnings and cash flow. The question, however, is whether this position can be sustained long term in view of their shrinking market share, and whether further investments should be made to boost growth.

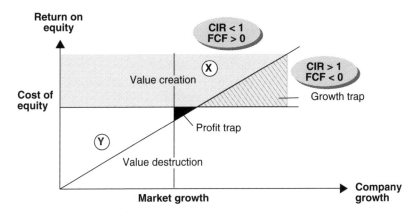

Figure 3.34: The Marakon profitability matrix.

Business unit Y, in the box at bottom left, is attractive neither from the point of view of the return on equity nor in terms of growth. It would be advisable to either restructure the unit or sell it. The same goes for business units in the little

---

[1] Marakon Associates (1981), p. 6.
[2] CIR = investment in equity/net income.

black triangle labelled 'profit trap', which, despite positive free cash flows, are not earning enough to cover their cost of capital. The situation is different for business units caught in the 'growth trap'. They are recouping their cost of capital, but are growing so fast that additional capital is having to be invested constantly. The mid- to long-term goal here has to be to reduce investments in order to move up to a position above the diagonal line.

There are other variants of the Marakon profitability matrix that are not dealt with here. All of them, however, have three inherent weaknesses which significantly impair their usefulness and any conclusions that might be derived:

- The matrices cannot be applied to business units that are shrinking.
- One of the components of the equity spread ratio is the classical, static return on equity figure derived from accounting data; the ratio therefore does not satisfy the requirements of value management.
- The assumption of a constant capital structure in order to define the diagonal line does not always accord with reality.

Consequently, we recommend that the Marakon profitability matrix be used, if so desired, at best as a supplement to the value portfolio we referred to at the start of this discussion. The growth view, which is lacking, should be handled in a separate, traditional portfolio – which, in any case, belongs in the context of strategic planning.

Value added portfolio

This portfolio from the Boston Consulting Group depicts the cash flow return on investment (CFROI) on the vertical axis. CFROI is defined as the gross cash flow earned by a business relative to capital employed.[3] The figure is calculated as the internal rate of return, which has four constituent elements:

- the gross assets as an initial outflow (replacement value of fixed assets plus net working capital and capitalised rental expenses less goodwill);
- gross cash flow (constant annual cash flow before taxes and rental expenses);
- the economic life of fixed assets (time taken to earn gross cash flows); and
- non-depreciating assets (residual asset value after expiry of its economic life).

Like the Marakon profitability matrix, the horizontal axis of the value added portfolio represents the growth of the business relative to the rate of growth of the industry as a whole. The most attractive place to be in this portfolio is in the box at the top right, where CFROI exceeds the total cost of capital and growth is above average. Different actions should be taken for units positioned in different parts of the portfolio.

---

[3] Lewis (1994), p. 40.

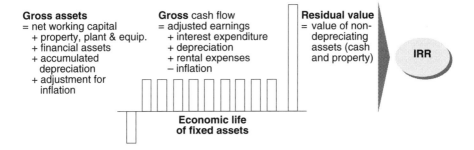

Figure 3.35: CFROI calculation.[4]

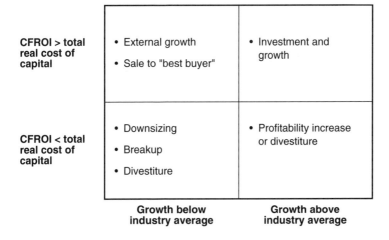

Figure 3.36: Boston Consulting Group's value added portfolio.[5]

Since CFROI is the pivotal point of the value added portfolio, it is this ratio which determines the advantages and drawbacks thereof. Unlike the static ROI figure used in the Marakon profitability matrix, the performance indicator used here does satisfy the demands of value management. CFROI is also easier to calculate than the shareholder value return, which can be determined only with the aid of a full-blown cash flow planning exercise. However, the approach has the drawback of assuming constant cash flows. This is why, in practice, fluctuating planned cash flows are being used more and more widely.

The residual value is defined only by non-depreciating assets, although, in our opinion, the use of the perpetuity method would come closer to determining

---

[4] Lewis (1994), pp. 40 ff.
[5] Lewis (1994), pp. 78 ff.

the value of business that is still in progress. Non-capitalised assets (e.g. relationships with customers, image etc.) are ignored as the calculation only involves balance sheet figures. A historical book value is used instead of the cash value for property, plant and equipment. CFROI is thus less incisive as an analysis tool than the shareholder value return indicator.

Value creation/cash flow portfolio[6]

The value creation/cash flow portfolio maps Economic Value Added (EVA) on the vertical axis. This metric is calculated for a period *t* as follows:[7]

$$EVA_t = OP_t - TCO_t \times WACC_t$$

where:

OP_t　　is the operating profit, after taxes/depreciation in period t
TCO_t　is total capital outstanding in period t
$WACC_t$ is the weighted average cost of capital for the period t.

Economic Value Added is an indicator devised by the American consulting firm Stern Stewart. It measures whether a business unit has earned its cost of capital, i.e. whether it has created value, during the previous reporting period.

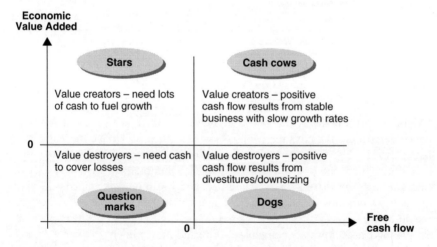

Figure 3.37: Höfner & Partner's value creation/cash flow portfolio.

---

[6] Höfner/Pohl (1994), p. 59.
[7] Stewart (1990b), pp. 118 ff.

The horizontal axis of the portfolio charts free cash flow. For each business unit, a circle is drawn whose diameter is proportional to the amount of capital invested in it. The four boxes in the portfolio assign business units to the classical categories 'stars', 'cash cows' etc. The box to aim for is at the top right.

Those business units with negative EVA need to be pushed upward in the portfolio by boosting operative cash flow (e.g. by means of cost cutting programs) or by reducing the amount of capital employed and the cost of capital. Divestiture is an option that may need to be considered for the 'dogs'. In our view, the recommendations for action that can be derived from this model are less clear than those produced by the other models outlined above. The reason is that, in this portfolio, both axes map value criteria in which operative cash flow is a significant component. As a result, the two indicators – EVA and free cash flow – are not mutually independent. It would have been better to use one of the axes to trace growth or strategic fit, as this would have added another independent and strategic component to the equation.

Other problems with this portfolio are rooted in the use of Economic Value Added. This metric is based on cash flow after depreciation; it thus contains an accounting measure. Furthermore, EVA involves a static, single-period observation with no reference to the future. In other words, EVA fails to meet two of the requirements value management places on controlling measures. One argument in favour of EVA is that it is easy to calculate. For this reason, we refer back to it in the section on 'Operative planning and controlling'.

Value creation matrix

The vertical axis of this matrix represents what is known as the final shareholder value return. This differs from the shareholder value return in that it is not calculated as an internal rate of return but as a kind of period-adjusted premium or discount on the value contribution and capital employed quotients relative to the total cost of capital:[8]

$$FSR = (1 + WACC) \cdot (VA/TCI)^{1/t} - 1$$

where:
FSR   is the final shareholder value return
VA   is the value added
TCI   is the total capital invested at the start
WACC is the weighted average cost of capital for total invested capital
t   is the forecast period in years.

---

[8] Reimann (1990), pp. 129 ff., Günther (1997), 366ff.

This yield formula assumes that the total capital employed at the start will, after *t* years, generate a final value whose cash value is value added to the company by the business unit:[9]

$$TCE \cdot (1 + FSR)^t = \text{final value} = VA(1 + WACC)^t$$

The calculation formula for the final shareholder value return can be derived from this formula by means of a mathematical transformation.

The ROI spread – the difference between the return on total investments and the weighted average cost of total capital – is shown on the horizontal axis. The assessments and recommendations for action applicable to the individual boxes are evident from the diagram.

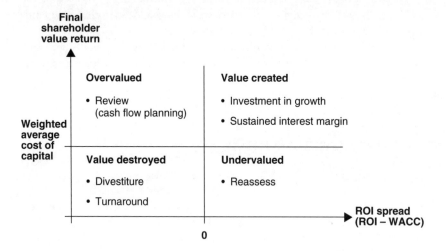

Figure 3.38: Value creation matrix.

Like the value creation/cash flow portfolio, the value creation matrix also maps two value criteria. One references the future and complies with value management requirements. The other, the ROI spread, is a static measure of current performance. This juxtaposition allows the information in the matrix to be used to draw conclusions about undervaluation and overvaluation and about the need to review cash flow planning. In our view, the statements made do not go far enough, however. A review of cash flow planning should be part of every planning process. Here again, therefore, the matrix would be more useful if a different criterion, such as growth or strategic fit, were plotted along the horizontal axis.

Having looked at four different value portfolios and matrices, it becomes clear that all of them have inherent drawbacks which appear to disqualify them

---

[9] Günther (1997), pp. 248 ff.

for use as the 'sole and exclusive' model. We therefore recommend that, at best, these portfolios/matrices be used to complement the value portfolio detailed in Chapter 3.2. The conclusions that can be drawn in the strategic planning process by using both our value portfolio and the classical market attractiveness/competitive position portfolio are of a superior quality. These conclusions can then, in turn, be used to formulate plans of action at corporate level and at the level of the business unit.

Operative planning and controlling

The operative planning process and operative controlling, like strategic planning, are also altered by the value management philosophy. The procedure that can be found in most companies remains unchanged, albeit the metrics and management variables used need to be adapted and/or complemented.

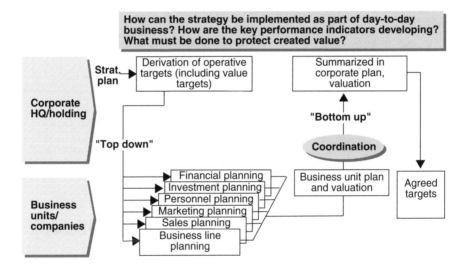

Figure 3.39: Operative planning process.

Many companies break their operative planning down into medium-term plans (around 3 years) and one-year plans. The procedure illustrated in the figure above is valid for either type of plan. Apart from having different durations, the two plans also differ in terms of level of detail and accuracy. The process plans and defines value metrics to be applied at various points. Operative targets therefore include value targets. Plans regarding the appropriate value drivers are added to the plans drawn up by the individual business units. The result of the entire process is to produce business plans at both corporate and business unit levels. The value-based metrics and management variables used in the process thus take on crucial significance.

Outline of the various value metrics

Right at the beginning of this section we would like to introduce a case example. Veba can safely be referred to as one of the pioneers of shareholder value management in continental Europe. Alongside business-specific and standard indicators, Veba uses two key metrics to determine value: CFROI and cash value added. We will compare the practical usefulness of these two metrics with that of other value metrics shortly. Before doing so, however, we would first like to provide an explanation of all the metrics and ratios that we have not yet defined (cf. the section on 'Strategic planning and controlling').

Business-specific indicators	Standard indicators	Value metrics
Presentation of typical operative control variables for parts of the company and strategic business units (reported monthly/ quarterly/ annually as appropriate)	Presentation of comparative results for parts of the company and strategic business units (SBUs, reported monthly)	Presentation of comparative value results for parts of the company and strategic business units (reported annually)

• Generation/purchase of electric power
 • Use of fuel to generate electricity
 • Price of chemical commodities
 • Manufacturing margin on petroleum
 • Retail stock turnover rate
 • ...
	• Sales
	 • Operating result
	 • Net interest income
	 • Operating income
	 • Non-operating result
	 • ...
		• **CFROI**
		 • **Cash value added (CVA)**
		 based on:
		    – Operating cash flow
		    – Gross investment base
		    – Net assets

Total: > 100	Total: < 10	Total: 2

Figure 3.40: Metrics used in Veba's planning and controlling processes.[10]

Cash value added (CVA)[11]

Cash value added is based on CFROI and identifies the increase in value earned on a cash flow basis over a period t:

$$CVA_t = (CFROI_t - \text{real cost of capital}_t) \cdot \text{gross assets}_{(t-1)}$$

---

[10] Veba AG (1996).
[11] Lewis (1994), pp. 125 ff.

The criticisms levelled at CFROI are therefore equally valid for this metric. Like Economic Value Added, CVA consequently indicates absolute value growth. At the same time, however, CVA reflects changes in the value of the company more precisely, for two reasons:

- Whereas EVA only looks at cash flow for a single year, the CFROI used to determine CVA includes several future periods in the calculation.
- The cash flow figure used to calculate EVA is determined after depreciation and therefore includes an accounting figure.

Market value added (MVA)

This metric is very similar to Economic Value Added and also originates from Stern & Stewart.[12] It is calculated as follows:

$$MVA_t = \text{total company value}_t - \text{capital outstanding},$$

MVA is, in effect, a variant of EVA that derives from a company's capitalised or market value. Accordingly, the total company value is defined as the market value of equity plus the book value of debt less marketable securities and plant under construction. Capital outstanding is calculated from total assets less non-interest-bearing short-term liabilities, marketable securities and plant under construction. This definition eliminates from the calculation those factors that do not belong to operative business. The cash value of rental and R&D expenses and cumulative depreciation is then added to capital outstanding.

Like EVA and CVA, MVA too calculates an absolute growth figure. Since market value is one of the components used in the formula, stock market price fluctuations have a considerable impact on MVA. As a result, this metric measures changes in shareholder value but not necessarily changes in the performance of a company.

Cash return on capital invested (CROCI)

The CROCI metric was devised by Deutsche Morgan Grenfell (DMG), an investment bank, and is explained here in lieu of a variety of similar ratios used by other investment banks. CROCI consists of the classical return on equity (ROE) corrected by five factors. These corrections substantially improve the indicator's correlation with market value. While the classical return on equity ratio has come in for heavy criticism and has a correlation coefficient of only 0.3 to 0.4, CROCI has a comparable coefficient of around 0.8.[13]

---

[12] Stewart (1990b), pp. 153 ff.
[13] Deutsche Morgan Grenfell (1997a), p. 1.

The following corrections are made to the calculation of return on equity:[14]

1   *Debt financing.* The classical figure for return on equity is replaced by the return on capital employed (ROCE), that is, pre-tax profits divided by total capital (of which equity is valued at current market rates).

2   *'Invisible' capital.* Three forms of 'invisible' capital are added to total capital. They are: a) depreciation on goodwill from an acquisition against reserves; b) the value of leased/movable property (leasing expenses are accordingly subtracted from cash flow); and c) non-capitalised intangible assets (such as the value of research and development projects). These corrections ensure that a realistic figure for tied capital is arrived at.

3   *Inflation.* The value of assets is adjusted for inflation in accordance with their average age and the rate of inflation. This adjustment corrects the fact that, otherwise, the numerator in the CROCI metric would contain a per-annum cash flow while the denominator would contain a stock variable. The average age of assets is estimated based on quotients made up of cumulative depreciation, corrected to account for growth effects, and current depreciation.[15]

4   *Depreciation.* Accounting values for depreciation are replaced here by depreciation figures that reflect the real service life of assets. Service life is calculated by three methods: a) as a quotient derived from depreciable gross fixed assets and current depreciation; b) as a quotient derived from depreciable gross fixed assets and maintenance investments; and c) by breaking assets down into around 20 different categories and estimating specific service life durations.

5   *Growth.* For a company in which capital employed is not growing significantly, the ratio of corporate value to total capital employed must correspond to the ratio of CROCI to the cost of capital. This can be illustrated by analogy to a fixed-interest security. Given an 8% coupon and a market interest rate of 10%, a bond offering 20% is being traded below par. Growth, however, obscures this clear relationship. An above-average ratio of corporate value to total capital can also be explained by overvaluation. To this end, Deutsche Morgan Grenfell compares CROCI with Economic Value Added, which measures value development subject to corrections for the growth of capital.

---

[14] Deutsche Morgan Grenfell (1997a), pp. 2 ff.
[15] For more details, see Deutsche Morgan Grenfell (1997a), pp. 6 ff.

In our view, the sheer volume of complicated corrections involved makes CROCI difficult to apply in corporate practice. It is difficult to communicate the end result, and calculation is laborious. Nevertheless, the main benefit of CROCI is its considerable accuracy, which is similar to that of shareholder value and shareholder value returns and is not based on forecast figures. Top management would therefore do well to pay attention to published CROCI figures and incorporate them in their decision-making processes.

Tobin's Q

The Q value is defined as the ratio between the market value of the total capital of a company or business unit and the cost of reproduction, i.e. the book value of total capital at present-day prices.[16] This is a modified form of market value/ book value ratio, since the denominator uses the book value at current prices instead of historical prices (i.e. the balance sheet values) for total capital. This corresponds to the gross investment base used in CFROI. The market value in the numerator is calculated in the same way as shareholder value, albeit using real free cash flows and the real (i.e. inflation-adjusted) cost of capital.

Q values greater than 1 indicate that the real market value, based on calculated shareholder value, is greater than the book value, and therefore that value is being increased for the company's owners.

The main difference between the Q value and the other metrics examined in this book is that the Q calculation uses real values. This is more difficult and, in economies where inflation is low and stable, adds little in terms of improved accuracy. The calculation of real cash flows is based on suppositions about the future rate of inflation which may turn out to be wrong. If nominal cash flows and the cost of capital are used, as in the shareholder value calculation, then the calculation of the cost of capital set forth in Chapter 3.1 implicitly assumes that future inflation will remain similar to past levels. In our opinion, this assumption is seldom less accurate than the one postulated for the Q value, and certainly does not justify the extra effort involved in calculation. We also see a further disadvantage in that Tobin's Q is an absolute value that is more difficult to communicate than yield values.

This multiplicity of value-based metrics and management variables – Deutsche Morgan Grenfell has fittingly referred to 'the war of the metrics' – begs the question: which ones should be used in practice? Table 3.9 compares and contrasts the metrics most widely used today and presents our recommendations as regards practical application.

---

[16] Reimann (1990), pp. 24 ff.

Table 3.8: Summary of value metrics.

	CFROI Cash flow return on investment [%])	CVA Cash value added [€]	CROCI Cash return on capital invested [%]	EVA Economic Value Added [€]	MVA Market value added [%]
Calculation	Internal rate of return on • Gross investment base • Gross cash flow • Service life of fixed assets • Residual asset value	Gross investment base multiplied by the difference between CFROI and the real cost of capital	Corrects the return on equity to account for: 1) Debt 2) "Invisible" capital 3) Inflation 4) Depreciation 5) Growth	Difference between operating profit and the product of capital outstanding and the weighted average cost of capital	Difference between the total value of the company (market capitalization + book value of debt) and capital employed
+	• Relatively easy to calculate	• Relatively easy to calculate • Better correlation to value creation than EVA	• Correlates well to market value	• Relatively easy to calculate	• Correlates well to market value • Relatively easy to calculate
–	• Correlation to market value is lower than for shareholder value or CROCI	• Correlation to value creation is lower than for shareholder value added	• Static; historical orientation • Extremely difficult to calculate	• Static; historical orientation • Cash flow includes depreciation	• Not applicable to business units/lines • Influenced by share price fluctuations
Recommended application	• Generally applicable if you can live with inherent inaccuracies	• Preference given to use of shareholder value added	• Refer to analysts' publications; do not bother calculating it yourself	• Can only be used as a supplement to forward-looking measures	• Only suitable for top management and entire companies

Table 3.8 (continued).

	Market capitalization [€]	Tobin's Q [absolute figure]	Shareholder value (added) [€]	Shareholder value return [%]	Final shareholder value return [%]
Calculation	Current share price multiplied by the number of shares	Quotient derived from market value of total capital (discounted free cash flows) and the gross investment base	Discounted cash flow less debt of capital plus non-essential operating capital	Internal rate of return on total capital employed, future cash flows and residual value	Transformation of quotients derived from value added and capital employed as period-specific premiums/discounts on the cost of capital
+	• Reflects market value of the company • Easy to calculate	• Establishes a ratio between shareholder value and capital employed	• Correlates well to market value • Forward-looking and dynamic	• Correlates well to market value • Forward-looking and dynamic • Takes account of capital employed	• Correlates well to market value • Forward-looking and dynamic • Takes account of capital employed
–	• Affected by share price fluctuations which do not always reflect company performance	• Difficult to calculate • Difficult to communicate as an absolute figure	• Bears no relation to current capital employed • Difficult to calculate • Difficult to communicate as an absolute figure	• Difficult to calculate • Assumes that free funds will be reinvested at the internal rate of return	• Difficult to calculate
Recommended application	• Only suitable for top management and entire companies • Useful when compared with market index and industry	• Preference given to the use of other metrics	• Only suitable for top management	• Generally applicable	• Generally applicable

Recommended system of metrics and management variables

Two criteria can be used to distinguish between the various systems of metrics and management variables: the nature of the management variables (cf. the system of metrics used by Veba); and the intended recipients who, on the basis of the information thus supplied, must perform deviation analyses and may need to take concrete action – and who may also be responsible for any undesirable developments. Given our belief that the focus should be on the recipients and what they need to do rather than on the nature of the metrics themselves, we generally recommend that the system of metrics used be varied according to the needs of their intended recipients. The example of metrics in a value-based management controlling system depicted in Fig. 3.41 is valid for a corporation that has a diversified array of business fields. The people in charge of the group – the management at corporate headquarters – will, as a rule, be supplied with information in the form of aggregated value indicators. Besides the forward-looking shareholder value and shareholder value return indicators, EVA, as a static value with a historical focus, is also applied as a useful supplement. The relevant figures are indicated for the group as a whole and for the business units individually. The trends in market capitalisation compared to the market index and the market capitalisation of the industry will also be of importance to corporate management.

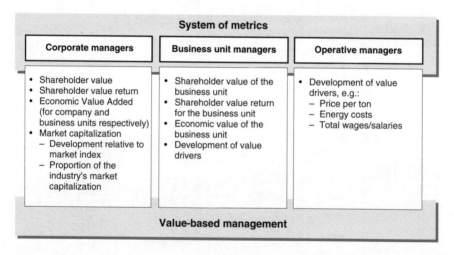

Figure 3.41: Recommended system of metrics – example.

With the exception of market capitalisation, the same figures are of relevance to the top managerial echelons in the business units, too – as far as they concern their own respective lines of business. These managers also need to know about the value drivers, i.e. those measures of success that exert the strongest influence on their business. And these value drivers are the only issue that is important for third-level (operative) management. Take, for example, a production manager at an aluminium plant. A sensitivity analysis (see Chapter 3.1) has found energy (electricity) consumption to be a significant value driver in production. It therefore follows that both energy costs and energy costs per ton of aluminium produced are important for the purposes of management control. The advantage of value drivers is that, for each business unit and its operational function, the most important metrics can be defined individually. Thus a small number of metrics are enough to provide each party concerned with solid information about value development; managers no longer find themselves wading through floods of irrelevant data.

For this system of operative planning metrics, actual data should be collated and the metrics calculated for precisely defined periods. Shareholder value added can be calculated on the basis of actual values, as explained in the section on strategic planning. The same section also clarifies how the shareholder value return can be calculated from actual data. The ideal solution would, of course, be to have these figures captured in a management information system that outputs them on a regular basis. This would allow deviation analyses to be performed as and when necessary and appropriate management actions to be inferred.

Investment planning and controlling

We have already stressed that investment planning and controlling are important as a means of controlling the allocation of funds. It is therefore only logical that value-based investment planning should play a key role in value management.

The aim should thus be to align investment policy in its entirety (planning, feasibility studies and controlling) with the interests of the shareholders. As a basic rule, only those investments are to be approved and implemented whose dynamic returns exceed the cost of capital – risk-adjusted for each business unit – and thereby create value for the company. Corporate practice shows that a value-based investment policy needs to include four major elements:

- Clearly defined procedural rules and areas of responsibility must exist for the planning of, application for and approval of investments.
- Investment appraisal must be dynamic and must be based on after-tax cash flows. A user-friendly PC-based tool should be deployed to simplify this task within the line organisation.
- The shareholder value-oriented cost of capital (see Chapter 3.1) must be applied as a uniform measure for all investments.
- All investments must be monitored and controlled *ex post* so that countermeasures can be applied, and sanction mechanisms enforced, should anything go wrong (e.g. cost overruns). New investment projects should also aim to enrich the company by adding new knowledge and experience.

Critics of the shareholder value philosophy may ask what is really new about such a value-based investment policy. After all, companies already make frequent use of dynamic investment appraisals. At least for large companies, this statement is undoubtedly true. However, the cost of capital is usually calculated on the basis of historical accounting data and not as an opportunity cost to the investor, unlike in the case of value management. Another innovative aspect is that calculation is based on cash flows. In practice, we have often encountered (dynamic) investment appraisals that were based on costs and earnings – along with the perennial problems concerning depreciation that we have already mentioned. Similar weaknesses exist in the way taxes are dealt with. Whereas value management unambiguously demands an after-tax assessment, many companies persist in calculating their investments before taxes.

Scope of validity

When a company wants to revise its existing investment guidelines, the first question to ask is: 'who do these guidelines apply to?'. Guidelines should apply to all business units – including participations in which the company holds the entrepreneurial reins. The scope of validity should be staked out as broadly as possible with regard to different types of investment, too, and should in all cases include the following types:

- *Investments in property, plant and equipment.* This includes all expenditure on goods and services that increase tangible fixed assets, e.g. the purchase of IT equipment or the construction of a building. These are the classical objects of investment planning and controlling.
- *Projects.* These include measures which, in some cases, create expenditure that does not need to be capitalised, such as a project to boost sales by increasing market coverage and providing extra advertising. The funds invested in these projects must satisfy the same criteria as investments in fixed assets. If no separate planning and controlling mechanisms exist for projects – as is the case in numerous companies – then the validity of the investment guidelines should be extended to include projects.
- *Participations/acquisitions.* The acquisition of a stake in the equity or share capital of a company or the increase of such a holding must naturally also fulfil the demands of value management. However, since the characteristic features of such transactions are markedly different from the other two types of investment (e.g. greater volume, involvement of top management only in most cases), a different procedure should be adopted.

Investments in property, plant and equipment should be subdivided into three categories: a) replacement investments; b) investments prescribed by law; and c) investments for purposes of expansion, adaptation and rationalisation. Different procedures should be adopted for each of these categories. In the case of an investment which simply involves replacing a machine, for example, the best possible time of replacement should be calculated. Where a company is required to make an investment in order to comply with statutory provisions, a dynamic investment appraisal is not absolutely necessary. The investment appraisal can be used here to compare various alternatives. However, in view of the company's legal obligations, the cost of capital cannot be used to determine whether the investment decision is positive or negative. For the third category, an exhaustive investment appraisal must be carried out in all cases. In line with our narrow interpretation of replacement investment, this category covers all such investments as lead to capacity expansion or more streamlined operation.

The investment planning and controlling process

As should be evident from the figure on the next page, this process ought to comprise four steps. Medium-term investment planning should draw up a rough forecast over a three-year period with the aim of coordinating this planning data with strategic, sales, results and liquidity planning. Every year, this exercise is then rolled over for the next three years. Medium-term investment planning is of particular importance in industries (such as the paper industry) which require very substantial investments to be made at extended intervals. In such cases, it is often advisable to adopt a longer planning period of perhaps five years.

Operative investment planning is drawn up each year for the following year and is more detailed. As a rule, this exercise will specify most investments individually. Flat-rate budgets tend to be estimated only for smaller amounts. The investment budget is harmonised with results and liquidity planning and then ratified by corporate management. Investment appraisals should be conducted in advance for major projects. The definition of major projects will vary from company to company and depend on the total investment volume.

Both medium-term and operative investment plans are to be worked out from the 'bottom up'. In other words, operative business units are to submit planning data which is then collated and examined by the controlling function.

The investment decision is a central element in value-based investment planning and controlling. The decision should be influenced by the following criteria:

- Different application and approval procedures should apply for different types and volumes of investment. Dynamic investment appraisals should not be performed for replacement investments, investments required by law or minor sums.
- As mentioned above, dynamic investment appraisals should always be based on after-tax cash flows and the risk-adjusted cost of capital (see also our case example).

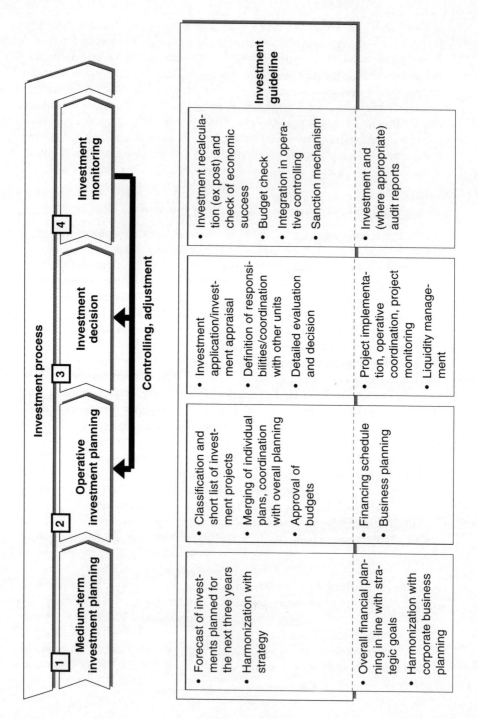

Figure 3.42: Overview of the investment process.

- Authority to decide the fate of investments must fit in with the corporate organisational structure. For instance, if regional office managers bear entrepreneurial responsibility and operate as profit centres, they can be afforded authority to decide on larger investment amounts than in cases where corporate headquarters keeps them on a tight rein and they have little autonomous responsibility.

Figure 3.43 outlines the process of applying for and deciding on a major investment. This, too, is a bottom-up process. Applications are submitted by those who wish to implement them, assisted by the investment controlling function if necessary. Upon receipt of an application, the latter department subjects it to plausibility checks.

The last step in the investment process is ongoing investment monitoring – an activity to which most companies fail to attach due importance. The aim of this activity is to verify whether planned expenditures are in fact adhered to and whether the savings or additional earnings projected actually materialise.

The frequency and extent of investment monitoring will depend on the procedure, i.e. the nature of the investment and the amount involved. In the case of major investments, for example, actual data should be fed into the feasibility study over a number of years in order to verify whether the investment is indeed creating value for the company. The results should also be linked to suitable sanctions for the applicant. For instance, the investment controlling department might demand written justification for any deviation. Serious departures from planning should be discussed at board level and affect the variable element of the person responsible's salary.

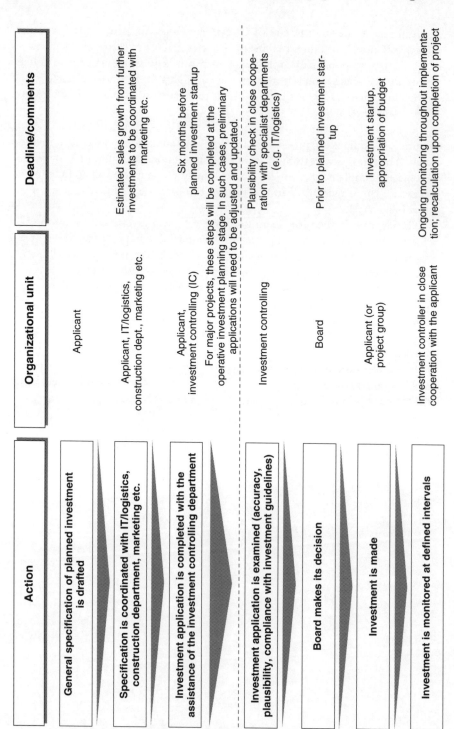

Figure 3.43: Investment application and decision.

Case example: Sanacorp Pharmahandel AG

Sanacorp, a pharmaceuticals wholesaler, converted its investment planning and controlling activities to the principles of value management some time ago. The key features of its new system are as follows:

- Procedures are clearly structured and assign responsibility unambiguously.
- Investment appraisals and the estimated cost of capital are fully in line with value management methodology.
- Investments are subject to systematic *ex post* monitoring. The results are linked to sanctions.

The section below takes a closer look at the second of these features, namely the system of dynamic, cash flow-based investment appraisal and the use of cost of capital as a metric.

Investment application and appraisal

At Sanacorp, appraisals for investments in expansion, streamlining and adaptation that exceed DM100,000 (approximately €50,000) are drawn up using an Excel-based PC tool. The file contains nine interrelated spreadsheets whose structure is illustrated in the figure below. All data that is relevant to the investment decision is included in the initial application.

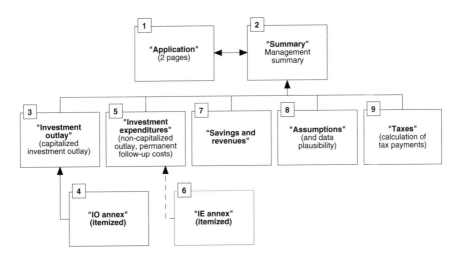

Figure 3.44: Investment appraisals and decisions at Sanacorp.

Spreadsheet no. 1 contains the application together with information of a general nature (e.g. applicant's name, description of the project, qualitative arguments etc.). Spreadsheet no. 2 is the key element of a dynamic investment appraisal which indicates the net present value of the investment and the internal rate of return. The future cash flows for the calculation are derived from spreadsheets 3, 5, 7 and 9 and are planned for 10 years; the perpetuity method is applied after this period. Spreadsheets 4, 6 and 8 serve to fill in the details, and substantiate the numbers. The tax effect of the investment is calculated in spreadsheet no. 9. To this end, the difference in the operating result that should be brought about by the investment is determined and then used as the basis for calculating the tax liability. The values required for this calculation are transferred automatically from the other spreadsheets.

Nominal cost of capital

Sanacorp currently puts its nominal, after-tax cost of capital at 8.5%. This figure applies both for its core business, pharmaceuticals wholesaling, and for its subsidiary lines, home care and supplier logistics, since the beta factors for these lines differ only slightly from each other. This cost of capital is calculated from the following components:

- The beta factor is 0.78 for core business and 0.85/0.91 for the other two lines. The method of calculation is the one described in Chapter 3.1.
- The risk premium for the stock market is estimated at 4.5% and the risk-free interest rate at 7%. Accordingly, the cost of shareholder capital is put at 10.5% for core business.
- A basic debt/equity ratio of 2/3 is assumed for the capital structure.
- The after-tax cost of debt capital (i.e. including the 'tax shield') is calculated as 4.9%.

This gives the company a hurdle rate based on modern financial theory to use in its investment appraisals. Investments with a positive net capital value calculated using this nominal cost of capital create value for the company.

3.4 Adapting compensation schemes

In Chapter 2 we stressed that compensation systems are a key factor in value-based company management. If one takes the idea of managers running the company in the best interests of the shareholders to its logical conclusion, it is only natural that the actors within the relevant company should be recompensed on the basis of incentive schemes designed to promote value creation. When assessing companies, professional investors and analysts are particularly keen to see benefits to investors linked to benefits to the employees.

Empirical evidence substantiates the efficiency of such a link. Various studies have shown a significant positive correlation between salaries with a sizeable variable component and improved company performance.[1] The reason for this is that managers who destroy value earn only below-average salaries in this kind of compensation system and thus tend to leave their company in the short to medium term.

It only really makes sense to apply genuinely value-based compensation models for decision-makers who have considerable influence on operational and strategic decisions. At the same time, the trend in recent years has been to delegate greater decision-making powers to autonomous organisational units under the control of global company targets. This tendency has also begun to make value-based incentive systems useful and, indeed, necessary for downstream levels of the corporate hierarchy. A substantial gap remains to be closed for the second, third and fourth levels of corporate management in particular. Value-based compensation systems are at least as important to these managers as they are to top-level management. The operative decisions of these managers regarding the implementation of company strategy have a far-reaching effect on the course of business.

Shareholder Value oriented compensation schemes have become a common instrument in stock exchange listed companies. Despite the difficulty in translating the creation of shareholder value in unlisted companies into metrics that can readily be used to influence compensation, value-based controlling tools can nevertheless be used to align even these managers' performance with the principles of value management.

Even so, one has to bear in mind that compensation becomes a more complex undertaking when one seeks to make use of the levers and incentives that effectively influence value. All the same, the success achieved in creating added value and the increased efficiency generated by less need for operative intervention, can more than justify the effort and expense involved in setting up a value-based system of compensation. This section examines four key aspects of the introduction of value-based compensation systems:

---

[1] Bernhardt *et al.* (1997), 90, Jernsen *et al.* (1990), pp. 139 ff.

- possible compensation systems and their impact;
- tailoring these systems to different levels of corporate hierarchy;
- requirements for implementation; and
- aids to implementation.

Systems and their impact

The principle behind value-based compensation

The principle behind value-based compensation is to link managers' salaries to value generation for the shareholders. A minimum threshold for company value expectations – the minimum interest rate to be paid on capital employed – must be set as a condition. The same methods and metrics should be used to measure compensation as are used throughout the entire value management concept.

Congruence between managers' incentive to maximise their own income and the maximisation of company value is most easily achieved by using identical reference variables – i.e. manager as a shareholder. By contrast, employed managerial staff who have full executive powers over the value of company assets must be offered a compensation package with a narrower band of fluctuation. The downside risk[2] in particular should be more strictly limited for them than for managers who own the company. Besides affording managers genuine participation in the company, value-based compensation systems can also be achieved by offering bonus payments linked to value-based reference variables.

Genuine participation models	Artificial participation models	Bonuses
• Vested equity title	• Simulation of equity title	• Compensation claim derived from a reference variable
Forms:	**Forms:**	**Forms:**
• (Employee) stock	• Stock appreciation rights	• EVA bonus
• Stock options	• Virtual shares	• SVA bonus
• Warrant-linked bonds		• Cost of capital bonus
• Convertible bonds		

Combined forms
• Link between bonus mechanisms and genuine/artificial participation models

Figure 3.45: Different types of value-based compensation.

---

[2] Downside risk is the term used here to denote the risk of an employed manager receiving only a low level of compensation.

Impact

When examining the impact of compensation systems quantitative (i.e. monetary) and qualitative impact, in addition to efficiency the parallel development of company value and compensation levels has to be regarded. A description of each of these effects is given below.

The quantitative impact includes the effect on the manager's salary in the narrower sense, the upside (profit) potential, the downside (loss) risk and the tax burden on the recipient. From the company's point of view, the effect on liquidity, income tax and costs is monitored. The qualitative aspects of such a system include the level of employee motivation, the time aspect of compensation and the degree to which the manager can directly influence the defined target metrics.

Detailed description and assessment

Genuine participation models: stocks

Giving employees a direct stake in the company, for example by offering them employee stocks, is a common way of motivating employees and contributing to their personal wealth. In the USA, 8.3% of total market capitalisation (around US $213 billion) is in the hands of employees who have been given shares as a variant form of participation-based compensation.[3] Employees at Lockheed, for example, receive between two and five times their annual salary in company shares. Nowadays, most of these shares are issued at below the company's current share price and are linked to exercise restrictions.

Where management – those people who are to a large extent responsible for overall performance – holds stocks it can be assumed that some form of shareholder value-based incentive does indeed exist. Management stocks can also be used as a form of payment that is directly linked to other target measures. However, to avoid blurring the distinction between employed executives and owner-managers, such stakes should not exceed the customary threshold of 3 to 5% of equity capital, or 20% in the case of highly innovative companies. The total proportion of capital made available each year should not exceed 1%. Following the idea of a minimum return for the company performance, a hurdle rate is only created by issuing shares at a higher selling price than the current quotation on the stock market or by restrictions on disposal. The difference between the selling price at the earliest possible selling date and the current share price then reflects the minimum return. If managers are required to delve into their own liquidity to finance the purchase of shares, this can be offset by a company loan, although it must be remembered that the employed executive would be liable for

---

[3] The National Centre for Employee Ownership (1997c).

income tax on gifts or discounted share prices or interest rates. One has to bear in mind that, depending on overall stock market performance, the manager's interest in equity capital could lead to losses or profits that have nothing to do with the destruction or creation of value as a result of management decisions. Accordingly, the direct incentive to apply value-based principles of management is relatively slight.

Stock options

Stock options are the classical instrument that tends to be linked most frequently to shareholder value-based executive compensation schemes. Such schemes grant a number of call options on the company's stock to managers as a variable component of their salary. The subscription price is usually equivalent to the current share price at the time the option is issued.[4] The subscription price should however, be higher then the current value to imply an anticipated minimum return (the 'hurdle rate', i.e. the company's cost of capital) for the period until the options may be exercised. These hurdle rates can be linked to the number of years until options are exercised or to the performance of an industry index.

> **Example:**
> Share price at the time of issue: €100
> Earliest exercise: after 5 years
> Expected minimum return on equity: 15%
> Base price: €201 = €100 × $(1 + 15\%)^4$

Along the same lines as hurdle rates for option prices, it is also possible to define ceilings. Ceilings set a limit on what a manager can earn. Options will normally reach maturity in the five to ten year range. The options used are of the American type, that is, they can be exercised on specified dates during the entire period to maturity and not only upon final maturity. The maturity dates set should be the set just after the day of publication of new company data to obviate the danger of insider conflicts. Furthermore, options should not be transferable, to preclude the possibility of selling them before maturity. The purchase and resale of a share should be the only path that leads to a return. If options are made available on a regular basis as part of a compensation package, the exercise price will always be determined by the current situation on the stock market. The company may grant a low-interest loan to finance the exercise price.

This kind of call option offers more or less unlimited upside potential. However, it should only be possible to exercise such an option once all options granted previously have been exercised. Adopting this approach effectively limits the downside risk to the manager should the value of the company (or its share

---

[4] Bernhardt *et al.* (1997), p. 89.

price) deteriorate. The alternative – with unlimited downside risk – is tantamount to giving the manager a put option. Should the company's share price fall, the supervisory board would exercise this option. To protect managers against the full risk of share price decline, fewer put options can be sold than the number of call options granted.

As an alternative to pure Stock options they can be granted in conjunction with warrant or convertible bonds, which is still necessary in some European countries due to legal restrictions. This method requires the manager to finance a bond on which the company pays interest and which must be repaid upon maturity. Warrant-linked options remain in existence even after exercise. Similarly, a bank or subsidiary of the company issues the bonds and then splits off the options rights and transfers them to the manager. This would indeed give employed executives pure options with no form of bond. Alternatively, the company can 'go short' and grant its managers purchase options under civil law. Should such options be exercised, the company could cover its obligations by buying its own shares on the stock market.

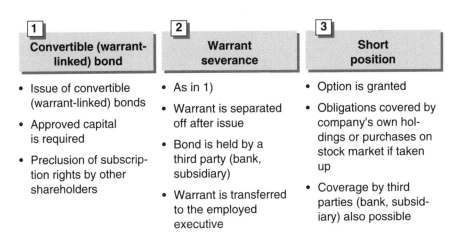

1 Convertible (warrant-linked) bond	2 Warrant severance	3 Short position
• Issue of convertible (warrant-linked) bonds • Approved capital is required • Preclusion of subscription rights by other shareholders	• As in 1) • Warrant is separated off after issue • Bond is held by a third party (bank, subsidiary) • Warrant is transferred to the employed executive	• Option is granted • Obligations covered by company's own holdings or purchases on stock market if taken up • Coverage by third parties (bank, subsidiary) also possible

Figure 3.46: Examples of option models that are legal in Germany.

This pure form of company stock options is only feasible for publicly traded companies. A substitute for unlisted companies can be achieved by the use of 'virtual' stocks (see below) that are linked to an internal method of corporate value determination.

Essentially, giving managers a stake in their company goes a long way toward aligning the interests of shareholders with those of the management. The limited risk on the one hand, coupled with substantial profit leverage with a long-term horizon on the other, largely cancels out the problems thrown up by the principal agency theory. A further benefit of stock options is that they do not weigh heavily on the company's cost or liquidity structure.

There is, however, a need for a more critical examination of options from the perspective of value management. Although they offer managers the same profit opportunities that are available to shareholders, movements in share prices are not determined exclusively by company financials. It would be misleading indeed to assume that the capital markets are so efficient that share prices reflect solely and exclusively company financials. A number of stock option models have been accused of being 'self-serving' on account of the high stock volumes involved and the need to exclude other shareholders from subscription rights. Nevertheless, if one ignores, for the time being, the question of what amounts are appropriate, the criticisms currently being levelled at this instrument by public opinion are unjustified.[5]

Convertible bonds

The basic principle of using convertible bonds as a value-based element of compensation is very similar to that of the warrant-linked option. The only difference is that loan capital is converted to share capital when the option is exercised. The bond as such thus ceases to exist once it has been exercised. If there is a share purchase premium it can be paid for, either out of company reserves or by the manager at the time of conversion, if necessary with the support of a company loan. Subscription prices and maturates can be varied in the same way as for warrant-linked options. The attraction of this variation on the same theme is the secure income yielded by the bond at an interest rate slightly below that of the bond market, plus the possibility of profits generated by exercising the option (which has no effect on liquidity). Paying for the share premium out of company reserves can further enhance potential profits from conversion. The guaranteed interest return thus covers the basic risk to which the employed executive is exposed, while the conversion option provides an incentive to create value. Since convertible bonds and warrant-linked options work in a virtually identical manner, both also exhibit the same benefits and drawbacks.

Artificial participation models

The classical methods of value-based compensation all involve share ownership for managers and therefore relate mostly to the situation of publicly traded stock corporations. However, it is also conceivable to link compensation to company value development without a direct interest in company equity. This can be done in the form of stock appreciation rights.

---

[5] The value of these non-transferable options should not be calculated using the customary Black-Scholes formula, precisely because the options are not transferable. Rather, their time value is determined by the internal value less interest for the period until the earliest point of exercise. Cf. Huddart (1996), p. 10.

Stock appreciation rights do not involve the ownership of shares by employed executives. The freely definable contractual agreement between employer and employee states instead that an amount will be paid out as a function of the change in the company's share price. The effect is thus similar to that of a share option. Here, too, hurdle rates and exercise restrictions can be built in. Stock appreciation rights are particularly well suited to situations where it is preferable to avoid including management in the body of shareholders.

All types of companies can use virtual shares since they do not depend on value calculations based on stock market prices. Instead, the company itself calculates how much it is worth. Ideally, this should be done using the shareholder value method, i.e. from a prospective point of view, taking account of cash flow figures and the risk-adjusted cost of capital. A virtual share of the equity capital of the company – a share that does not exist for all legal purposes – is apportioned to the manager. The value of this virtual share then increases in line with the calculated development of company value. This added value can either be paid out in cash on an ongoing basis (e.g. after a no-exercise period), or be drawn on by the manager, or be paid out when the manager leaves the company.

The fact that the method is based on an internal measure of value creation which itself is based on capitalised value shields it from the criticism that managers might harvest unmerited windfalls or losses if the stock market rallies or crashes. At the same time, the approach requires the introduction of an elaborate system of value determination whose calculation method must be contractually defined. Equally, external auditors should examine the calculation method itself, all value estimates and the cost of capital. If the internal value calculation is based on forecast cash flows, it is appropriate to introduce penalties for failure to meet cash flow targets from the previous planning exercise.

Bonuses

The most flexible, versatile and universally applicable form of variable compensation is the bonus. A bonus consists of an (annual) payment that is linked to predefined, value-based reference variables. Bonuses can also be defined by what are known as 'management by objectives' (MBO) systems and be subject to a qualitative end-of-period assessment. For the first, second and (depending on the size of the company) third levels of management, the considerable autonomy granted to the employees makes it advisable to peg bonuses to fixed amounts such as percentages of result measures.

The reference variable(s) used and the mechanism by which personal bonus proportions are calculated are key factors here. Any of the metrics used in the calculation methods for value-based compensation systems are in theory suitable as reference variables. The metrics selected, however, should as closely as possible reflect the sphere of responsibility and influence of the executive concerned. Best of all are reference variables that are based on net cash flows after tax (net operating profit less adjusted taxes, or NOPLAT) within a given manager's scope of responsibility.

If it is possible to calculate capital invested for this sphere of responsibility, the modified form of Economic Value Added (EVA)[6] lends itself. A personal percentage rate allows executives to share in value actually created – that is, over and above the cost of capital – in their respective areas. Alternatively, the return on capital employed (ROCE) can also be used. The important thing, here again, is to establish a hurdle rate that is equivalent to the risk-adjusted minimum return for each executive's sphere of influence.

Bonus models allow value-based incentive systems to be formulated even for parts of a company for which it is not possible to draw up cash flow statements based on income and expenditure. The value drivers used for modelling purposes and in value-based controlling can, for example, serve as reference variables. The relative sensitivities of these value drivers can be used to calculate the change in company value. Where this kind of shareholder value calculation model[7] is in place, direct changes in corporate value can be defined as executive targets and reflected in the compensation system.

Example:

Sales manager:
2% share in the value created for the company as a whole by changes within his/her sphere of responsibility

Value creation levers[8]
Revenues: 6.7 Expenditures: –5.7

Change:

Investment in sales support systems at a cost of €1 million p.a.
= 0.1% of total expenditures

Expected increase in revenues:
€1.2 million p.a. = 0.1% of total revenues

Impact on company value (subject to shareholder value calculation):
Total company value prior to change: €1.5 billion

Change from investment in sales support systems:
$0.1\% \times -5.7 \times €1.5 \text{ billion} = -€8.55 \text{ million}$

Change from increase in revenues:
$+0.1\% \times 6.7 \times €1.5 \text{ billion} = €10.05 \text{ million}$

Total impact: €1.5 million (= 0.1% of company value)

Sales manager's share: $2\% \times €1.5 \text{ million} = €30,000$

---

[6] Stewart (1990b), pp. 118 ff.

[7] Cf. the section entitled "Identifying value drivers" in Chapter 3.1.

[8] Lever: a 1% change in p.a. revenues adds 6.7% to the value of the company.

The variety of forms in which bonuses can be framed makes them not only the most widely applicable but also the most flexible instrument. They can just as well be applied even for third and fourth-level management, and adapted annually to changes in corporate policy in conjunction with a 'management by objectives' arrangement. The only requirement is that a value-based system of controlling and corporate valuation must be in place. Traditional methods of controlling with static, historical focus are unsuitable.

To what extent bonuses satisfy the demands of shareholder value depends on the reference variables and mechanisms used. Key aspects include the relationship to accounting numbers that leave no room to 'massage' valuation figures and the need to take account of specific minimum returns in the form of the cost of capital.[9]

Combined forms

Different value-based systems can be interlinked to achieve useful global effects that accurately reflect individual spheres of responsibility – by distinguishing between compensation for components that are influenced individually and collectively, for example. A positive year for the company as a whole can, for instance, be recompensed in line with the ROCE figure, while poor NOPLAT performance within a given manager's field of jurisdiction is also reflected (see Fig. 3.47). The profits generated by this pool can then be paid out partly in cash and partly in convertible bonds.

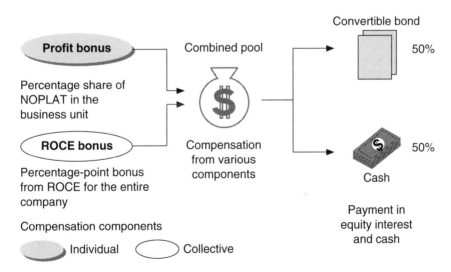

Figure 3.47: Example of a combined compensation system.

---

[9] cf. Chapter 2.5.

The most useful and most widespread combinations of the methods outlined above are links between bonus systems and some form of participation scheme. The two systems can exist independently of one another or in an upstream-downstream configuration. In the latter case, part of the claims arising from the bonus systems can be realised in the form of participation rights. This transforms the bonus system, which is essentially a single-period system, into a multi-period system.

Summary of compensation schemes

The sheer variety of value-based incentive schemes that are possible enables suitable forms to be devised for just about any level of company management. The main challenge lies in adapting these schemes so that they align with real spheres of responsibility. Inappropriate incentives that bear no relation to a manager's own scope of operation are hardly likely to provide sufficient incentive. Nor do they line up with the need to cultivate entrepreneurial initiative among managers that will cause them to create value for the company.

From this, it should be evident that systems of participation which make up the lion's share of the overall salary package can only be usefully applied for managers who bear substantial responsibility for the overall performance of a company.

Astute combinations of individual and collective reference variables, single-period and multi-period elements, and direct and indirect components are the key factor of success in developing an effective value-based compensation system. And it is important to remember that such systems need not be restricted to top management.

Tailoring schemes to different hierarchy levels

An efficient value-based compensation system will do more than merely link executive pay with the development of company value (and hence, in the narrowest sense, of shareholder benefit). Such a system will exercise three major functions for the managerial staff concerned. Firstly, it will provide extrinsic motivation and encourage dedication. Secondly, it will provide pecuniary compensation for work done. Thirdly, it should guide the actions taken by management. The mechanism of the compensation system should be designed in a way that, when managers are called upon to decide between alternative courses of action, the choice that will positively impact their own personal income is at the same time the right course of action in the company's best interests. The critical task is therefore defining the right components, mechanisms and variable elements for each level of the corporate hierarchy.

Company-specific incentive schemes, insofar as they are not intended as catch-all wealth creation schemes for the entire workforce, can be used at most down to the fourth level of management below the executive board.[10] This will, of course, depend on the organisation. In modern, flat hierarchies – which are also the ones best suited to value-based compensation – it may make sense not to go below second-level management. The criterion for deciding whether a significant proportion of someone's pay should be variable and value-based is the extent of their decision-making freedoms and their managerial powers. Employees who have no room to take autonomous decisions, who take decisions based only on strictly defined conditions or who have no authority to issue instructions should not in large measure be recompensed on the basis of entrepreneurial incentive schemes. Their incentive systems should instead be purely performance-oriented, i.e. related to the quantity and quality of the work they do. The rule of thumb is that around 1% of the people in large organisations and no more than 10% of the people in smaller, flatter, innovative organisations are genuine candidates for entrepreneurial compensation.

Design dimensions

The main design dimensions that need to be coordinated for executive compensation systems are:

- the amount and proportion of the variable components;
- the reference variables used for assessment;
- the modes and mechanisms established; and
- the form of payment.

Amounts/proportions

The salary amount paid out will essentially be determined by comparable market salaries. Variable components must differ in line with varying levels of responsibility. The further down the hierarchy a manager is and the less responsibility is borne, the lower should be the variable component, which can ultimately range from 5% to 80% of the fixed component. Even here, however, upward variations may be in order depending on the competitive context. Top management compensation systems in emerging businesses, which imply significant entrepreneurial acting, can reach variable components far beyond 100% of the fixed salary. In these cases a high likelihood for a consistent positive bonus is assumed to ensure an appropriate salary. In many European countries, those proportions of pay that are genuinely variable are relatively small (see Chapter 2.5).

In order to create incentives worthy of the name, these variable components need to be increased. Higher variable components tend to get an enthusiastic reception from managerial staff who are truly dedicated and willing to perform, provided that they are linked to the opportunity of increasing personal earnings.

---

[10] This designation will naturally vary according to corporate form.

Seniority and differences in the importance of certain fields of responsibility can be impounded not only in the amount paid out as a fixed salary but also by the use of different levers (percentages of the relevant reference variables).

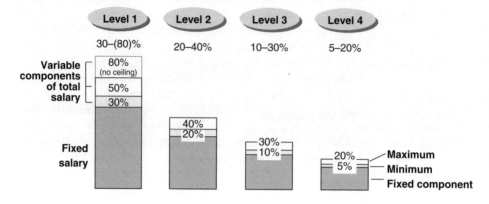

Figure 3.48: Variable compensation components at different hierarchy levels.

When modelling variable compensation systems, attention must be paid to the expected value and to minimum and maximum compensation levels. The expected value corresponds to the statistical average of variable remuneration relative to the development of reference variables over time. The minimum level is usually the fixed salary. If the fixed salary is particularly low, the expected value must be taken into account here, too, in order to prevent cases of acute hardship. A ceiling can be put at the top end of the scale.

Congruence between salary impact and target performance

How well a system of compensation works will depend on whether the incentive to act afforded by that system harmonises with what will maximise the value of the company. As described above, this is determined largely by the choice of reference variables, but also by the degree of congruence between movements in salary and company value. The leverage offered by a compensation component must bear sensible relation to the development of the reference variable.

As illustrated in Fig. 3.49, normal market salaries and fluctuation corridors need to be juxtaposed with possible developments for the said reference variables. Should a reference variable experience average development, i.e. if only the cost of capital is recouped, the linked compensation element must increase only at a below-average rate. The amount, reference variables, proportions and mechanisms must all be designed such that, if company value develops only in line with the specific cost of capital, compensation will remain below the market average. If strategic targets for returns are achieved, the employees concerned should be recompensed on a par with the market average. In this case, strategic return targets should not stray too far away from minimum returns. If exceptional increases in value creation are achieved, salaries should also be allowed to reach exceptional, one-off peaks.

Caps or ceilings on maximum salaries generally tend to be counterproductive – at least if they are set too low, i.e. below an amount that is double the fixed salary element. Such ceilings may nevertheless be useful for third- and fourth-level management. Fixed salaries should be structured to ensure that downside risks are limited to an extent commensurate with the position of the employee concerned. But there is nothing to prevent top management from having lower fixed salaries than downstream executives, provided that the expected minimum top-level salary remains sufficiently far above the fixed second-level salary once compensation mechanisms and multi-period payments have been taken into account.

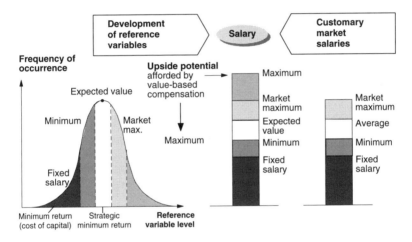

Figure 3.49: Congruence between target corridors.

Reference variables

The choice of reference variables for value-based compensation components is the key factor that determines the efficiency of such a compensation system. A system which combines collective and individual effects is generally the most efficient solution. Figure 3.50 provides an overview of the collective and individual reference variables that can be used. Collective components are characterised by the fact that reference variables are influenced by various decision-makers – classical examples being profit, Economic Value Added for the company as a whole, or the share price. Collective components must relate to the overall company or at least to a sizeable entity such as a business unit. Essentially, the ideal variables are shareholder value added (according to the DCF method) as the basis for calculating the value of virtual shares, as well as modified EVA (Economic Value Added before depreciation) and (C)ROCE [(cash) return on capital employed].[11] Empirical studies have found that total company value based on the DCF method correlates best with share price performance and management actions.

The reference variable for the genuine and artificial participation systems described above (shares, stock options, stock appreciation rights etc.) are already defined in the system; they can all be subsumed under the heading of collective incentive systems. Bonus systems are best suited for use as individual components, for which there are a multiplicity of alternative reference variables that cannot be dealt with exhaustively here. Basically, any of the variables covered in the chapter on controlling metrics are suitable for compensation incentives, especially value drivers and cash flow measures. Whatever the case, the variables chosen must satisfy the demands of shareholder value. This means that they must focus on cash flows while accounting for the cost of capital and the time value of money and looking ahead to the future. The figure calculated for capital employed is the critical factor for all return variables. Asset-intensive companies with heavily depreciated or obsolete plant will, as stated in Chapter 3.1, have to determine the replacement value in order to calculate tied capital. Yield-oriented variables are thus particularly easy to apply to businesses with short-term assets or financial assets for which current valuation is possible.

Compensation components	Reference object	Reference variables	
Collective	Entire company or jointly managed units	• Share price • Shareholder value (calculated) • Shareholder value added • EVA • (C)ROCE • Cost of capital	
Individual	Units for which individual responsibility is borne	• All value drivers • EVA • (C)ROCE • Cash flow surplus • NOPLAT • EBITD	**within sphere of responsibility**

Figure 3.50: Collective and individual reference variables.

---

[11] For compensation systems, the critical factors in these two variables are the cost of capital, investment expenditure and depreciation. This can be particularly problematic when trying to delimit units that are managed separately. Depreciation, which cannot be included in genuine value-based calculations, is incorporated in the calculation in the form of planned investment expenditure. Planning for future investment behaviour must therefore be well thought out with a view to monetary depreciation. A compromise is often arrived at by using EVA including depreciation. If this is done, adjustments will be necessary to account for depreciation that only exists on the balance sheet, e.g. where the actual service life departs substantially from the standard period defined for fiscal purposes.

Modes and mechanisms

The mechanism used in the compensation system traces the path from an absolute figure for a reference variable (or the change in that variable) to the impact on someone's salary. Numerous variations are possible, depending to a large extent on which reference variables are selected. Fundamental distinctions are drawn between methods that use absolute values (e.g. EVA), percentage changes (e.g. CROCE) and deviations from target values respectively.

In the case of absolute values, a percentage is defined in a similar manner to the familiar management bonuses derived from annual net profits. The advantage of absolute values is that absolute figures also reflect differences in size between different fields of responsibility, for example.

A reference to percentage figures (e.g. CROCE) or to a rate of change can be achieved by paying a certain amount per percentage point. This approach evens out any differences in the size of fields of responsibility. Such an approach can, for example, make sense where the absolute amount of the reference variables used for the compensation system cannot be influenced because it has been fixed by an external decision. In such cases, it is easy to generate hurdle rates and progressive compensation growth. A table of concrete amounts per percentage point is also crystal clear and can thus be a powerful tool for employee motivation.

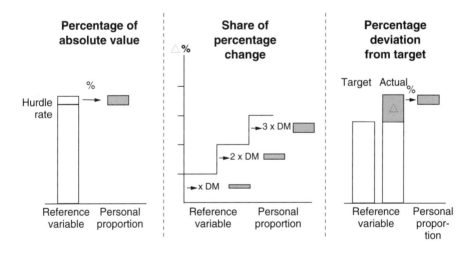

Figure 3.51: Overview of mechanisms.

Value management seeks to create value and be able to measure it in the future. Consequently, much valuation work – above all for unlisted companies – must be done on the basis of forecast or planning figures. This is the case, for instance, when the value of a company is calculated based on the DCF method or when cash flows are estimated. Compensation systems founded on forecast figures alone cannot measure actual performance. For this reason, penalties must be built into planning-based systems. Such penalties can take the form of withholding the premium for value actually created or compensating premiums deriving from other reference variables if planned targets are not achieved. Conversely, additional percentage points can be added progressively if targets are exceeded.

Compensation, smoothing, additional payments and expiry

It is perfectly feasible for the incentive given by a system of compensation to lead to undesirable courses of actions and give rise to the problem of moral hazard.[12] This can involve measures to optimise individual units that fail to optimise the company as a whole, as well as false allocation of profit/cost to a certain period. Such effects can occur as a result of the deliberate 'massaging' of a reference variable for an individual period, or of 'cosmetic surgery' performed on results by exploiting the leeway inherent in valuation methods. Problems of this nature can be avoided largely, but never entirely, by the careful choice of reference variables, hurdle rates and ceilings.

Ensuring that collective and individual compensation components balance each other out over a given period, for example, precludes the problem of 'self-optimisation' at the expense of the company as a whole (see Fig. 3.52). The same end can also be achieved by a points system which converts the reference variable values achieved into points as a function of the extent to which targets are achieved (credit points for performance, debit points for underperformance). In this way, credit and debit points accumulated from different components can also balance each other out. Claims for actual payment are then determined by converting total points into a salary figure.

Payment

As a rule, variable compensation claims result in annual cash payments. However, payment can also be made in the form of company shares or convertible bonds, for example. This would provide a further incentive to create value. The beneficiaries can, if they wish, sell these shares and thereby determine their own cash inflow. The exercise of options and virtual bonds can also be linked to the time at which a person leaves the company. If payment claims expire when a person leaves the company, this creates an incentive to maximise company value

---

[12] 'Moral hazard' is the term describing the phenomenon whereby the freedoms granted by a compensation system are exploited for personal gain to the neglect or detriment of the company's interests.

as quickly as possible, thereby creating value for the company's shareholders in the short term rather than nurturing the temptation to indulge in overly optimistic planning.

Spreading payment claims across several years and offering multi-period compensation can also help ensure a certain continuity in corporate development. With a view to the aim of increasing the value of the company over the long term, this is eminently recommendable. In the USA, over half of the larger companies avail themselves of this deferred payment facility.[13]

Similarly, staggering the disbursement of variable compensation claims across a number of years can be used to offset positive results in previous years against negative results in later years. However, this should never lead to a situation where the employee actually owes payments to the company. The result is a limited but singularly effective downside risk which prevents people from maximising short-term profits in one year and then running up losses in the next. This kind of multi-period compensation is well suited to extremely volatile businesses, enabling them to prevent employees from creaming off income by shifting business transactions into good years and leaving the shareholders to foot the bill for subsequent performance troughs.

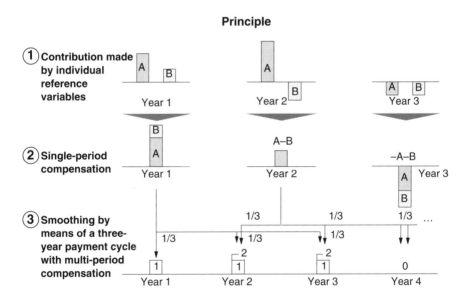

Figure 3.52: Compensation, smoothing, multi-period payment.

---

[13] Unpublished study of 27 "Dow Jones Industrial" companies, 1997, quoted in: Luck (1997), p. 78.

Adaptation criteria

The design dimensions described above should be used to adapt the compensation system for different levels of the hierarchy on the basis of several criteria: the degree of influence within a field of responsibility; the congruence between compensation and target metric behaviour; and the balance between individual and collective reference variables.

Degree of influence

When working out the individual components of a compensation system, adaptations for various hierarchic levels and fields of responsibility must be tailored very carefully to the scope of influence and responsibility of the individual manager. Compensation should be linked only to those variables that the manager can genuinely influence. In other words, interference from other managers outside the unit or area for which a given manager has to answer must be excluded. Furthermore, it must be possible to exert a considerable influence on the chosen reference variables by means of entrepreneurial activity. (Price changes resulting from fluctuations in the exchange rate would, for example, represent a singularly inappropriate reference variable.) One of the most frequent criticisms levelled at participation-oriented compensation systems (stock options etc.) is that managers receive compensation for market changes over which they exercise no influence whatsoever. Basing compensation systems on company development as a figure relative to that of an industry index or a reference group of competitors can offset this weakness. This procedure can be equated with the definition of a hurdle rate based on the risk-adjusted cost of capital.

Defining reference variables becomes a simpler matter in organisations whose structure consists of clearly delimited units that are market players in their own right and have separate cost accounting. Cash flows can be calculated for most such profit centres. Economic cash flow can, for instance, be calculated for the market segment for which a unit is responsible, for target customers or for the profit centre itself. A more suitable measure would be the return on capital employed (ROCE). This, however, is more difficult to calculate, since assigning capital employed to different business units is often fraught with problems. Such an approach would only appear to make sense where business unit managers themselves can influence how capital-intensive their operations are.

Yet another option for defining reference variables is to use the value drivers and value creation strategies defined for the business units (the classical example

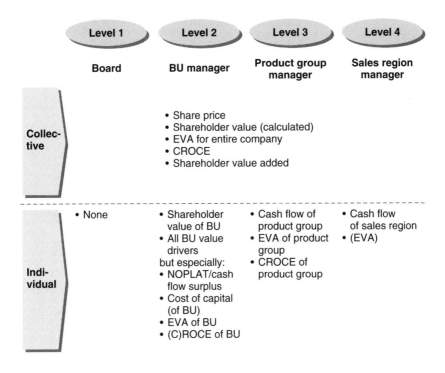

Figure 3.53: Reference variables and spheres of responsibility (example).

would be increases in gross margins). Figure 3.53 shows an example of reference variables that differ according to the sphere of responsibility.

The cash flow orientation to which we have so far given precedence in the compensation system applies in particular for corporate divisions that reflect the typical structure of a profit centre. However, it is also possible to measure the contribution made to value creation by certain internal departments on the basis of their value drivers. For the finance department, for example, this can be done using the cost of financing and the financial structure. The chief financial officer, for instance, should be measured against the absolute cost of capital.[14] It is the CFO who is responsible for keeping the interest paid on total capital to a necessary minimum. The tools with which this figure can be optimised are the structure of financing, liquidity management and the amount of interest paid on, or the opportunity cost of, equity capital.

---

[14] The cost of debt can be posted as an actual item of expenditure. For listed companies, the cost of equity can be determined by using fictitious interest rates based on CAPM; cf. Chapter 3.1.

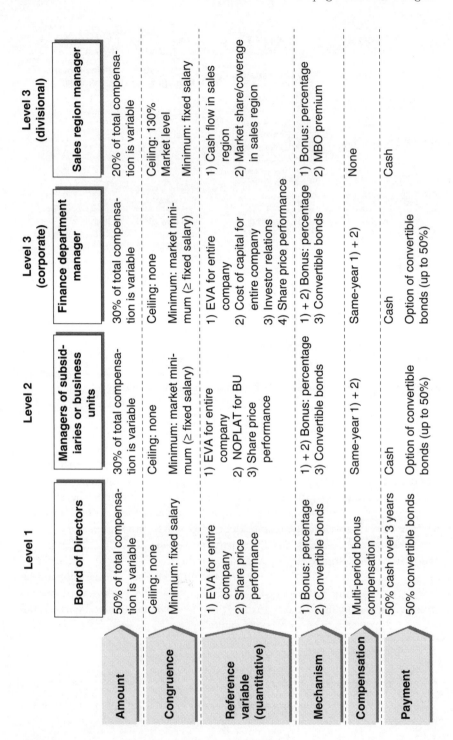

	Level 1 **Board of Directors**	Level 2 **Managers of subsidiaries or business units**	Level 3 (corporate) **Finance department manager**	Level 3 (divisional) **Sales region manager**
Amount	50% of total compensation is variable	30% of total compensation is variable	30% of total compensation is variable	20% of total compensation is variable
Congruence	Ceiling: none Minimum: fixed salary	Ceiling: none Minimum: market minimum (≥ fixed salary)	Ceiling: none Minimum: market minimum (≥ fixed salary)	Ceiling: 130% Market level Minimum: fixed salary
Reference variable (quantitative)	1) EVA for entire company 2) Share price performance	1) EVA for entire company 2) NOPLAT for BU 3) Share price performance	1) EVA for entire company 2) Cost of capital for entire company 3) Investor relations 4) Share price performance	1) Cash flow in sales region 2) Market share/coverage in sales region
Mechanism	1) Bonus: percentage 2) Convertible bonds	1) + 2) Bonus: percentage 3) Convertible bonds	1) + 2) Bonus: percentage 3) Convertible bonds	1) Bonus: percentage 2) MBO premium
Compensation	Multi-period bonus compensation	Same-year 1) + 2)	Same-year 1) + 2)	None
Payment	50% cash over 3 years 50% convertible bonds	Cash Option of convertible bonds (up to 50%)	Cash Option of convertible bonds (up to 50%)	Cash

Figure 3.54: Forms of implementation at various levels – example.

Balancing individual and collective incentives

Links to measures of collective performance reinforce cooperation and prevent competition within the company. They can, however, also be a breeding ground for passivity or the neglect of units or entities for which no one feels responsible (e.g. overhead costs, unassigned customer segments etc.).

Individual reference variables trace only a person's individual scope of responsibility or the effect of that person's actions. Compensation systems based on individual reference variables are a direct source of motivation and guidance, but can at the same time produce undesirable results such as partial optimisation, inefficiency, lead to competition, or fruitless discussions about who is responsible for what. Within a project organisation whose tasks have a strong team emphasis, individual incentives can actually be counterproductive.

The rule of thumb is therefore to combine both individual and collective components in incentive schemes. The two components should not be measured against the same variable, however. Instead, one should logically follow on from the other. The factor determining the individual incentive could, for example, be NOPLAT, while EBITD (gross cash flow) could be taken as the collective reference variable. Figure 3.54 takes the top three management levels of a publicly traded company to illustrate the design dimensions available for the compensation system.

Requirements for implementation

Organisational, formal and process-related requirements must be met to facilitate the practical introduction of value-based compensation systems. Figure 3.55 outlines the individual requirements.

Delimitation of units as separate market players

The preceding sections have already highlighted the fact that clearly delimited spheres of responsibility that are reflected in internal accounting units are an implicit prerequisite for value management. Within any given business unit, the most important resources can be structured independently by the management of that business unit, i.e. in terms of their nature, quantity and purchase price. Moreover, the output produced by this business unit should have a market with its own autonomous price setting mechanism. These minimum requirements open up the opportunity of correctly applying the tools of value-based controlling while, at the same time, affording the manager genuine freedom to act on strategic and operative matters in order to create value.

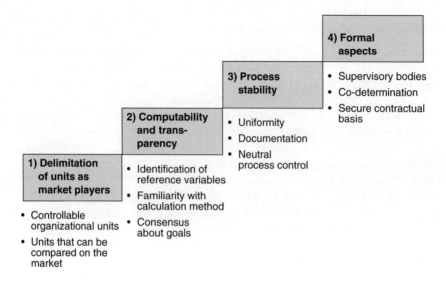

Figure 3.55: Requirements.

Computability and transparency

Internal accounting departments must collate valid data and supply it to the units not only at the end of the year, but more frequently so that real control can be exercised. The demands of the compensation system do not, however, go beyond those of value-based controlling. It is important to ensure transparency and consensus among managers regarding the tools of controlling and the compensation reference variables to be used. This is especially true for the internal calculation of company value. The definition of hurdle rates and the cost of capital – as the basis on which value creation is to be assessed – must also have the full backing of all concerned. Ideally, these compensation goals should be defined and ratified in the context of coordinated business planning.

Process stability

The compensation process must be uniform for all beneficiaries. The identification of targets, the monitoring of compliance and the method adopted must all be defined on a standardised basis (see Fig. 3.56). The personnel department is the process owner in this case. The parties involved in determining the benchmark figures for the compensation system will vary depending on the structure and legal form of the company. For downstream levels of the hierarchy, this will usually be done by the managers responsible on the next highest level, in conjunction with the personnel department. It is the latter's task to ensure that salary levels, compensation systems and framework processes within the company are homogenised. In most cases, the employee council and the executives' representative body will merely have the right to be informed, since the beneficiaries of a value-based system of compensation will, by definition, all be managerial employees.

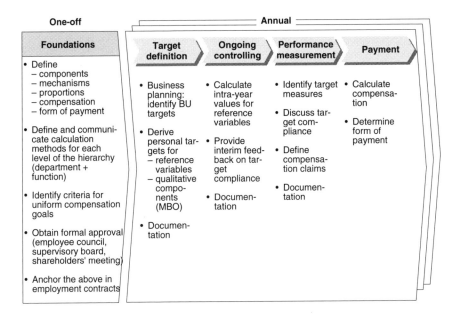

One-off	Annual			
Foundations	**Target definition**	**Ongoing controlling**	**Performance measurement**	**Payment**
• Define – components – mechanisms – proportions – compensation – form of payment • Define and communicate calculation methods for each level of the hierarchy (department + function) • Identify criteria for uniform compensation goals • Obtain formal approval (employee council, supervisory board, shareholders' meeting) • Anchor the above in employment contracts	• Business planning: identify BU targets • Derive personal targets for – reference variables – qualitative components (MBO) • Documentation	• Calculate intra-year values for reference variables • Provide interim feedback on target compliance • Documentation	• Identify target measures • Discuss target compliance • Define compensation claims • Documentation	• Calculate compensation • Determine form of payment

Figure 3.56: The value-based compensation process.

Formal aspects

Determining the amount of compensation to be paid to top management is a matter for the supervisory board and, where appropriate, for the shareholders' or annual general meeting. Genuine equity participation will normally require a resolution by the annual general meeting if the scheme necessitates a conditional increase in capital stock. Shareholders' associations attach considerable importance to imposing realistic caps on top management compensation, and will often demand that the issue be explained, and voted on, at the annual general meeting.

Since there is virtually no limit to the creativity with which participatory compensation schemes can be put together, tax effects for both the company and beneficiary should be clarified in advance on the basis of binding information supplied by the relevant fiscal authorities. Finally, compensation agreements only formally take effect when they are appended in writing to the contract of employment. This is important for identification of the calculation base and of the criteria for assessing achievement of the targets defined.

Implementation aids

The main challenge to implementation is the need to secure the acceptance of all interested and directly affected parties and to keep the effort involved in switching to the new system within manageable limits. Figure 3.57 summarises the key points to be considered when designing and introducing a compensation system.

Design	Introduction
• All beneficiaries should enjoy salary growth in the startup phase	• Define a multi-period process
• Parallel development of salaries and business performance will benefit corporate value in the long term	• Redefinition must be possible
	• Introduce scheme only once value-based controlling tools are in place
• Use a simple principle that is readily comprehensible to shareholders, the public and the employees	• Obtain support and legitimization from external compensation advisers
• Adapt to existing compensation components (MBO system, management bonuses)	• Apply concerted communication
	(• Set up a compensation committee)
• Offer market-oriented salary levels	

Figure 3.57: Implementation aids.

Design

Compensation systems always go down well with the beneficiaries if they go hand in hand with an effective pay rise. A system can be introduced in one of several ways. One option is for customary salary increases to be applied only to the variable component of compensation, with the result that this variable component grows over the years. If the new value-based system is introduced during a phase when company value is expected to increase at above-average rates, scarcely any of the beneficiaries will be tempted to resist the offer of a more powerful salary lever.

The principle that salary and corporate development should plot parallel courses, above all in times of below-average value growth, is the argument that is most widely accepted by shareholders. And the golden rule for every compensation system is: the simpler, the better. The acid test of simplicity is whether the scheme is easily understood by the beneficiaries and by external observers. Internal value determination methods may be ever so sophisticated in order to take due account of each and every delimitation, as dictated by the principles of value management. Nonetheless, the basic structures at least must always be easy to explain. In our view, any system containing more than three elements of variable compensation is too complicated.

Since most companies already work with variable compensation components along the lines of MBO agreements or discretionary management bonuses, it is easy enough, during the transitional period, simply to incorporate value-based reference variables in the catalogue of MBO targets. Equally, the element of subjective decision-making that is inherent in the MBO system can most certainly be put to good use for non-measurable performance that nevertheless creates value.

The introductory phase

The introduction of a value-based compensation system is a process that will extend over several reporting periods. Reference variables, proportions and mechanisms will need to be tried out over several periods, and may need to be redefined.

Above all, such systems will only work if they are sufficiently transparent and can win the confidence of internal and external observers alike. Given this situation, it must also be possible to make changes during the introductory phase. It may not exactly be standard practice in relation to systems of compensation, but it can be a good idea to set up project teams, including the beneficiaries themselves, and even to hold a series of introductory seminars. Such seminars lend themselves particularly in the case of downstream levels of the hierarchy, if they have not hitherto been involved in designing the system.

It makes sense to have something of a time lag between the introduction of value-based controlling systems and the introduction of corresponding compensation systems. This provides a breathing space in which the company can get a secure handle on the calculation of the relevant management and reference variables, and come to terms with their application.

A common practice in the USA – and one we would also recommend to other companies – is the creation of a compensation committee for top management and executive employees. This committee represents all relevant interest groups: the supervisory board, the shareholders, the management, and an external compensation adviser. Each year, this committee decides on the components and the amount of management compensation, and its decisions are binding for all other bodies within the company.

When a company sets about far-reaching changes to its systems of compensation, it is advisable to enlist the aid of reputable and professional external consultants – not only to ensure internal acceptance and external legitimisation. Having a neutral moderator during the coordination phase is just as important as having external assistance on designing the ingredients of the system (amounts, calculation methods etc.) with reference to comparable systems already in existence on the market.

The result of these aspects of value management will be a compensation system that motivates both managers and their staff to act in line with value-based principles – a move which, in particular, accommodates the demand for more performance-oriented compensation that is widely advocated by professional investors.

3.5 Informing stakeholders and shareholders; developing investor relations

Of all stakeholders, the investors are the ones who probably play the most important role. It is they who decide on what funding is made available to the company. And, if returns are poor, they may well withdraw their money and invest it in more profitable undertakings. This chapter is intended as a guideline for the development and conduct of value-based investor relations. Having laid this foundation, we shall then examine the goals pursued by investor relations activities and look at the target groups on which a company needs to focus. The bulk of the chapter, however, concerns itself with what goes into the successful development of investor relations programs and the procedure that needs to be adopted. The chapter concludes with a brief case example to flesh out the theory of investor relations.

Investor relations as a crucial communication tool for value management

Investor relations is a term that is often bandied around. But what exactly does it mean?

Investors will only be interested in and invest in a company if it promises to be an attractive – i.e. profitable – investment. It must therefore be possible to put a value on a company in some way so that an informed decision can be taken. This is precisely where investor relations come into play. A stock corporation's investor relations activities should supply the financial community with the information it needs to be able to assess the company. Investor relations is not a one-off information exercise: it is a long-term process of positive opinion-building, a process which begins in the run up to an initial public offering and continues *ad infinitum* thereafter. The fact that between around 10 and 15% of a company's value development is these days ascribed to the influence of professional investor relations makes this ongoing process all the more critical. Investor relations evidently has a decisive contribution to make to the sustained and fair valuation of a company.

The USA is the most advanced and proactive – some might even say aggressive – investor relations market in the world. In Europe the UK is still far ahead of continental European countries. Compared with the USA and the UK, the practice of investor relations in France, Germany or Italy has long been conspicuous by its absence. Reasons for this country-specific development include the relatively underdeveloped share culture and the fact that stocks are not particularly popular among private investors. In Germany, in the wake of World War II, the major corporations – Lufthansa, RWE, Volkswagen etc. – were either largely or entirely in the hands of the public sector. Where there is only one major shareholder, there is no immediate need for a broadly based flow of information. As a major shareholder the state will, in any case, be involved in any decisions taken by such companies. At the same time, many companies have in the past subscribed to the erroneous belief that investors by and large base their decisions on the observation of historical returns. And a further weakness has been the inordinate confidence often placed in the ability of commercial banks' retail customer departments to act as sales brokers. Thus the task of publicising company-internal decisions and the changes that would ensue has often been delegated to third parties. Consequently, many companies have effectively fore-gone their chance to actively penetrate the investor market.

Notwithstanding, Europe has in recent years witnessed a significant change for the better as investor relations has become recognised as an opportunity to communicate information that is highly relevant to the investment community. Taking a look at this development, there have been three reasons for this turn of events, some of which we touched on in Chapter 1:

• Competition for capital as a factor of production is growing and is increas-ingly being played out on the global capital markets.
• The number of institutional investors who have higher expectations is on the rise.
• The proportion of foreign investors, e.g. in Germany, having stagnated be-tween 1990 and 1996, is now picking up again.[1]

If anyone was harbouring doubts that investor relations stop at the country's border, these were swept away in July 1998. It was then that the London Stock Exchange and the Frankfurt-based Deutsche Börse, Europe's two largest stock markets, announced that they had formed a strategic alliance. Against this back-drop, publicly traded European companies are increasingly being compelled to satisfy the growing thirst for information that is indicative of investor groups who themselves are in the throes of transition. The situation calls for stepped-up activities and greater professionalism in corporate investor relations. Both aspects are evidently lacking; the consequences for listed companies are, accord-ingly, negative.

Our intention here is to provide a detailed explanation of the following as-pects of investor relations programs:

• What are the goals pursued by investor relations?
• What tools are available (target group orientation, communication tools, forms of organisation, scoring models)?
• How can investor relations programs be applied?
• What does investor relations look like in practice?

---

[1] Dürr (1995), pp. 3 ff.

Defining and pursuing goals

The overriding goal of investor relations is to safeguard and communicate the attractiveness of the company as a profitable object for investment. The company uses specific tools (see below) in an attempt to align the company's share value with the 'true' value of the company and to avoid overvaluation or undervaluation on the capital market. There are four aspects to this primary goal, the key elements of which are outlined in Fig. 3.58.

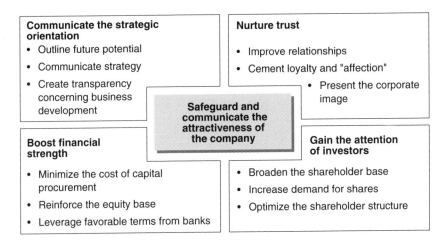

Figure 3.58: The goals of investor relations activities.[2]

Each company has to translate these goals and their various constituents into operational reality in accordance with its own particular situation. Only then will the measures applied take on a concrete form that can ultimately be measured as part of an investor relations program.

It is interesting to note the importance the financial community attaches to these goals, as evidenced in Fig. 3.59. Efforts to communicate the company's strategic orientation and to nurture an atmosphere of fundamental trust are seen to have a comparatively significant impact.

In a value management context, it is not difficult to understand why the first of these two points is expected to have such considerable impact. Investors do not base their decisions solely on the basis of the historical information contained in the balance sheet and the income statement, both of which retroactively represent the earning power of the company. Statements concerning the future strategy of the company are far more likely to influence their investment decisions, especially if mostly qualitative arguments are supplemented by more

---

[2] IRES (1991), Chapter 2.2.2.

concrete, quantitative explanations, as is standard practice especially in North America. By European standards, the German Veba AG is something of a paragon of virtue as far as information about corporate strategy is concerned: the company is unusually candid in its disclosure of future sales, results and investments projections, each of which is broken down by division.

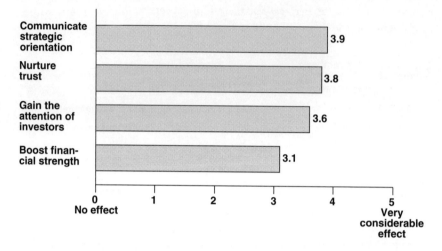

Figure 3.59: How investor relations goals affect the financial community.[3]

The considerable significance attached to efforts to nurture trust shows that investor relations is never a one-off exercise, but is rather a continuous process whose successes are achieved over the medium to long term. Shareholders who can rely on the fact that they will receive the relevant information quickly and comprehensively will reward companies that do so. Companies which, in extreme cases, have been plunged into crisis situations, and have then been able plausibly to articulate both the causes and their strategies for surmounting these crises, have found that a positive base of investor trust has helped them to weather the storm more easily than companies who, hitherto, have presented themselves to investors more or less as a 'black box'.

Targeting information to specific groups

Investor relations is a strategy communication that has its roots in financial expertise. Having defined its goals and objectives, the next step that is necessary to the successful introduction and continuation of an investor relations program is to identify the relevant target groups. Essentially, investor behaviour is akin to

---

[3] IRES (1991), Chapter 2.2.2.

that of the demand side of the consumer goods market. Information, be it rational or emotional, will miss its mark if it does not satisfy the requirements of its target group and will render the program inefficient from the ground up.

The target group for investor relations is the financial community as a whole. This community in turn is made up of financial analysts, representatives of the business press and rating agencies, all of whom act as multipliers and opinion leaders for the capital market. The company itself and these multipliers then seek directly to influence the investment decisions taken by individual investors. This relationship is illustrated by the figure below.

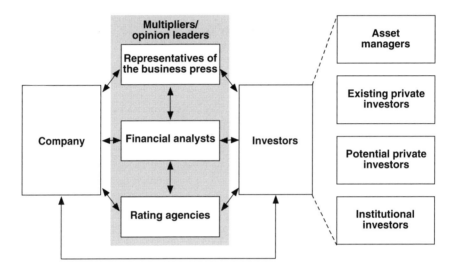

Figure 3.60: Target groups for investor relations.

Of the target groups listed, two in particular occupy a pre-eminent position: financial analysts and institutional investors. Both groups are highly specialised in the fields they respectively monitor; both have access to a wealth of detailed expertise. Every day, all around the globe, data on companies, industries, markets, stock market performance, interest rate and currency trends, and political developments are recorded, analysed, and assessed in terms of their bearing on investment decisions. Logically, therefore, both groups have far more exacting information needs than, say, private investors – especially with regard to the medium-term activities and strategic orientation of a company. Foreign institutional investors in particular, whose influence in domestic companies is growing, are putting pressure on the top management to change their information policies. This attitude is conditioned by the more widespread tradition of active investor relations in their home countries and the higher expectations and demands that such an environment instils. However, private investors too are by no means uninteresting as a target group.

The 1990s has seen continental Europe following the privatisation route taken by the UK in the 1980s. With major IPOs in Germany, shares are gaining greater popularity as a capital investment for private investors. In 1996, the total number of private investors rose by 15% to its present figure of some 5.2 million. This development is being fuelled in part by the flotation of former state-owned companies, as federal government seeks to fill the holes in the national budget by selling off large numbers of hitherto publicly owned shares. Examples of this trend include Deutsche Telekom AG (with an issue volume of around DM 21 billion in 1996) and Deutsche Lufthansa AG (around DM 5 billion in 1997). One of the largest IPO's in Europe took place in 1997, when the state-owned France Telecom offered its shares in Paris and New York. Almost 3.9 million individual investors bought shares, according to the government, generating approximately FFr 42 billion. The IPO made France Telecom the biggest French company in terms of market capitalisation.

Yet there is a further factor that is making private investors more attractive as a target group: as a rule, private investors do not tend to reshuffle their securities portfolios so often and in many cases have an emotional tie with a particular company. As a result, private investors can have a stabilising influence on share prices.

Figure 3.61 summarises the relative importance of the various target groups from the company's point of view.

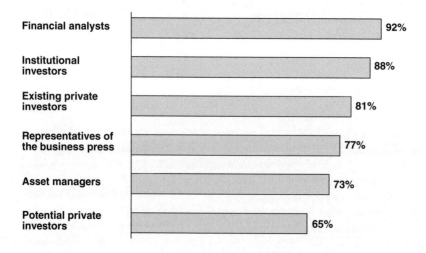

Figure 3.61: Importance of the various investor relations target groups.[4]

---

[4] IRES (1991), Chapter 2.2.4.

It is certainly not easy to identify target groups. Yet this is an extremely important task, and one which must be done differently for individual groups. Market research methods can be used to identify the data and facts that isolate a given target group; on this basis, their specific requirements can be pinpointed. The principal results of this exercise, which will form the basis on which to design a company's investor relations program, are as follows:

- The individual company can prioritise the various target groups for its own purposes.
- The key contacts in each group can be named (which institutional investors, who are the people to contact?).
- The information needs and expectations of each group can be identified.

Successfully developing and conducting investor relations

Once the goals have been set and the relevant target groups identified, it is time to design a suitable program of investor relations. To do so, four main aspects must be examined:

- the appropriate use of alternative communication tools;
- the establishment of investor relations as a corporate function;
- the conversion of the company's accounting principles; and
- the permanent implementation of scoring models to evaluate investor relations.

The section that follows focuses in particular on the uses of the various communication instruments, as their impact will depend to a large extent on the company's relationship with the addressee.

Making appropriate use of alternative communication tools

For the purposes of investor relations, tools of communication can be divided into direct and indirect means of addressing the intended recipient. To satisfy the information requirements and fuel the information impact of all target groups, there is in practice always a need to bundle various forms of direct and indirect communication. Of the indirect means available, annual reports are regarded as singularly important. Of the direct means, presentations and one-on-one meetings are felt to carry most weight. Figure 3.62 outlines the various tools and their comparative importance to investors.

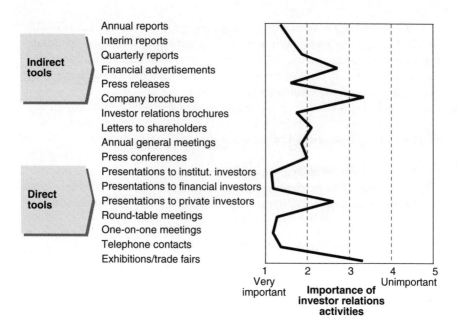

Figure 3.62: Tools of communication and their importance to investors.[5]

Tools of indirect communication

Indirect tools of communication are traditionally the most widely and frequently used methods. Most are targeted primarily at existing and potential private investors, since this group cannot be addressed collectively with any degree of certainty, which makes direct communication very difficult. In view of the considerable importance of annual reports to the information behaviour of investors, as shown in Fig. 3.62, it is worthwhile taking a closer look at this medium. However, this should not be construed as meaning that the other tools referred to do not have their rightful place within a comprehensive program of investor relations.

One result of today's more exacting demands for information has been a radical change in expectations concerning the structure of annual reports. Until recently, annual reports were pretty uninformative affairs, tending rather towards obfuscation and high levels of aggregation. Their purpose was merely to satisfy statutory disclosure requirements. One major German food company provided a fine example. The company's annual report for the fiscal year in 1996 resembled more of an advertising brochure than a medium of information tailored to the needs of investor relations. Although the company had gross external sales of over DM 50 billion, the relatively paltry sum of DM 6 billion appeared in the

---

[5] Günther/Otterbein (1996), p. 410.

income statement – presumably because the consolidated group was treated separately from the parent company. There was no detailed information about sales and results by segment, nor any statement of cash flows. In fairness, it should be said that this is no longer the rule: much has now changed for the better. Such changes have been reinforced by prizes awarded for disclosure practices. The 'Investor Relations Magazine' in the UK, for example, awards a prize for the best annual report each year. SmithKline Beecham won the award in 1998 just beating British Petroleum and Cadbury Schweppes.

From the point of view of investor relations, what requirements should an annual report satisfy? First we need to look at the content to be communicated. The focus of investor interest is divided between historical information on the one hand and the future development of the company on the other. Figure 3.63 lists the most important issues that must be detailed. However, the points listed here are not confined to annual reports alone. On the contrary, they remain equally valid for the contents of all forms of indirect and direct communication. At the same time, Fig. 3.63 in its entirety represents the maximum requirement or best-case scenario. Accordingly, the exact composition will vary as a function of each company's cost/benefit considerations.

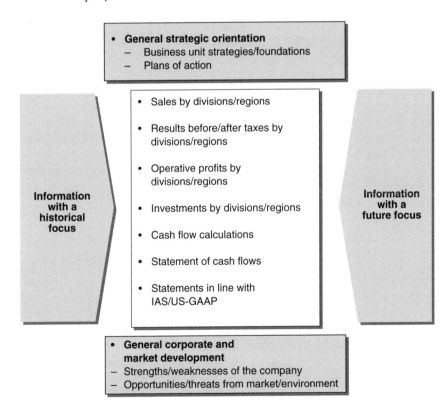

Figure 3.63: What investors expect to see in annual reports.

Yet content alone is not the only issue. Other important factors include the structure and layout of the annual report. The figures must be easy to interpret if they are to leave a lasting impression with the investor. The challenge to companies is actively to market the benefit arising from a presentation of their past business successes and future potential, and to do this in as attractive a form as possible. Annual reports are, after all, all too often seen as a company's calling card. This being the case, the structure of the text and image material – colour, typeface, pictures, graphics, layout, paper, volume and other relevant factors – plays a key role. Equally, it is important to ensure that annual reports 'speak the right language'. Well-structured, readily comprehensible sentence structures and clear, careful wording are of paramount importance.

Biannual and quarterly reports should also be published in addition to annual reports. Since 1990, the German Stock Market Law has prescribed that at least one interim report must be published in each fiscal year. Unlike in the USA, quarterly reports are not compulsory in Germany. They are, however, an opportunity for information disclosure that companies would do well to exploit. Interim and quarterly reports should avoid focusing too heavily on domestic issues, and should also address investors abroad.

One vast topic that is ignored entirely by the study on which Fig. 3.62 is based, is the issue of new media, which is growing in importance in the context of investor relations. Let us briefly examine these new media now.

The potential afforded by new media should be put to good use for investor relations activities. Nowadays, it is taken for granted that the current annual report, the latest news on corporate developments or today's share price will all be posted on the Internet. This medium gives companies an opportunity to supply up-to-date information that is of relevance to a wider group of investors. Another advantage is the comparatively high degree of interaction that can be achieved with new media. Whereas someone who is reading a brochure will very seldom take the trouble to submit active feedback, the chances of eliciting such a response are far greater when all it takes is a mouse-click or an e-mail. Statistical analyses, such as the number of 'virtual visits' to the company's Website, can also be generated very easily.

Tools of direct communication

Direct communication tools can be brought into play wherever a group of addressees can be identified unambiguously. Presentations to financial analysts and institutional investors are an exceptionally important aspect of investor relations activities, a fact attested to by the target groups themselves (see Fig. 3.62). Such events give companies a chance to engage their target groups in direct dialogue in order to provide them with exactly the information they want. A survey conducted found that 90% of companies stage presentations for institutional investors several times a year in Germany, while 86% do the same abroad. The figures are more or less the same for the financial analysts' target group.[6]

Thorough preparation and professional presentation are the key to the success of these events. As a rule, no more than 15 to 20 people should be in attendance, and presentations should be held as close as possible to the publication of annual or interim results. It is also advisable to meet with selected financial analysts or institutional investors beforehand, for two reasons. One is to underscore in advance the importance of such presentations; the other is to ensure that the subsequent presentation genuinely matches the existing need for information. The presentation itself will usually be a fairly formal affair followed by a lengthy, perhaps more informal discussion. To clinch the success of such presentations, we strongly recommend that top management play an active role. Finally, it is also important that background material, such as the latest annual and interim reports and copies of the presentation documents, be handed out to participants.

Selected institutional investors who operate as major capital backers should be catered for, in the context of one-on-one meetings. This setting will allow their information needs to be serviced more fully, while at the same time leaving room to deal with sensitive issues that are best not tackled in open presentations. One-on-one meetings should be held at least once or twice a year.

Companies whose investors have a wide geographical spread – companies whose shares are quoted on foreign stock exchanges, for example, or where significant foreign investors already exist or are on the horizon – should provide local support to these groups. It should be obvious that regional events ought to be held in the appropriate financial centres. These events are referred to by the banking and investment community as 'roadshows'. When Daimler Benz and Chrysler announced their global merger a worldwide roadshow was set up. In the course of 50 one-on-one meetings, presentations and telephone calls, more than 1200 institutional investors were addressed.[7]

With all tools of direct communication, it is important to recognise and make provision for regional aspects and cultural considerations. This applies less to the content of the information – the facts, figures, strategies and company and market developments that are required by domestic and foreign investors alike – and more to the form in which this information is communicated. In America, such communication tends to be very straight and to-the-point. People are therefore usually very open to one-on-one meetings. This costs a company more time and money; but the up-front investment is appreciated by financial analysts and investors alike, since ongoing dialogue creates a forum in which to service their specific information requirements on a far more detailed level. The situation in Asia, for instance, is completely different. In this part of the world, presentations are more effective, as one-on-one contact is often not immediately forthcoming

---

[6] Günther/Otterbein (1996), p. 408.

[7] Gentz (1998), B1.

and a less direct approach is generally preferred. Here, communication and *rapprochement* tend to occur one small step at a time. It is therefore all the more important to provide exhaustive documentation that can be examined *ex post* by the people who attend such presentations.

Establishing investor relations as a corporate function

Given the supreme importance of investor relations to the sustained and accurate valuation of companies, it is recommended for investor relations to be established as a corporate function in its own right. Nevertheless, hands-on experience shows there to be considerable room for improvement in this quarter, too. It is still by no means common for companies to set up a separate organisational unit under the heading 'Investor Relations'. In many cases, the relevant activities are handled by the staff of the finance or public relations departments alongside their other tasks. Studies in Germany and the United Kingdom confirm this practice. Only about 50% of the companies surveyed in the two countries have a dedicated investor relations department or a full-time investor relations manager.[8] 22% of respondent companies in Germany have two or three full-time managers for this area.[9] We are nevertheless expecting this relatively poor showing to change for the better in the near future.

Factors which influence the recruitment of an investor relations manager include the size of the company, a generally positive attitude toward investor relations on the part of top management, and quotation on overseas stock exchanges. When its stocks were first listed on the New York Stock Exchange in 1993, Daimler-Benz AG, for example, set up a local investor relations office in order to establish direct personal contact with local target groups.

How should a company set up and equip its investor relations department?

The first step is to define the position of the new unit within the organisation and establish the reporting lines. In practice, the investor relations department will usually belong to either corporate finance or the public relations office. In the former case it will report to the CFO, in the latter case usually to the CEO. Most European companies set up their investor relations departments as part of their finance units – as is the case at Glaxo Wellcome and France Telecom, for example, where investor relations reports to the chief financial officer.

We would refrain from any general recommendation about whether the new department should be attached to the one function rather than the other. This decision has to be left to each company. The most important thing is that the investor relations department should satisfy two conditions. The first is that it must report directly to top management. This fact alone will document the importance of investor relations both within the company and to the outside world. Secondly, interaction between finance and accounting, public relations and in-

---

[8] Marston (1996), p. 477.
[9] Deutsche Morgan Grenfell (1996), p. 29.

vestor relations must be made to work smoothly. A closer examination of this demand naturally raises the question of the job description and requirements profile of an investor relations manager.

The tasks assigned to an investor relations manager are many and varied, as can be seen from the issues we have already dealt with. They range from designing the investor relations program to overseeing its implementation. This will involve activities such as surveying the shareholder structure, organising the annual general meeting, assuming responsibility for annual and interim reports, and holding regular presentations to financial analysts. In addition to routine tasks, the ability to respond to unusual events concerning the company – mergers and acquisitions, or even accidents at work, for example – is a further key aspect of the manager's work.

The breadth of this portfolio is reflected in the requirements profile for an investor relations manager. The need is for all-rounders rather than specialists – people who are just as at home fielding questions about funding, financial analysis and the stock markets as they are dealing with marketing and public relations issues. Analytical and conceptual skills are also a must. At the same time, investor relations managers should be excellent communicators who are capable of developing internal and external networks.

Not every stock corporation will set up a fully-fledged investor relations department. An alternative solution is to outsource these activities, in part or in full, to external service providers. This can be a particularly attractive option to small and medium-sized companies who do not themselves have sufficient financial and/or human resources. However, even companies who are preparing to go public or have long since been listed on the stock exchange are increasingly availing themselves of such external services in order to take advantage of other people's experience and expertise in the design, implementation and permanent controlling of investor relations programs. As we have already stressed, investor relations is not a one-off assignment but an ongoing process. All activities conducted under the umbrella of investor relations will need to be reviewed on a regular basis and adapted to changes in investors' information requirements.

Converting the company's accounting principles

Investor relations programs can only succeed if a company's end-of-year financial statements provide information that is useful and relevant. This means tailoring the contents to the needs of the recipients, i.e. the investors. More and more of these investors come from international and/or institutional backgrounds; and their appetite for information is increasingly putting pressure on companies to adopt internationally used and accepted standards of accounting. The objective must be to produce annual financial statements that can usefully be compared beyond national borders. This trend is forcing European companies to realign the long-term focus of their accounting practices. The German Commercial Code (HGB), in particular, leaves open a variety of options and alternative valuation methods that can be used to influence yearly results.

To comply with international standards, accounting can in principle adhere to one of two systems: the International Accounting Standards (IAS) and the US' Generally Accepted Accounting Principles (US-GAAP). Any and every European company that wants to be listed in the USA is required to produce parallel balance sheets in accordance with US-GAAP. The end-of-year results arrived at by the two systems – e.g. HGB and US-GAAP – differ considerably. This is clearly illustrated by Daimler-Benz AG's flotation on the New York Stock Exchange in 1993. On the balance sheet prepared according to the HGB principles, the group posted an annual net profit of around DM 600 million. The parallel statement prepared in line with US-GAAP, however, recorded a loss of around DM 1.9 billion. Taking a look at the United Kingdom we can observe discrepancies between the UK- and the US-GAAP of a similar magnitude. In 1998, the profit of Cadbury Schweppes for the Financial Year from continuing operations, net of tax, (per UK GAAP) amounted to £355 million. On the basis of the US-GAAP method the profit decreased to £257 million, especially due to adjustments in the amortisation of goodwill and trademarks. Investors will therefore naturally want to know which system best and most truthfully represents the economic situation and attractiveness of a company. Without going into the respective benefits and drawbacks of the two sets of principles, calls for parallel statements to be abolished and replaced by a single, compulsory system would appear to be justified. Other companies, such as Bayer AG, draw up parallel balance sheets in compliance with IAS principles. At the present time, this is a requirement for foreign companies that are quoted on the London Stock Exchange. Although heavily outweighed by US-GAAP, the International Accounting Standards are essentially the only truly international set of principles currently in existence, albeit they have never been completely finalised. Further standardisation is to be finally completed. As soon as this milestone has been put into force, IAS-compliant statements are accepted for quotation on any stock exchange anywhere in the world. According to the Security Exchange Commission (SEC), this would also include the US stock market. In effect, then, this move would significantly further the cause of uniform information quality in corporate accounting.

Using scoring models to evaluate investor relations

Investor relations activities should be designed to communicate the attractiveness of a company to the chosen target groups. One way of achieving this end is by using scoring models. Scoring models help to keep a record of and evaluate a company's investor relations activities. This should be done at regular intervals in order to identify either positive or negative developments.

Deutsche Morgan Grenfell has formulated a scoring model that provides a rather comprehensive assessment of a company's investor relations work. In five categories, the way in which investor relations is organised, the nature of the related activities, and the quality and transparency of the data published is investigated and evaluated (see Fig. 3.64).

Investor relations scoring model			
	Yes	In part	No
1. Size of IR department • Existence of IR department/full-time manager • 2-3 full-time IR managers •			
2. Immediate access to top management and data • Direct line of reporting to CFO/CEO • Direct access to budget and strategic planning •			
3. Activities of IR department • Fast and up-to-date publication of data • Two major presentations per year •			
4. Detail, quality and up-to-date nature of reporting • Sales by division • Informative cash flow statement •			
5. Purpose and frequency of performance reporting • Publication of medium-term performance figures • Semi-annual publication of performance figures •			
Total score			
Weighting factor			
Total IR score			

Figure 3.64: Scoring model to evaluate investor relations.[10]

These five categories are broken down into 25 variants, each of which is scored individually. The result offers a clear, detailed assessment of a company's investor relations performance. When interpreting the results, however, it is important to remember that their accuracy will, to some extent, be limited by the subjective nature of the evaluation.

A study of 99 publicly traded German companies yielded an average score of around 44%. DAX companies, with an average of 60%, returned significantly above-average results. What this means is that not even half of all the companies surveyed satisfy the criteria for a comprehensive investor relations program. By comparison, the average investor relations score for companies in the United Kingdom and Sweden was put at around 85%. This disparity clearly highlights, despite the tangible improvements made in recent years, the persisting need,

[10] Deutsche Morgan Grenfell (1996), p. 29.

especially for German companies, to catch up with the UK and Anglo-Saxon-influenced countries in Scandinavia.

Average investor relations scores	
• 99 companies	44.2%
• DAX	60.0%
• Non-DAX	39.9%
• Chemicals and pharmaceuticals	72.3%
• Automotive and transport	54.2%
• Utilities	49.8%
• Steel	49.7%
• Electronics	40.5%
• Construction	33.7%
• Consumer and retail	32.5%
• Mechanical engineering	31.4%

Figure 3.65: Investor relations scores at German companies.[11]

The study also confirms another hypothesis, where companies operating in industries with a pronounced international focus, tend to show a better quality of investor relations than those confined primarily to domestic markets. Chemicals and pharmaceuticals, for example, and the automotive and transport industries are way ahead of sectors such as the construction industry, consumer goods and retail. The reasons for this is that foreign investor groups expect far more by way of detailed information, and accordingly exert pressure on the information policies of multinational companies. The results of the study are summarised in Fig. 3.65.

---

[11] Deutsche Morgan Grenfell (1996), p. 30.

Implementing investor relations programs in three stages

An investor relations program can be introduced along classical project lines in three stages: current status analysis, drafting of a concept, and implementation.

Stage 1 involves an inventory exercise. The objective is to identify the current status regarding the nature, extent and quality of existing investor relations activities within the company. This exercise will reveal existing weaknesses and pinpoint any gaps relative to the firm's competitors. To get this analysis moving, we recommend a procedure involving both internal and external company investigation criteria. The focus of internal analysis will initially be on what are known as 'belief audits' among top management. Belief audits consist of interviews, which record top management's attitude toward and acceptance of investor relations. The ongoing support of top management is, after all, extremely important if the outward expression of investor relations is ever to succeed. Investor relations programs can only be implemented top-down with the full backing of top management.

The internal inventorying exercise also evaluates the investor relations department itself and the degree to which it is integrated in top management. At the same time, the tools of communication used to date, the existing financial policy and structure, and the rules that currently govern shareholding and voting rights must also be noted.

Outside the company, image analyses should be conducted among existing target groups in order to identify what information is required, and to find out whether people know about the investor relations activities already in place and how they rate them. A performance comparison with relevant competitor companies and best-practice companies should also be carried out. The results of this first stage will thus clearly indicate where the company is currently at in terms of its investor relations activities.

These results lay the foundation for stage 2, the design of an investor relations program that will optimise the company's position within the financial community. This stage will involve working through all the points described in detail in the main body of this chapter. One additional point that also needs to be defined is the issue of training requirements, and a suitable training program. The extent to which training is necessary will depend on how much needs to be changed; this information can be derived from the results of the inventory exercise and the ensuing concept. Stage 2 culminates in an endorsement of the investor relations program by top management.

The crucial factor of success once any program has been fully designed is, of course, that it be implemented rigorously within the organisation. This is especially true of investor relations programs. Value must be created systematically across all entrepreneurial levels. Commensurate changes in the behaviour of everyone involved must be achieved by the appropriate opinion leaders, and by a series of well-planned measures.

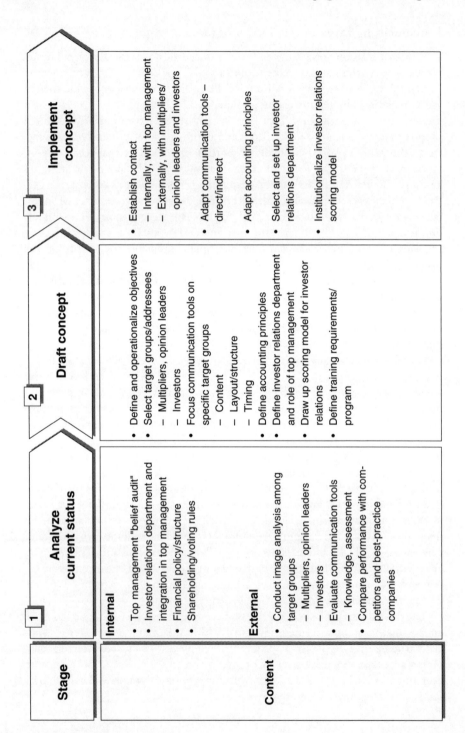

Figure 3.66: Project outline for implementing investor relations.

Stage 3 consists of precisely this gradual introduction of the concept within the company itself and in its surrounding environment. A lot of work is needed to secure internal acceptance. A neutral consultant can be invaluable in reinforcing the credibility of the program, a task that becomes easier the more that top management clearly articulates its unequivocal backing. Internal mechanisms are to be adapted in such a way that the information required by investor relations can be retrieved without significantly adding to the burden of work. Investor relations activities are institutionalised by anchoring them in a specific department. In addition, control mechanisms must be introduced that can monitor both qualitative and quantitative performance measures. On an external front, initial contact must also be established with the target groups identified. Here again, high-profile top management involvement is of paramount importance.

Example of investor relations at Model, Inc.

Model, Inc. is an international player in the beverages production market. The company's shares have been listed on the Frankfurt Stock Exchange since 1987, and at the London Stock Exchange since 1996. Since 1994, Model, Inc. has been pursuing a rather significant program of investor relations activities. As far as the shareholder structure is concerned, substantial capital flows in from institutional investors, but a considerable capital stock is owned by small private investors. In addition, over the past few years, the company's shares have increasingly caught the eye of overseas investors.

The investor relations program at Model, Inc. is based on three key elements. As shown in Fig. 3.67, these elements are: identification of the relevant target group; selection of suitable communication tools for each target group; and definition of supplementary and supportive activities.

Target group	Communication tools	Supplementary tools/activities

• **Institutional investors**
  – DWS Deutsche Gesellschaft für Wertpapiersparen
  – Deutsche Asset Management GmbH
  – Fidelity Investments
  – Templeton Global Strategic Services
  – Union-Investment
• **Financial analysts**
  – DB Research
  – Dresdner International Research Institute
  – J.P. Morgan
  – Merrill Lynch
  – United Bank of Switzerland
• **Private investors**
	• **Direct communication**
	  – Presentations to institutional investors in Frankfurt and London involving top management
	  – One-on-one meetings on the premises of selected institutional investors
	  – Meetings with financial analysts
	  – Telephone conferences
	• **Indirect communication**
	  – Annual/interim/quarterly reports
	  – Annual general meeting
	  – Financial advertisements in Financial Times, Handelsblatt
	  – Company fact book
		• Creation of a second full-time manager position
		  – Reporting directly to CEO
		  – Separate budget responsibility
		• Database of (potential) investors and financial analysts
		• Scoring model to evaluate investor relations

Figure 3.67: Overview of investor relations at Model, Inc.

Identification of target groups

Owing to the size of the Model, Inc. holding company, a special level of direct and intensive service is given to five particular institutional investors and their fund managers. These five are DWS Deutsche Gesellschaft für Wertpapiersparen mbH, Deutsche Asset Management GmbH, Fidelity Investments, Templeton Global Strategic Services and Union-Investment. All of these institutions are based in either Frankfurt or London. At the same time, care is also provided for other important investors who are not listed in the figure. Meanwhile, five financial analysis firms are also of considerable interest to Model, Inc., namely: DB Research, the Dresdner International Research Institute, and the analysts at J.P. Morgan, Merrill Lynch and United Bank of Switzerland. Lower priority is given to servicing other addresses. Finally, Model, Inc. has also developed a focus on its last target group, namely private investors, who already hold a considerable proportion of the company's shares.

Selection of communication tools

To service its chosen target groups, Model, Inc. has compiled a catalogue of measures containing numerous tools of direct and indirect communication. Together, these measures combine to make up a comprehensive strategy of investor relations communication.

Presentations to institutional investors take pride of place among the tools of direct communication. These presentations are held in Frankfurt and London; and the presence of top managers underscores the importance of these events on each occasion. Other tools of direct communication include one-on-one meetings on the premises of the selected institutional investors listed above, as well as meetings with financial analysts and the use of telephone conferences.

Within the framework of its indirect communication activities, Model, Inc. has taken full advantage of the facilities available to it for providing a constant stream of up-to-date information. Over and above the annual and interim reports required by law, Model, Inc. also publishes a quarterly report. Furthermore, the company holds an annual general meeting, places financial advertisements in two leading business dailies, the British 'Financial Times' and the German 'Handelsblatt', and circulates a 'Company Fact Book' containing everything the investor needs to know about the past performance and future development of Model, Inc.

At this point, allow us to digress to a different example, which illustrates how the detailed contents of financial reports can be prepared. The case in point concerns Cadbury Schweppes, a company which, in our opinion, does a good job of satisfying investors' varying needs for information. The annual report contains 150 pages and is dedicated to the management of value. The financial ratios and stream analysis, for instance, divides corporate data such as sales, trading profit, operating assets etc. between the company's segments beverages and confectionery (see Fig. 3.68). At the same time, earnings and dividends per ordinary share, interest and dividend cover, as well as the gearing ratio are provided.

Financial Ratios and Stream Analysis			1998	1997	1996
Earnings per	– Basic	pence	35.0	68.7	34.1
ordinary share	– Diluted	pence	34.5	68.0	33.8
	– Underlying	pence	39.4	37.2	34.1
Dividends per ordinary share		pence	19.0	18.0	17.0
Interest cover		times	11.7	10.0	6.4
Dividend cover		times	2.1	2.1	2.0
Gearing ratio		%	27	37	92
Sales	Beverages	£m	1,937	1,953	1,954
	Discounted operations	£m	–	47	921
	Confectionery	£m	2,169	2,220	2,240
Trading profit	Beverages	£m	362	342	321
	Discounted operations	£m	–	4	124
	Confectionery	£m	280	282	267
Operating assets	Beverages	£m	260	273	255
	Discounted operations	£m	–	–	214
	Confectionery	£m	1,002	1,041	1,028
Trading margin	Beverages	%	18.7	17.5	16.4
	Confectionery	%	12.9	12.7	11.9
Operating asset	Beverages	times	7.3	7.4	6.7
turnover	Confectionery	times	2.1	2.2	2.2

Figure 3.68: Cadbury Schweppes' financial ratios and stream analysis 1998.[12]

Definition of supplementary tools and activities

To support and apply its chosen tools of communication, Model, Inc. began by taking a bold and decisive organisational step: it added a second full-time employee to its investor relations department. The department itself reports to the chief executive officer and has a budget of its own. Over the years, Model, Inc. has also built up an extensive database of potential and existing investors. The database contains a very detailed set of criteria defining target groups, including, for example, who the main contact persons are for each group (contact person, age, career development, address etc.), and what information is required and expected by each group. To round things off, Model, Inc. also operates a scoring model to keep track of investor relations activities and assess their impact over the long term.

In effect, the above discourse simply reiterates the key criteria to be borne in mind if a company truly wants to operate a successful system of investor relations. Alongside the 'hard aspects' of value management – the arithmetic, the value creation programs and the necessary adaptations to management and compensation systems that we have already examined – the response of the financial community at large will also determine the success of a company's value management program. The investor relations concept outlined above ensures that this piece of the puzzle, too, can be designed professionally and implemented effectively.

---

[12] Cadbury Schweppes (1998), pp. 80 ff.

4 Using Growth To Leverage Value Creation

4.1 Why growth?

In Europe, growth is the subject of heated debate. Against the background of familiar statistics, this comes as no surprise. From an economic viewpoint, growth figures must be seen in relation to unemployment and government debt. The relevant historical figures for Europe paint a noticeably grim picture:

- Real rates of (GDP) growth in Europe halved between 1992 and 1996 to a mere 1.5% or so, compared with the 3% achieved between 1986 and 1990.
- Unemployment in Europe grew from around 14 million in 1991 to around 19 million in 1996.
- Government debt as a percentage of Gross National Product rose from 44% in 1991 to 64% in 1996.

Whether the forecasts for Europe's future hold water or not, the fact of the matter is that European growth lags far behind that of the Asia-Pacific region in particular. Annual GDP growth calculations make the discrepancy crystal clear: annual growth for the key nations in the Asia-Pacific region is expected to average out at 7.3% (1994–2000), compared with a figure of only around 2.2% for Germany (1996–2002). These figures do not, however, account for the possible structural effects of the severe stock market turbulence in 1997/1998. Figure 4.1 illustrates these Prognos growth forecasts.

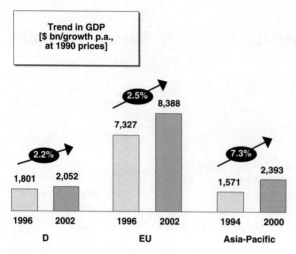

Figure 4.1: GDP growth forecasts.[1]

From the point of view of business, too, growth is an indispensable prerequisite if companies are to create value and thus achieve success: growing companies can invest in new jobs, develop better products and services (if not, they would not grow), procure more deliveries from their suppliers, and generally contribute to greater prosperity. Companies who fail to observe the principles of value management will, in time, lose their ability to compete in the international arena. Their business foundation will be eroded; the destruction of wealth, income and jobs will be the consequence.

Value management and growth therefore belong together. There are a number of causal links in this relationship:

- Only companies that are growing gain market share and secure for themselves the advantages of market leadership.
- Cash flow growth raises a company's self-financing capability and can thus contribute to cutting the cost of capital. Above all, however, growing companies attract more investors than stagnant ones.
- Growing companies attract top-performing, high-quality employees, who in turn can be the driver for further investment thrusts.

These causal links can be established for all groups who have an interest in the company. Figure 4.2 illustrates the reciprocal relationships that exist between growth – quantified here as 'free cash flows' – and the various stakeholders (employees, customers, suppliers, outside capital backers, shareholders, and the government).

---

[1] Prognos (1996), Prognos (1997); selected Asian countries: China, Hong Kong, Indonesia, Malaysia, Singapore, South Korea, Taiwan, Thailand.

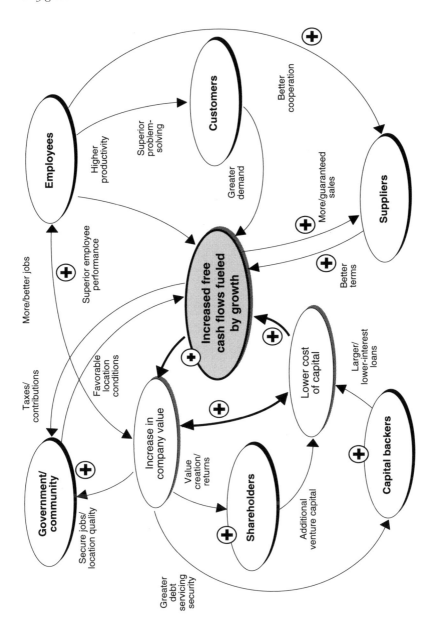

Figure 4.2: Stakeholders and value-based management.

There is also empirical evidence that companies run along value-based management lines can achieve above-average growth rates. A European study conducted by Roland Berger & Partners (see Fig. 4.3) has found that such companies:

* achieve sales growth that is around two times the average level;
* record markedly faster growth in the number of employees; and
* experience greater investment and cash flow growth.

GROWTH RATES (CAGR) p.a., 1993-1997	VALUE-MANAGED COMPANIES	CONTROL GROUP
Sales	11.9%	6.0%
Employees	8.1%	1.6%
Investments	10.9%	7.8%
Cash flow	14.6%	10.0%

Figure 4.3: Growth rates for value-managed companies and a control group in Europe (1993–1994).

To summarise the above findings:

* Corporate growth is essential for macroeconomic reasons in order to achieve improved prosperity.
* Corporate growth is essential for business reasons in order to provide the basis for value creation.

4.2 Value management through strategic growth management

What conclusions can be drawn from empirical studies? Consistent growth is the long-term basis for increasing company value. At the same time, however, this growth must be accompanied by the establishment of barriers to entry. Companies need to focus on 'share, speed and scale':

- They must grow more strongly than their competitors in order to increase their market share.
- They must be faster than their competitors, securing growth by means of barriers to entry.
- They must achieve cost leadership and optimise investment by achieving economies of scale.

The value portfolio analysis displayed earlier in the book – the quadrant for 'stars that fit the corporate vision' – defines the appropriate, growth-based strategy. This strategy does more than merely cater to the interests of shareholders by maximising value for them. Here we see the very close relationship between the shareholder and stakeholder approaches. The shareholder value concept is often accused of achieving only short-term optimisation by improving intra-year quarterly results. This is far too narrow an assessment, and one which does not do justice to the situation. Provided that the shareholder value concept is applied correctly and is shielded from what are often socio-politically motivated claims, the criticism that the whole approach is innately myopic is neither justified nor tenable with regard to the methods used: shareholder value puts a value on the performance of companies or business units based on the sum of their discounted future cash flows. Consequently, even long-term growth strategies associated with heavy initial investments can, given commensurate returns, contribute more to shareholder value than investment-shy measures to maximise short-term profits.

Whatever the case, shareholder value-based corporate management as it is practised in Europe has little to do with the 'quarterly earnings and dividends' that are so often (and erroneously?) associated with it. On the contrary, this approach contributes to a clearly-defined corporate orientation that charts a course toward value-based growth.

- Taking market returns as the measure of success puts pressure on companies to achieve profitability, forcing them to develop forward-looking and therefore creative growth projects and activities.
- At the same time, companies cannot rest on past laurels: yesterday's profits are no guarantee of the future allocation of investment funds.

In our view, at least the medium-term – if not long-term – strategic orientation of the value management concept, especially given the need to corner market share and raise barriers to entry by giving the company a value orientation, upholds the interests of all stakeholders.

An entrepreneurial course that focuses on growth generates value for all stakeholders, whose contributions in turn support the progress of growth. The result is therefore a 'boomerang effect' with subsequent stakeholder returns:

- A value orientation satisfies the needs of the customers.
- Shareholders see the value of the capital they have invested increase.
- Strict value orientation secures a high quality of employment for the workforce.
- Suppliers have better prospects for selling their wares.
- The government benefits from the steady flow of local contributions (taxes, levies etc.).
- Growth provides capital backers from outside the company with funding opportunities that yield an acceptable payback.

'Stakeholder inputs' arise from the stakeholders' commitment to and activities involving the company. For example:

- Customers buy more and/or bring in comparatively higher revenues.
- Shareholders are more willing to invest when the cost of capital is lower.
- Employees are more productive at lower cost and make their contribution to processes of innovation.
- Suppliers offer preferred-customer arrangements on relatively favourable terms.
- The government makes a better contribution to infrastructure.
- Capital backers ensure that plenty of funds are available to finance growth.

Figure 4.4 illustrates this 'boomerang effect', consisting of stakeholder returns and stakeholder inputs.

The translation of this concept for integrated growth and value management into an operational strategy that can be implemented on a practical level consists of three steps:

- definition and implementation of the growth strategy by making use of the growth-based 'toolbox';
- safeguarding growth by raising barriers to entry; and
- developing a comprehensive concept for effective and efficient stakeholder management.

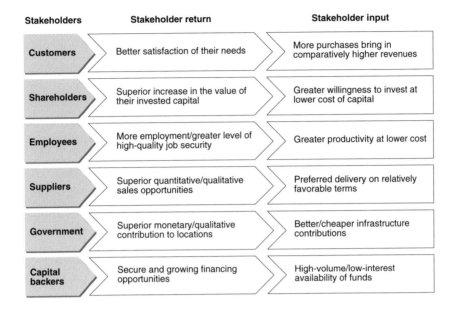

Figure 4.4: The 'boomerang effect' in stakeholder management.

Defining and implementing the growth strategy

The 'toolbox' with which growth can be achieved consistently is fairly extensive. We will restrict ourselves to a detailed examination of just a few individual tools: product innovation management, sales activation, regional expansion, acquisitions, and new areas of business.

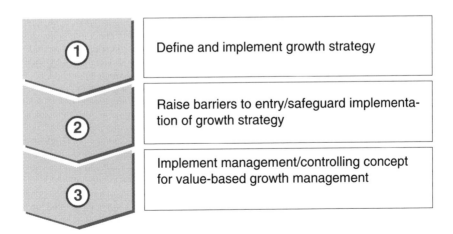

Figure 4.5: Three steps to integrated growth management.

Product innovation management

Growth is realised through the workings of the market. Hence, it can only be achieved by companies whose new products and services set them apart and qualify them for growth.

The process of innovation must be both effective and efficient, and must be organised accordingly. To do so, the individual phases in the process must be harmonised and coordinated. 'Innovation is a process of decision-making and implementation.'[2]

- Innovation has to be fuelled by ideas and motivation (the initiative phase).
- 'The problem' must be defined. Goals are to be fixed for an innovation project.
- Innovative alternatives need to be tracked down. This requires both a knowledge of the market and an environment that is conducive to creative free thinking.
- Technical implementation will initially involve interaction between research and development, marketing and other sources of expertise in the product development process, before moving on to the production phase.
- The resultant new products must be marketed.

Both corporate culture and the working environment must leave room for innovation. Teamwork, genuinely open communication, and resource availability are just some of the crucial prerequisites. Nevertheless, experience shows that there are still a few places in which this free and creative environment for product development needs to be 'nailed down'. These places should be staked out by clear procedures for go/no-go decisions, clarity concerning strategic intentions, discipline with regard to open decisions, transparency in respect of costs and available resources, and so on.

What alternatives can be deployed in order to realise growth opportunities? In their German book entitled 'Wachstum mit Gewinn' ('Profitable Growth'), Wiezorek and Wallinger provide a number of tools for this purpose to which we refer in Table 4.1. The table introduces a series of tools for product and service innovation strategies, outlines the approach adopted by each strategy, and provides examples.

---

[2] Hauschildt (1992), p. 277.

Product/service innovation strategy	Approach	Examples
New product segments/ categories	New markets/market segments opened up by "genuine" innovations	• Persil Megaperls • LC 1 yoghurt
"Tailor-made" series production	Standardized product modules combined to form "tailor-made" solutions	• Swatch watches
Portfolio expansion	Service program expanded by differentiating strategies (covering more market segments)	• Club Med
Line extension	Using brand names for new product groups	• Nivea
Brand cooperation	Combined brand presentation (advertising, products etc.)	•Schöller/Mövenpick ice cream •Opel Corsa and Nescafé
Licensing	Enhanced brand awareness and revenues from the transfer of licensing rights	• Etienne Aigner/ Gerry Weber
Add-on services	Customer loyalty and differentiation achieved through consulting, maintenance, financing, training etc.	• Financing programs for automobile producers

Table 4.1: Examples of innovative products/services.[3]

Sales activation

Sales activation or client relationship programs are of supreme importance in terms of the contribution they can make to growth:

- It is far more expensive to win a new customer than to keep an existing customer – measured in terms of lost sales revenues and profits and the cost of acquiring a new customer.
- Lost customers act as 'negative opinion leaders' and thus have a direct impact on other existing or potential customers.

Roland Berger & Partners have seen considerable success in working together with their clients to implement the 'Sales up' activation program. Several major airlines, for example, have been able to realise disproportionate increases in sales in key markets. 'Sales up' is essentially a two-pronged strategy, focusing on:

- The consistent increase in sales figures, substantial improvements in product and service awareness and presentation of a more sharply defined company profile toward primary and secondary customers. All this centres around a more rigorous market orientation, higher quantitative revenues and, above

---

[3] Based on Wiezoreck/Wallinger (1997), pp. 21-81.

all, making one's products and services the 'number one topic of conversation' on the market.

- Improved market coverage thanks to the structured, consistent and unambiguous assignment of markets and customers, the analysis and prioritisation of customer potential, the setting of sales targets, the implementation of one's own sales activation measures, the targeted deployment of resources and, above all, the regular measurement of performance.

Our primary focus is on sales performance; organisational and cost-cutting aspects are of secondary importance. No changes are made to products or prices. And the assumption is made that products/services are perfectly comparable with those of competitors. The main aim is to create a transparent overview of sales potential and to deploy sales resources where they are likely to be most profitable.

The first step is to segment a market by delivery channels. Customers (or customer groups) must then be subjected to a thorough analysis. Only those customers who are found to have genuine sales activation potential are selected for the program. On the basis of current (monthly) sales figures and the completed potential analysis (i.e. 'What is possible?'), targets are defined. Following on from this analysis, six key questions must be answered about activities that can be applied in the short term. Sales resources are then channelled accordingly with a view to increasing market coverage (see also Fig. 4.6):

- Which existing customers harbour significant sales potential?
- Which sales-boosting ideas will impress our customers?
- How can we activate our internal sales personnel?
- How can we pragmatically adapt our incentive schemes?
- Are we actually reaching the decision-makers?
- Which new customers should we contact?

In other words, the starting point for sales activation is to increase market presence where this is inadequate, to tighten up 'loose' customer contacts, to actively apply sales activation programs, to tangibly improve after-sales service, and to eliminate any other weak links in the sales chain. The results speak for themselves: sales growth of up to 30% and more is eminently realistic.

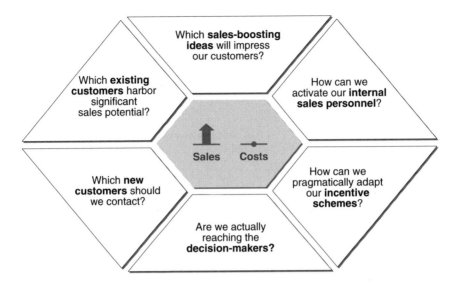

Figure 4.6: Key questions to ask for a sales activation program.

Regional expansion

There is no need at this point to look into the motives for growth based on regional expansion, that is, the aim of making sales in new markets. The relevant keywords are either dealt with in the document supplied or are self-explanatory: globalisation, triad, European Union, etc.

If a company's potential for growth is already exhausted or if it would be too expensive to achieve marginal sales growth in established regions, the possibility of expanding into new regions should be investigated and, where appropriate, initiated. There can be no 'one-size-fits-all' approach to this kind of strategy: market entry will always depend on global and/or local aspects that are very specific to each individual industry.[4]

What are the possible options for penetrating new markets? Here again, a reasonable analysis of the targeted depth and breadth of value creation will be needed. The company must decide to what extent it intends to commit itself to a new region.[5] Does it wish 'merely' to set up sales activities? Should production be relocated, in part or in full? To what extent should research and development activities be established in the new region? What administrative instances and functions will have to be set up locally? And so the list goes on.

The definition of a strategy thus requires answers to numerous questions, all of which will always relate to the company-specific division of labour and degree

---

[4] See also Rall (1997), pp. 53 ff.
[5] See also the example of Böringer Ingelheim quoted in Liebrecht (1988).

of decentralisation, and always with a view to potential synergies (through centralisation).

Regional expansion can be assisted by a wide range of tools, of which the following are but a few:

- development of sales activities with no additional facilities, such as the company's own sales team or a representation;
- market penetration by means of alliances and joint ventures;
- development of a company-owned infrastructure for research and development, production facilities etc. by founding a subsidiary company; and
- acquisition of a company or companies.

A detailed analysis of the business in question is imperative when deciding which measures to apply in order to tap new regional markets, to what extent and in what order.

For the sake of completeness, we will also briefly touch on two further approaches to growth – acquisitions and new areas of business – albeit without going into any depth on either subject.

Acquisitions

By presenting company acquisitions as a tool for use in value-based growth strategies at this point, we are consciously taking a limited view of the various purposes that can be served by mergers and acquisitions. Here we merely define the requirements for value-based acquisition strategies:

- In this context, acquisitions can never be pushed through 'at all costs'. Any and every acquisition must fit in with corporate strategy and must pay its way by earning the cost of the capital invested in it. What we are looking for is 'stars that fit the corporate vision'.
- The same applies to potential 'hostile takeovers'. Even moves to buy out competitors in order to remove capacity from the market must be subject to the principles of value management.

Provided due consideration is given to these factors, pursuing external growth by means of acquisitions undoubtedly offers certain advantages:[6] economies of scale, the transfer of existing technological and management expertise, and value creation through the restructuring and modified utilisation of assets. There is also the added benefit of acquiring complementary products, technologies or 'know-how'.

Rather than re-examine the steps involved in mergers and acquisitions, we would at this point simply refer the reader to existing literature on the subject.[7]

---

[6] See also Rappaport (1986), pp. 134 ff.

[7] e.g. Zimmerer (1993), pp. 4294 ff.

Potential candidates for acquisition should, of course, first be exposed to the DCF method of valuation.

New areas of business

In our treatment of the value portfolio in Chapter 3, we examined the strategies of 'stars that fit the corporate vision', focusing on the intensification of core businesses. Any redefinition of corporate strategy – i.e. by including new areas of business in the portfolio – must be linked to clearly defined conditions. Above all, in line with the doctrine of value orientation, returns must exceed the cost of capital. The incorporation of new areas of business must be preceded by a systematic analysis along the lines of the following questions:

- Is the potential for growth in those core businesses in which we master the factors of success really limited, or could further potential be tapped by regional expansion, rigorous innovation management or other, similar measures?
- Will the returns generated by the new business cover its cost of capital and hence the additional risk?
- Does expanding into this line of business give us the chance to corner a significant share of the market in order, from there, to develop a strong competitive position?
- If growth is to be realised by means of new or additional lines of business, can the approaches to internal and external growth referred to above be applied subsequently?

The above is no more than a rough sketch of a number of tools in the growth strategy toolbox. The second step in our integrated approach to growth management is now to see how barriers to entry can be raised.

Raising barriers to entry

Barriers to entry to a market are conditions or factors that are established or promoted in an industry/market which cause other companies to refrain from investing in or entering them although they may appear to be attractive or profitable. In other words, the aim is to protect one's own market coverage, access to important customers and relevant delivery channels etc. in such a way that 'me too' suppliers are put off by the new or further commitment they would be required to make. The market leaders, the biggest and/or the first companies in an industry will necessarily seek to protect themselves so that they can reap the rewards of their innovations, cause marginal unit costs to decline, dictate the industry trends or secure other competitive advantages. Barriers to entry are therefore a necessary but, in themselves, not a sufficient condition for the long-term profitability of an industry. The established companies who raise these barriers thus take advantage of their ability to cut prices to what is known as the 'limit price' to thwart the efforts of potential new entrants to the market. As a result, new companies would have to swallow very high start-up losses.

Barriers to entry must be reinforced by the strategy adopted. They should be backed up by the integrated value management approach – a conscious policy of stakeholder management. If this is done, successful companies will be able not only to frighten off would-be competitors: they will also be able to extend their lead over existing competitors. Value-based stakeholder management therefore aims in particular to protect targeted growth by erecting and reinforcing barriers to market entry.

Along the lines expounded by Porter, we would highlight the following specific barriers to entry: economies of scale; customer loyalty thanks to product differentiation; brand identity; switchover costs/capacity; access to capital; access to delivery channels; absolute cost benefits; and the regulation of supplier integration. Figure 4.7 summarises these barriers to entry and the particular stakeholders involved in each case.[8]

Barriers to entry	Degree of influence from stakeholder value management				
	Customers	Employees	Suppliers	Capital backers	Govt.
• Economies of scale					
• Customer loyalty (through product differentiation)	+	+ +	+		
• Brand identity	+	+ +			
• Switching costs	+ +	+			
• Better access to necessary capital				+ +	
• Access to delivery channels		+			
• Absolute cost advantages					
– Edge in experience curve		+ +			
– Better access to raw materials			+		
– Low-cost product design	+	+ +	+		
• Regulation (controls, license applications)					+ +
• Supplier integration			+ +		

+ + Considerable influence   + Some influence

Figure 4.7: Barriers to entry that can be influenced by stakeholder management.

There is, therefore, a link between the development of barriers to entry and the management of interest groups. Only those companies that succeed in anchoring such a rigorous approach to stakeholder management in their corporate policy will be able to safeguard the strategy on which the dynamics of growth depends.

---

[8] Cf. Porter (1988), pp. 60 ff.

Let us take the example of product development to explain. Barriers to market entry can, for example, seek:

- To achieve substantially greater customer benefits by specifically differentiating the company's products/services from those of its existing or potential competitors, i.e. the company should offer customers better 'user economics' than its competitors
- To achieve cost leadership by means of low-cost product design, favourable access to the necessary raw materials or similar measures.

In the product development process, it is therefore the employees, the customers and the suppliers who are to be 'managed' systematically, for example by integrating customers in product development ('partnering'), by raising the level of employee qualification/motivation, or by integrating suppliers in the development process.

Developing a stakeholder management strategy

Wherever possible, the principle of integrating stakeholders in the growth process and mobilising them as a force to create value should always be based on a 'win-win' approach: both the company and the stakeholders must stand to benefit from mutual involvement.

In this case, stakeholders can be mobilised along simple, logical lines as summed up by the following four questions:

- What contribution can stakeholders make to value-based growth? The potential contribution of each interest group should be defined.
- How can we motivate stakeholders to maximise their contribution? The need here is to identify the stakeholders' target systems, their preferences, and the levers that can activate these preferences.
- What action must we take to accomplish this goal? Plans of action to mobilise stakeholders must be implemented.
- How can we measure the anticipated effects? A system of key ratios by which to measure and monitor success must be put in place.

Given suitable 'management', each stakeholder will contribute to growth.

- Customers make a major contribution to growth. They are the cornerstone of all growth that is based on sales activation and innovative stimuli.
- Employees support value-based growth by high levels of productivity, continual improvements, contributions to development etc. all growth that is based on sales activation and innovative stimuli.
- Suppliers can offer high levels of material productivity and make contributions to innovation.

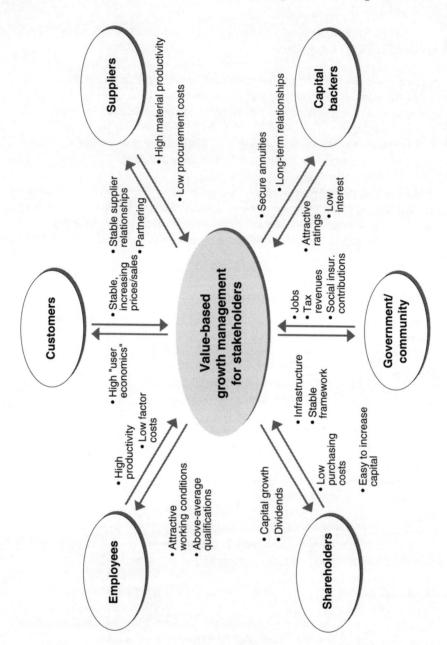

Figure 4.8: Mobilising stakeholders for value-based growth.

- Shareholders and banks are a source of capital (on favourable terms) to fund growth.
- The government can lay the foundation for growth by providing the necessary infrastructure and suitable framework conditions.

How stakeholders are motivated to make their respective contributions to company growth must be tailored to their various preferences and goals, and those of their representatives. Employees and trade unions, for instance, will have a keen eye for levels of qualification and attractive working conditions. Customers, on the other hand, will be motivated by maximised 'user economics'. The different approaches for each stakeholder group are depicted in Fig. 4.8.

Answering the question of what action or actions a company must take to get the stakeholders 'on board' conveniently brings us to the issue of value drivers for the various activities.

Where the need is to optimise user economics, i.e. the primary control variable as far as customer contributions are concerned, company activities will have to centre around the following levers: their innovative strengths must be greater than those of their competitors, so that customers benefit more from their new and innovative products than from those of the competition. Customers who consume the company's products or use their services thus obtain a higher level of 'value added'. The same applies to the cost/benefit ratio, in which context the image attached to a purchased product is of particular importance. An obvious value driver is the level of service provided to the customer.

The more accurately a company can quantify the user economics it offers to its customers, the easier it is to interpret the control variable. Let us take an example from the field of technical services. The management – i.e. the construction and maintenance – of facilities that combine to form a network is often handled by external service providers. Both manufacturers and operators avail themselves of the services of third-party maintenance companies. One need only think of computer or telephone networks, filling station networks, travel ticket sales facilities for local public transport, or any number of similar facilities. Technical service providers have at their disposal a number of control variables with which to satisfy their customers as best as possible. Two examples should help to clarify the issue. A high level of network availability/network security avoids downtime for the objects in question and eliminates their inherent risks. From the customer's viewpoint, 'user economics' in this case consists of less downtime, less sales losses to competitors, greater customer satisfaction, and more regular customers. Customers can measure their user economics in very concrete terms, e.g. as revenue losses resulting from an hour's or a day's downtime. The control variables available to the technical service provider are the high quality of service, short throughput times thanks to innovative process concepts (such as call centres, intelligent scheduling and assembly concepts that are closely linked to logistical services), and other such features. And, like their customers, the service providers too can measure these variables to quantify their performance. They can measure availability, compliance with response times, error and complaint quotas, productivity ratios for assembly staff etc.

Shareholders can serve as a second example. They will be concerned about the following value drivers: free cash flow must be greater than for comparable commitments; and equity capital turnover must exceed that of competitor companies, ideally in conjunction with minimised risks. Above all, the company's information and communication behaviour must be superior in terms of investor relations quality. The control variable for shareholders is shareholder value. This, too, should be higher than for the competition to ensure that shareholders are attracted to the company. As far as the company itself is concerned, this aspect of stakeholder management involves attempting to keep the cost of capital down to a minimum.

We have already seen that the workforce is an important stakeholder group. Value drivers of relevance to this group include increases in the level of employment (which, when measured as volume times income, also constitutes the control variable for this group), income per unit of employment, better work processes and a level of qualification/motivation that surpasses that offered by competitor companies.

To secure the active participation of suppliers in a value-based growth strategy, they must be assured of specific sales quotas for higher volumes and at higher margins. Above all, however, suppliers must be integrated in the company's own processes in a more systematic way than is the case at competitor firms. The results for the supplier will be higher order volumes which offer sustained relationships and ensure greater business stability and continuity.

What activity-based value drivers serve to motivate outside capital backers? The answer is simply the expected financing budgets, with the opportunities these offer to reap returns, plus a stable financing structure with low credit risk.

The government, the sixth stakeholder, can in most cases be enlisted to support value-based growth only indirectly, insofar as high employment potential – the provision of highly-qualified jobs – holds out the promise of commensurate fiscal contributions, while the ecological efficiency of the company also contributes to the general well-being of the community.

In this way, the various activity-based control variables can be defined on the basis of economic benefits to each specific interest group for the purposes of value-based growth management.

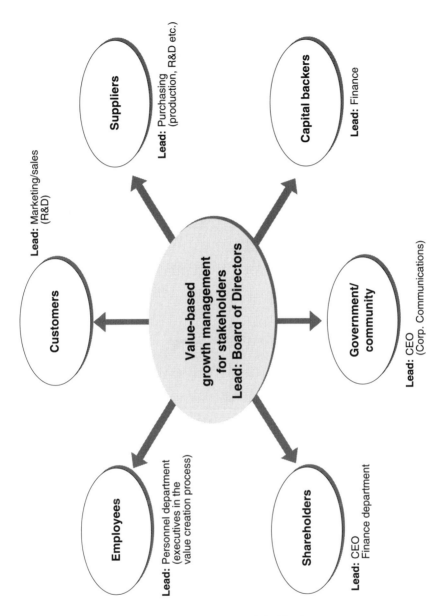

Figure 4.9: Who is responsible for the various stakeholders?

Controlling concept for value-based growth

If the process of recruiting the stakeholders to support this growth policy is to be managed consistently, a company must clearly define who is responsible for what stakeholder-related outputs, control variables and value drivers. Figure 4.9 illustrates our proposal.

In order to map these control variables and output metrics and their related fields of responsibility onto a controlling system, we suggest that a scorecard be used to measure and sustain progress. The scorecard should centre around those control variables which drive value and growth, and which thus require regular monitoring. Figure 4.10 lists these variables.

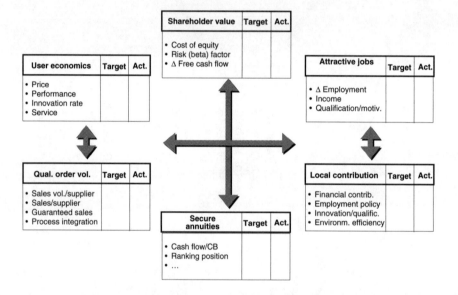

Figure 4.10: Scorecards for measuring value drivers and growth drivers.

The basic premises of a scorecard system are simple:

- 'If you don't measure it, it won't improve'. The goals defined in the strategy are broken down and expressed as ratios in order to further implementation, and promote acceptance.
- A comprehensive view must be taken: the customary narrow focus on financial data is extended to include other key control fields.

The original 'balanced scorecard'[9] system assumes a four-level management system, including the financial perspective, the customers' perspective, internal proc-

---

[9] Kaplan/Norton (1997).

esses, and learning and development. The company model is mapped out in these terms in order to ensure more successful implementation and measurement.

Here, we have simply applied the notion of the scorecard to the control of stakeholder activities and communication policy in the sense used in investor relations.

To manage the stakeholders successfully, quantified targets must be set for the value and growth drivers listed. These drivers must be monitored over time. To recap:

- Growth is necessary: we outlined the positive successes achieved by growing companies.
- Value management is strategic growth management. From a pragmatic point of view, there is no contradiction between the interests of the shareholders and those of the stakeholders. We detailed approaches to the realisation of growth targets.
- 'Stakeholder management' – the management practice of systematically setting and realising interest group-specific targets – is an important aspect of growth policy. We proposed the use of scorecards.

The chapter that follows deals with the practical outworking of a value-based strategy via the medium of consistent transformation management.

5 Transformation Processes To Realise And Consolidate Value Management

The most important prerequisite for the sustained, long-term realisation of a value management strategy is to initiate a company-wide process of culture change – to change the way the company thinks. This means transforming every aspect of the company and all levels of the workforce into a hive of value-oriented activity. The following steps are involved:

- a comprehensive, in-depth restructuring and reorientation of the company, not only on the practical level of strategies, structures and systems, but – above all – also on a mental plane;
- bringing about a genuine change in the mindset of executives and employees; and
- activating and developing the skills needed to think and act in line with the principles of value management.

Corporate transformation is by nature a 'holistic' approach, and one that links four key task complexes. These are: putting the company in a position to tap new businesses or areas of business; reengineering the company's core processes and methods; integrating and developing the skills of all employees right from the outset; and effecting a change which leads to value-based actions.

This chapter devotes itself to the task of designing an effective and efficient process of transformation. To this end, we shall examine the objectives and factors of success of transformation processes before presenting a three-tiered project strategy for 'value-based transformation' and describing how such a process can be managed.

The concept of value-based management should be made sustainable. 'Good' transformations will deliver significant improvements. A few examples of the results already achieved in such projects suffice to demonstrate both the differences and the similarities between the goals that a transformation process can pursue:

- fast/short-term increases in marketing power through the management/control of resources in market-related activities which, in turn, are based on the introduction of customer-specific quality management systems and the implementation of a flexible, customer-oriented system of personnel deployment;
- sustained increases in productivity by defining a customer-oriented business system, including target processes and the division of labour;

- establishing a competitive structural, management and systems concept by implementing lean, performance-oriented management, drawing up a structural concept and a management system in line with target processes, and designing an integrated IT strategy; and
- developing a customer-oriented corporate culture by mobilising employees through a program of training, communication, teamwork, the development of a company-specific change management concept, and a significant improvement in performance/competitive orientation.

5.1 Establishing a value mindset: the goals of transformation

We would not dispute the fact that German companies in particular have, in recent years, been forced to undergo extensive and often painful processes of restructuring and realignment. Nor, however, would we dispute the fact that these measures and programs have focused predominantly on the cost side and have, by and large, not had a sufficiently broad outlook to truly be a source of new, innovation-driven growth.

The principles of value management can only be established throughout all levels of a company by throwing conventional thinking patterns overboard and thereby facilitating a fundamental transformation of the entire company. Unless companies succeed in nurturing a culture of entrepreneurial, value-based action on all corporate levels that is far more clearly focused on customer benefit and evidences a far more process-oriented approach to the handling of business transactions than is currently the case, they will remain unable to consolidate their market position and thereby ensure the continued creation of value over the long term.

One pressing concern is the need to develop and apply customer orientation across the board and to design operational activities so that they create benefit for the customer. Traditional methods of organisation and operation are no longer capable of providing customers with a superior quality of service.

- Functional organisational structures are known to lead to the fragmentation of working processes, causing a general understanding of internal and external customers' perspectives to be lost along the way.
- Decentralising responsibility for results runs the risk of putting the interests of individual units before those of the company as a whole.
- Centralising responsibility for results can distance the company from its market and its customers.

Corporate transformations that aim to create value are therefore an exercise in asking fundamental questions and reorienting the strategic and operative activities of a company. What is at stake is the need to redefine a company's strategy, organisation and management culture (simultaneously, if possible), to attain time, cost, quality and innovation leadership, and thereby to achieve sustained increases in the growth and value of the company.

Corporate transformation thus means implementing uniform changes across all corporate levels and all modes of activity. It does not involve tinkering with a bit here and a bit there. It is not a matter of repairing or fine-tuning. It is a matter of creating something entirely new, with several objectives:

- to increase the benefit to customers and develop/build up new businesses;
- to exploit market potential and competitive advantages by means of innovative business systems;
- to realise top levels of operative performance by means of process innovation;
- to design the requisite changes in the behaviour and attitudes of management and employees on all levels; and
- to thereby firmly establish the value creation program throughout the company.

In other words, corporate transformation seeks to advance the company as a whole, opening up new solutions, new businesses, new modes of behaviour, new ways of working. Unlike so many other management methods, transformation does not deal with isolated weak points: it aims to move the entire company forward. The aim is as much to cultivate new ways of doing things as to come up with new solutions to problems and new business opportunities. Consequently, correctly managing a process of corporate transformation means linking the tasks of portfolio restructuring and innovation together in order to create value for the company. This interrelationship is illustrated in Fig. 5.1.

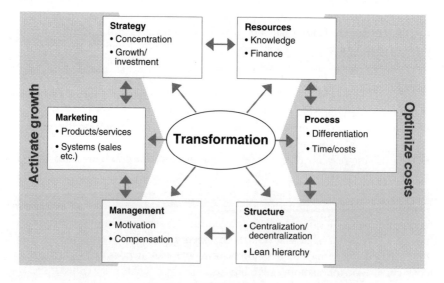

Figure 5.1: Transformation links innovation with restructuring.

A link must therefore be established between two levels if value-based corporate transformation is to succeed:

- the instrumental level, i.e. the level at which vision is defined and put into operational practice, where the need to act and alternative courses of action

are recognised, modelled and communicated, and where professional measures management comes into play; and
- the mental level, i.e. where the necessary change of mindset is set in motion by the interactive involvement of the workforce, integrating them in and winning their backing for the process of change, and training them to develop new skills.

In the context of value creation programs, the goals of a transformation process must be seen from the viewpoint of an analysis of the current status, the defined objectives and the introduction of change management. In other words:

- The value performance of the company or its business units must be determined.
- Value creation measures must be identified.
- Value growth must be quantified.
- Management and controlling systems must be reoriented.
- Change management must be inaugurated and established.

5.2 Factors of success: the cornerstones of transformation

During attempts to establish value management programs by means of corporate transformation exercises, the same mistakes are made time and again. Although it is true that each company has its own unique 'transformation history', the prime movers nevertheless follow the same general principles that are always indicative of successful transformation management. If one puts the sources of success in some sort of order, seven key 'factors of success' stand out.

- the setting of ambitious goals that see transformation as a quantum leap in pursuit of a clearly defined corporate vision;
- the mobilisation of as much of the workforce as possible by means of interdivisional and cross-hierarchy teams and workgroups;
- simplicity – the ability to come up with uncomplicated concepts that are easy to communicate;
- performance-oriented work, since regular measurement and harmonisation with defined targets is the only way to enable deviations to be corrected and countermeasures taken. Moreover, as the saying goes: 'If you don't measure it, it won't improve';
- the setting of realistic target deadlines to avoid a demotivating effect;
- the nurture of trust by actively involving employee/personnel councils and communicating openly and honestly; and
- employee training: skills cannot be issued by decree.

The transformation efforts of many companies stumble at the following hurdles:

- They cling to tried and trusted 'recipes'.
- They settle for programs which cut costs and improve efficiency in the short term but which lack any real orientation toward the future and/or innovation.
- They lack the courage to make far-reaching changes for fear of the conflicts that will inevitably ensue.

Only if what is often the fateful balance between persistence and the need for change can effectively be destabilised, can a company receive the sudden jolt that is a necessary precursor to transformation.

The 'rules of the game' outlined above are essential to the efficient management of the transformation process. In principle, they apply for large companies and small companies, for service providers and industrial firms alike. There will naturally be an element of company-specific redesign. Communication concerning the transformation process and the results achieved will, for example, be a more complex task for large companies than for small ones. Conversely, small companies will usually find it considerably more difficult to put together competent composite teams and free up the necessary staffing capacity.

5.3 Three-phase transformation projects

A corporate transformation is a pragmatic approach to the fast but far-reaching improvement of a company's value. The crucial issue is that transformation should target the entire company and therefore significantly improve the overall value of the company by:

- achieving a better market position and greater customer orientation;
- raising performance in terms of both time and quality; and
- improving the cost position and results.

Corporate transformation is a conscious *tour de force* whose aim is to get the whole of the company and the entire workforce moving forward, setting new standards in the process. The very cornerstone of such a transformation thus has to be a fundamental, innovative rethinking of the business system, accompanied by the wholesale mobilisation of the workforce.

It is important to define the strategic direction of thrust to enable innovative processes to be developed and introduced for the defined business units and areas. Rapid implementation of the measures drawn up to create value must be coupled with the aspect of mobilisation.

Mobilising each and every employee is the key factor of success in enterprise-wide transformation and, hence, in any sustained increase in corporate value. It is therefore of crucial importance that all employees go along with the journey, that new developments be communicated to them and that they play an active role in the work of creating value. Such widespread involvement can, however, naturally only be achieved gradually.

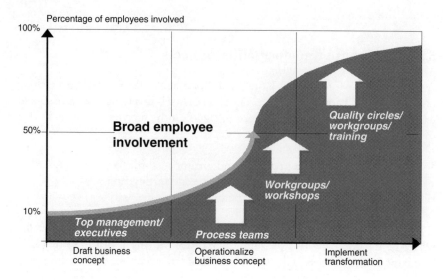

Figure 5.2: Transformation through mobilisation.

Apart from getting people actively involved in various teams and workgroups, efforts to integrate the entire workforce should be accompanied by

- a training offensive; and
- a broadly based communication offensive.

The keys to a transformation that will successfully implement a value creation program translate into a three-phase plan of attack:

Phase 1 operationalises the instrumental level. This is where an understanding of the business economics of the business areas is gained and the value of the individual businesses is identified. The critical questions in this phase are:

- Which business areas and issues are the key to improving efficiency, cutting costs and deepening market penetration? What are the relevant fields of innovation?
- What level of potential do they possess? What are the most important, value-driving ratios and metrics?

Phase 2 is the pivotal point of efforts to implement a value creation program in a company. The focus here is on developing the value creation program itself and establishing the link between strategic value growth and operative improvement measures, which must be drawn up in dialogue with the people concerned. Phase 2 also sets up the link between the instrumental and mental levels as the basis on which value management can be 'lived out'.

Phase 3 serves to establish the value creation program for the long term. Besides fine-tuning the measures already defined and adding supplementary measures where necessary, the aim of this phase is to initialise the process of involving all employees throughout the company. This means initiating the process of change management so that carefully targeted measures actively involve everyone in the company and bring about an effective paradigm shift. Once the project has got off the ground, backed by the full energies and dedicated commitment of corporate management, it is important at this stage to carry out a focused inventory exercise in order to be able to define the key thrust of subsequent activities and find a common line of orientation. To coordinate teams and workgroups, it is essential at this stage to have tight project management that produces quick results and provides a long-term grounding for the transformation process as it now begins to be expanded throughout the company. Figure 5.3 outlines the three phases.

Individual descriptions of each phase of transformation are provided below.

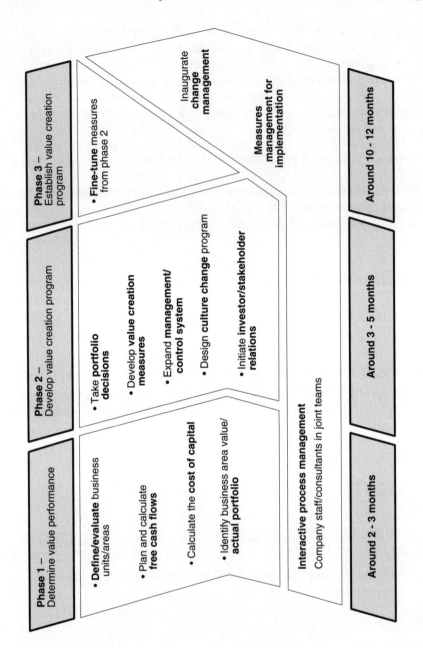

Figure 5.3: A simple, three-phase approach to value creation projects.

Phase 1: Determine value performance

The purpose of phase 1 of the value creation program is to determine the value performance of the individual businesses or strategic business units and thereby to lay the foundation for the entire value creation program.

To start with, all parties concerned need to gain an understanding of the business economics of the relevant business fields as the basis on which to identify and define the key performance indicators. Here, it is important to use these indicators and additional information to assess the value of the individual units or fields and position them within the value portfolio. This step results in each business unit being designated a 'star' or a 'dog', whereupon specific measures can be drawn up.

It is crucial to the success of the value management program to draw up a uniform, methodical concept containing the definition of cash flow and how it is calculated, taking account of the cost of capital/discount factor calculations, and calculating the internal rate of return on capital for the various business units.

Alongside these strategic/instrumental steps, it is important to set the points for interaction with the workforce by working together with selected employees right from the beginning. Results will be accepted and adopted more willingly if they are the fruit of work done together; implementation, too, will proceed significantly faster.

The use of interdisciplinary workgroups and teams dedicated to specific tasks enables earnings and cost drivers to be identified and cash flow statements to be drawn up jointly for each specific business unit. This kind of employee involvement yields a two-fold benefit: it makes sure that internal expertise is used, while allowing team members to act as multipliers for the value management program.

The requirements for the widespread and efficient integration of employees are as follows:

- From the word go, project design must enable as many task areas as possible to be handled by interdivisional project teams.
- Staff must receive training from an early stage.

This kind of interactive approach creates a climate conducive to a positive attitude toward necessary changes: since they themselves have to get to grips with the problems, employees will gain a better understanding of these problems and become convinced that the goals defined are the right ones, and that change is both needed and can be mastered. Above all, however, this approach ensures that the full extent of business-specific knowledge flows into risk calculations, for example, or into the calculation of cash flow drivers in the business units.

The results of phase 1 of the project form a solid basis for the value-based management of the business portfolio. The following individual results are achieved by phase 1:

- The position of each business unit in the value portfolio is determined; core business areas are defined; 'stars' and 'dogs' are identified.
- Actual shareholder value is calculated; figures for the value of the company as a whole and the value of the business units individually are made available.
- The framework of available funding for strategic measures is staked out; free cash flows in the business units are calculated; financial leeway within the entire company or group is defined.
- The 'bare bones' structure of strategic and operative metrics of relevance to management and controlling is set in place.
- The interactive approach directly involves a large number of employees. These people serve as the basis for the enterprise-wide transformation program, since this can now be built on a shared basic understanding of value-based management. Initial options for improvement will already have been worked out and can be made ready for implementation.

Figure 5.4 summarises phase 1.

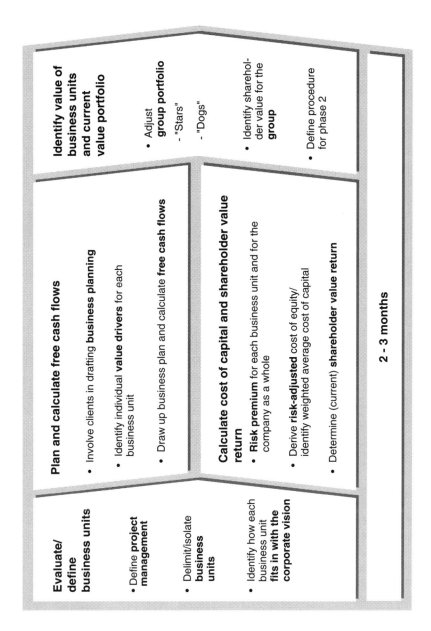

Figure 5.4: Phase 1 of the project at a glance.

Phase 2: Develop value creation programs

The objective of phase 2 is to develop and operationalise a company-specific value creation program.

During this phase, operationalising activities will involve fleshing out the details of actions and improvement measures to be taken for the individual business units, preparing for implementation and, at the same time, gauging the likely impact on the shareholders and other stakeholders. Since the ultimate aim is complete corporate transformation, more employees will be integrated in phase 2 of the program, while preparations are made for further steps in which the program of culture change is to take effect.

The program of measures must take concrete shape and the management and controlling system must be extended if value management is to be modelled effectively. Given that 'if you don't measure it, it won't improve', there should be no problem incorporating the value-based management variables in the system of controlling already in place.

As shown in Fig. 5.5, phase 2 is equally crucial to the issue of change management. Change management and corporate transformation must first be preceded by a wide-scale training offensive to enable large numbers of employees to play an intelligent part. Target group-specific training sessions should be set up to transfer methodological expertise and teach group moderation techniques, creativity techniques, project management and, of course, behavioural training.

This training will allow a considerable number of staff to be involved in action teams and play a specific role in project work. In the course of their work, they, in turn, will approach other colleagues and inform them about project objectives and procedures.

The results of phase 2 lay the foundation for fast, systematic implementation. Phase 2 achieves the following individual results:

- Strategic and operative value creation measures are defined and prepared for implementation.
- The necessary expansions to management and controlling systems are developed.
- Investor and stakeholder relations programs are designed or further developed.
- Interactive project work combines with the training program to set the points for a necessary culture change toward value-based thinking and action throughout the company.

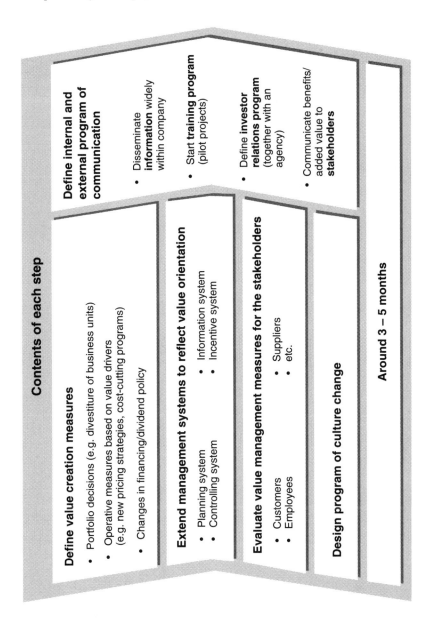

Figure 5.5: Phase 2 of the project at a glance.

Phase 3: Establish the value creation program

The most important requirement for the successful, long-term implementation of a value management program – one which realises value creation measures, changes systems and implements a new investor and stakeholder relations strategy – is the establishment of a culture change program within the company.

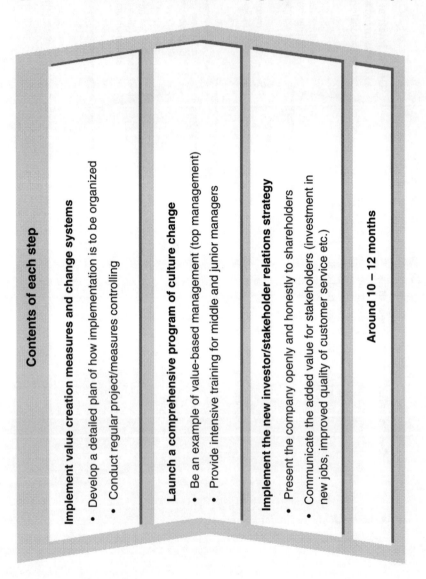

Contents of each step

Implement value creation measures and change systems
- Develop a detailed plan of how implementation is to be organized
- Conduct regular project/measures controlling

Launch a comprehensive program of culture change
- Be an example of value-based management (top management)
- Provide intensive training for middle and junior managers

Implement the new investor/stakeholder relations strategy
- Present the company openly and honestly to shareholders
- Communicate the added value for stakeholders (investment in new jobs, improved quality of customer service etc.)

Around 10 – 12 months

Figure 5.6: Phase 3 of the project at a glance.

Three simple but important conditions for successful transformation management must be observed:

- *'Commitment'*: managers and executives must be convinced of what they are doing and prove this through renewed commitment and active participation.
- *'Involvement'*: employees must be 'mobilised' and actively involved in the process of transformation.
- *'Facilitating'*: an effective, implementation-focused transformation organisation is needed to support the transformation process.

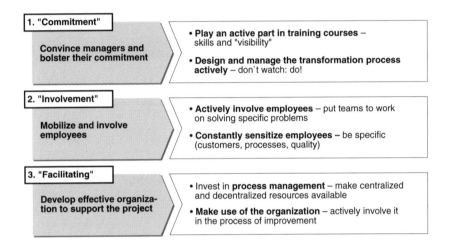

Figure 5.7: Three conditions of successful transformation.

Operationalised target concepts must be introduced on a broad front through a system of transformation management that is tailored to the company's situation. Transformation has two legs to stand on: one is an effective, implementation-focused project organisation; the other is process management, which enables migration strategies to be drawn up for the measures defined and allows implementation to be usefully accompanied. In this context, Fig. 5.8 outlines the key elements of change management.

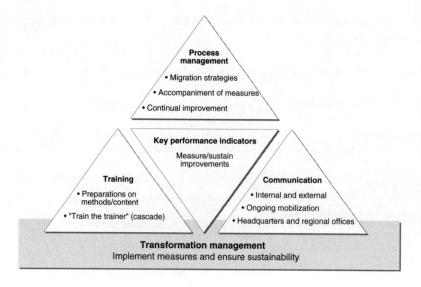

Figure 5.8: Elements of the change management program.

Change always brings uncertainty. Bearing this in mind, it is important to keep the entire workforce well informed. Active communication builds trust and prevents rumour-mongering. Every tool of communication available to the company should be used to this end. In addition to secondary communication channels such as in-house magazines, bulletin boards, employee meetings, posters and the like, communication cascades are the instrument of choice for involving staff in in-depth discussions in small groups (with no more than 20 to 25 participants) and registering what those affected by the measures have to say for themselves. These events also force managers to show their face within the company and actively to come to terms with suggestions made by employees.

Our experience of the communication cascade depicted in Fig. 5.9 has been thoroughly positive.

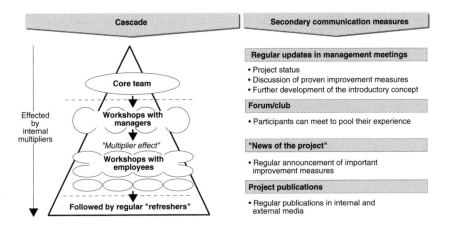

Figure 5.9: A communication cascade in change management.

It will only be possible to sensitise and enable all employees across all levels of the hierarchy if the process of transformation is underpinned by a comprehensive training offensive. To speed up this process and reach as much of the workforce as possible, the concept of 'training the trainer' has frequently proved to be invaluable. 'Training the trainer' means what it says: internal staff are taught to become trainers in their own right and can then provide defined training courses to other employees. One key advantage of this concept is the inherent multiplier effect: a large number of internal trainers can be trained; and they, in turn, can train a large number of their colleagues. Equally, the use of internal trainers underscores the fact that corporate transformation is not a 'one-off project' but is 'here to stay'.

From the very beginning one must reckon with a prolonged period of time for the program of culture change and the process of transformation to take effect, if lasting changes are to be achieved and a willingness to change established. The challenge to the people managing a transformation process is thus to sustain interest in, commitment to and motivation for the project on all levels of the company.

Impassioned appeals alone are not enough. There are also several other essential ingredients:

- Communication must be understood to be genuine dialogue in which sensitivity to individual fears and ideas can be cultivated.
- Even unpleasant measures have to be implemented rigorously.
- In critical situations, it must always be possible to report successes.

In the long run, the value management philosophy will only become flesh and blood if employees are given the opportunity to actively shape and implement measures within the framework of action teams and workgroups. This also requires the clear and unequivocal commitment of top management, expressed in a management lifestyle which consciously models and supports the implementation of the measures defined.

5.4 Organising successful transformation projects

In view of the complexity of a value management program and the transformation process, project management is extremely important. The project organisation must satisfy two essential requirements: it must be simple, manageable and easy to communicate; and it must be based on a clear breakdown of tasks and responsibilities. One useful option is to have a three-tiered structure with a steering committee as the ultimate decision-making body, a core team for operative activity management, and action teams/workgroups to handle specific tasks.

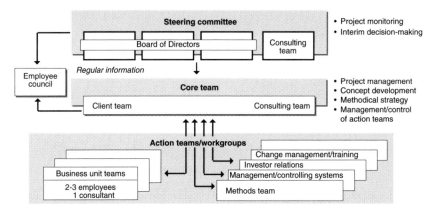

Figure 5.10: Project management in a value management project.

Team composition, and who is responsible for what, must be defined clearly and carefully:

- *Steering committee*: the steering committee, which is usually made up of the board of directors and top management, is responsible for:
  - defining overall goals;
  - delegating decision-making and implementational responsibilities in keeping with requirements;
  - evaluating the project;
  - decisively tearing down barriers to change; and
  - managing enterprise-wide communication.

Again, given the importance of the value management project and the transformation process, the steering committee will need to keep in close touch with project developments and must therefore meet at regular intervals – every two weeks during key project phases.

- *Core team*: the core team is responsible for:
  - overall project management;
  - coordinating the project teams;
  - ensuring that the overall concept dovetails; and
  - motivating team members and, where necessary, assuming a coaching function.

This means that it is essential to have the company's best and most highly qualified performers involved.

Exacting demands will be placed on core team members. They will require social skills and the ability to communicate across all corporate levels. They will need a firm grasp of methods and a thorough knowledge of the company and its 'key players'.

- *Action teams/workgroups*: action teams are set up to deal with individual issues and, in particular, to implement defined measures.

The project organisation will naturally have to be adapted to the specific conditions surrounding the project and the company in question. There is virtually no limit to the conceivable permutations. One option, for example, is to appoint sponsors who ensure that their teams get to work under ideal conditions and pave the way to networks of relationships. Even so, specific 'team factors of success' exist that are also crucial to the overall success of the project:

- Teamwork as a factor of success:
  - The right personnel mix is needed – a combination of skills and hierarchies that is a representative cross-section of the company and provides overall control for the project.
  - Strong and capable leadership personalities must be involved.
  - Team spirit must be fostered around active involvement and joint activity.

- Targets as a factor of success:
  - The focus must be on process innovation; teams should not 'run aground' in the status quo.
  - Targets should be measurable/quantifiable wherever possible.

- Specific approaches as a factor of success:
  - Analyses must be robust and should not be swamped by too much detail.
  - Reporting should be simple and uncomplicated.
  - 'Benefit tracking' – the measurement and communication of successes – should be a regular exercise.

- Leveraging work as a factor of success:
  - Teams should not work in isolation but should channel their results into the business units.
  - Analysis and the development of solutions should act as catalysts.

When choosing team members, one important point should always be remembered. The 'yes, but' faction will never bring about change. That is why it is important to have team members with a 'why not?' attitude, so that new ideas can be not only conceived of but also fleshed out and implemented (see Fig. 5.11).

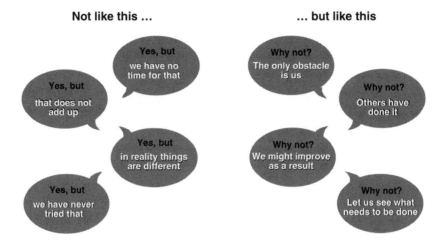

Figure 5.11: Transformation: not like this … but like this!

5.5 The bottom line: transformation makes value management feasible

Transformation *is* possible. It will, however, require clear guiding principles and a powerful, effective organisation. Even then, transformation will be no easy task. The 'prime movers' in a company are important here: they are the only people who can push ahead with transformation and secure its place in the company. Similarly, it is important to continue to mobilise the company via a program of communication and training etc. Our experience suggests that this is best done in a structured manner, however: a positive, open environment is needed – but so is a clear direction. Tight project management, too, is of the essence – at least for the first two phases of the project. And the involvement of a broad selection of employees will widen the base of 'active transformers' – a sure way to success.

Successful transformation lays a firm foundation for sustained value creation in the company:

- Portfolio decisions have been taken and are already being implemented.
- Operative measures to create value are beginning to take effect.
- Management and controlling systems are expanded and extended in line with value management principles.
- Innovative compensation models provide both management and staff with an incentive to act in the best interests of the shareholders.
- The successes of the value management program can be communicated on a broad front, both inside and outside the company.

The most positive effects for the company and its shareholders will be increases in the company's value and share price, easier access to capital as a result and, in cases where parts of the company are sold off, the realisation of higher levels of revenue (see Fig. 5.12). At the same time, thanks to the stakeholder management approach, this form of optimisation will not benefit the shareholders at the expense of the other stakeholders.

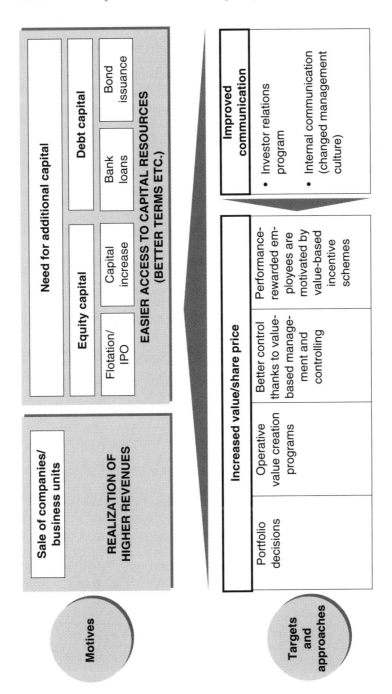

Figure 5.12: The fruits of a successful transformation project.

Publishers and Authors

DR. STEFAN BÖTZEL, born 1960, is a Principal at Roland Berger & Partners. His key responsibilities include value management/value creation and corporate transformation. After commercial training, studies in business management (at Kiel and St. Gallen) and a two-year university assistantship, Stefan Bötzel joined Roland Berger & Partners in Hamburg in 1993. As part of an empirical study, his dissertation investigated the ways in which individual companies can manipulate their financial statements in order to 'paper over' crisis situations within the company, and devised new tools to enable analysts to identify these tricks. Stefan Bötzel is heavily involved in product development at Roland Berger & Partners.

ANDREAS SCHWILLING was born in Meerbusch, Lower Rhine, in 1965. He graduated from the University of St. Gallen with a masters degree in business administration, and went on to complete an MBA with a specialisation in finance and a concentration in policy studies at the University of Chicago Graduate School of Business. Andreas Schwilling was employed by Roland Berger & Partner GmbH International Management Consultants in Munich in 1992. He has been a Principal of the company since early 1997 and focuses primarily on value management. His industry experience and expertise mainly lies in the transport and retail industries.

JÜRGEN A. HAMMERSCHICK was born in Frankfurt in 1964. He began his career by training as an industrial clerk at ITT-Automotiv before completing a course of studies in business administration. He later earned a post-graduate degree as an investment analyst (DVFA) at the Technical University of Darmstadt. Jürgen Hammerschick joined Roland Berger & Partners as a consultant in 1992; since 1996, he has held a post as project manager at the company's Frankfurt office. The major thrust of his consulting activities has been in the areas of restructuring, transformation and strategy.

ANGELIKA HEINZ, born in Munich in 1969, graduated from the University of Regensburg and the Ecole Superieur de Commerce, Marseille–Provence. She studied business administration with a major in corporate finance and strategy. Having gained initial international experience during study periods in France, the USA and Central America, she joined Roland Berger & Partners in 1996. The focus of her consulting work was on value management and strategy. Angelika Heinz now is Vice President, Corporate Finance & Investor Relations at MediGene AG, a German biopharmaceutical company.

DR. CHRISTIAN KOCH was born in Burg in 1971. He studied business administration at the European Business School in Oestrich-Winkel and philosophy, literature and law at the correspondence university of Hagen. Since 1996, Christian Koch has worked as a consultant for Roland Berger & Partners, International Management Consultants. His consulting activities centre around corporate finance, value management and mergers & acquisitions. He completed his doctoral thesis on 'real options in corporate acquisition projects'.

ANDREAS KÖNIG, born in Kempten in 1965, learned the trade of a bank clerk before studying business administration at the University of Erlangen-Nuremberg, majoring in strategic corporate management, accounting and banking. He joined Roland Berger & Partners banking in 1994 and has served as project manager since 1998. Andreas König has been involved in developing value management products and has successfully completed numerous consulting projects in this field.

MICHAEL KUEMMERLE was born in Heidelberg in 1969. He completed his studies in business administration at the University of Bayreuth, majoring in public finance, bank management and marketing, and came to Roland Berger & Partners in Munich in 1995. Michael Kuemmerle is Senior Consultant, with a key emphasis on investor relations in the context of value management.

Bibliography

Ackermann, J. (1996): Wieviel Gewinn für wen?, in: *Dossier Neue Züricher Zeitung: Shareholder Value*, pp. 9–12.

Adams, M. (1997): Corporate Governance: Vertragen sich die deutsche Unternehmensverfassung und das Shareholder-Prinzip?, in: *Zeitschrift für Betriebswirtschaft*, special edition 4/97, pp. 21–30.

Amihud, Y./Murgia, M. (1997): Dividends, taxes and signaling: evidence from Germany, in: *Journal of Finance*, March. Internet.

Ballwieser, W. (1984): Bestimmung des Kapitalisierungszinsfußes, in: Peemöller, V.H.: *Handbuch der Unternehmensbewertung*. Landsberg, pp. 1–9.

Benner, C. H. (1997): Equity Phoria, Entering New Territory, Deutsche Morgan Grenfell. Frankfurt am Main.

Bernhardt, W./Witt P. (1997): Stock Options und Shareholder Value, in: *ZfB-Zeitschrift für Betriebswirtschaft*, 67.Jhg., pp. 85–101.

Blumberg, C./Helling, N. (1996): Die Bewertung mittelständischer Unternehmen: ein Vergleich, in: *M&A-Review*, October, S. pp. 432–436.

Bodie, Z./Kane, A./Marcus A. J. (1989): *Investments*. Homewood/Boston.

Brealey, R./Myers, S. (1996): *Principles of Corporate Finance*, 5th edition. New York.

Bühner, R. (1989): Möglichkeiten der unternehmerischen Gehaltsvereinbarung für das Top-Management, in: *Der Betrieb*, issue 44/3, November, Vol. 42, pp. 2181–2186.

Bühner, R. (1990): *Das Management-Wert-Konzept*. Stuttgart.

Cadbury Schweppes (1998): Annual Report and Form 20 F.

Chamberlain, K./Campell, R. (1995): Creating Shareholder Value, in: *New Zealand Manufacturer*.

Coopers & Lybrand International (1997): Wertorientierte Unternehmensführung. Frankfurt am Main.

Copeland, T./Koller, T./Murrin, J. (1990): Valuation. New York.

Deutsches Aktieninstitut e.V. (1997): DAI-Factbook: Statistiken, Analysen und Grafiken zu Aktionären, Aktiengesellschaften und Börsen. Frankfurt am Main.

Deutsche Morgan Grenfell (1996): Shareholder Value in Deutschland, December.

Deutsche Morgan Grenfell (1997a): Running the Numbers – The CROCI Book, July–September.

Deutsche Morgan Grenfell (1997b): Der Shareholder-Value-Report. Frankfurt am Main.

Deutsche Morgan Grenfell (1997c): Equity Phoria. Frankfurt am Main.

Domann, Rita (1995): Deutschland, in: Mennel/Förster, *Steuern*, 28th delivery, 1995.

Donaldson, G. (1984): *Managing Corporate Wealth*. New York.

Doppler, K./Lauterburg, C. (1995): *Change Management*, 4th edition. Frankfurt am Main.

Drukarczyk, J. (1993): *Theorie und Politik der Finanzierung*, 2nd edition. Munich.

Drukarczyk, J. (1996): *Unternehmensbewertung*. Munich.

Dürr, M. (1995): *Investor Relations, 2*. Auflage. Munich/Vienna.

Easterbrook, F.H. (1984): Two Agency-Cost Explanations of Dividends, in: *AER*, Vol. 74, pp.650–659.

Egon Zehnder International (1997): Durchschnittliches Einkommen von Vorstandsmitgliedern 1997, in: *Blick durch die Wirtschaft*, 06.03.1998.

Eicker, A. (1996): Unternehmens-Value muß Manager-Value sein, in: *Handelsblatt*, 20.12.1996.

Eschenbach, R./Kuenesch, H. (1994): *Strategische Konzepte: Management-Ansätze von Ansoff bis Ulrich*. Stuttgart.

Fischer, G./Wilhelm, W. (1995):Test-Gelände – Manager sollten nach Leistung bezahlt werden – aber keiner weiß, wie Leistung zu bemessen ist, in: *Manager Magazin*, September, pp. 231–241.

Fisher, J. (1995): How effective executive compensation plans work, in: *ABI/INFORM – American Management Association/CMA Magazine*, Vol. 69, No. 5, pp. 36–39.

Freund, W. (1995): *Generationenwechsel im Mittelstand, Institut für Mittelstandsforschung*. Bonn.

Gentz, M. (1998): IR-Herausforderungen bei einem globalen Merger, in: *Börsenzeitung*, 03.12.98, p. B1.

Gentz, M. (1999): DaimlerChryler Investoren- und Analystenkonferenz, 31.03.1999.

Gomez, P. (1993): *Wertmanagement: Vernetzte Strategien für Unternehmen im Wandel*. Düsseldorf.

Greenhill, R. (1990): *Performance related Pay for the 1990s*, 2nd edition. Cambridge.

Gudono (o. J.): The role of executive compensation schemes and stock ownership in corporate strategy: How they affect performance. Internet.

Günther, T. (1997): *Unternehmenswertorientiertes Controlling*. Munich.

Günther, Th./Otterbein, S. (1996): Die Gestaltung der Investor Relations am Beispiel führender deutscher Aktiengesellschaften, in: *Zeitschrift für Betriebswirtschaftslehre*, Vol. 6, pp. 389–417.

Hamel, G. (1997): Killer strategies that make shareholders rich, in: *Fortune*, June, pp. 22–34.

Hauschildt, J. (1992): *Innovationsmanagement*. Munich.

Hax, A. C./Majluf, N. S. (1984): *Strategic Management, an integrative perspective*. New Jersey.

Hax, A. C./Majluf, N. S. (1984): *Strategic Management: An integrative Perspective*. Englewood Cliffs.

Hax, A. C./Majluf, N. S. (1991): *Strategisches Management: Ein integratives Konzept aus dem MIT*. Frankfurt am Main.

Heinz, A./Koch C. (1997): Wege zum effizienten Wertmanagement, in: *Blick durch die Wirtschaft*, 02.05.1997.

Helbling, C. (1991): *Unternehmensbewertung und Steuern*, 6th edition. Düsseldorf.

HFA-Stellungnahme (1983): Grundsätze zur Durchführung von Unternehmensbewertungen, in: *Wpg*, Vol. 36., pp. 469–480.

Höfner, K./Pohl, A. (1994): Wertsteigerungstechniken für das Geschäftsfeld- und Beteiligungsportfolio, in: Höfner, K./Pohl, A. (Hrsg.): *Wertsteigerungs-Management – Das Shareholder Value-Konzept: Methoden und erfolgreiche Beispiele*. Frankfurt am Main.

Hören, M. von (1997): Managmentvergütung 1996: Ergebnisse einer Unternehmensbefragung, in: *Personal*, January, pp. 37–40.

Hören, M. v. (1996): Managementvergütung 1996: Ergebnisse einer Unternehmensbefragung, in: *Personal*, January, pp. 4–7.

Hostettler, S. (1996): Führen mit EVA!, in: *Der Organisator*, March, pp. 36–38.

Huddart, S./Lang, M. (1996): Employee stock option exercises – An empirical analysis, in: *Journal of Accounting & Economics*, No. 21, pp. 5–43.

IMF (1996): Balance of Payments Statistics Yearbook.

IMF (1997a): International Financial Statistics Yearbook.

IMF (1997b): World Economic Outlook, May.

IMF (1997c): World Economic Outlook, October.

IRES (1991): Investor Relations von Aktiengesellschaften: Bewertungen und Erwartungen. Düsseldorf.

Jensen, M. C./Murphy, K. J. (1990): CEO Incentives – It's not how much you pay, but how, in: *Harvard Business Review*, May-June, pp. 138–153.

Johanson, D. R. (1997a): Stock options, phantom stock, and other non-ESOP equity incentive plans, in: *The Stock options book* (NCEO).

Johanson, D. R. (1997b): Statutory stock options, in: *The Stock options book* (NCEO).

Justin, M./Randall, T. (1996): Eli Lilly is making shareholders rich. How? By linking pay to EVA., in: *Fortune*, September. Internet.

Kaplan, R. S./Norton, D. P. (1997): *Balanced scorecard: Strategien erfolgreich umsetzen*. Stuttgart.

Krüger, W./Schwarz, G. (1997): Strategische Stimmigkeit von Erfolgsfaktoren und Erfolgspotentialen, in: Hahn, D./Taylor, B. (Hrsg.): *Strategische Unternehmungsplanung, strategische Unternehmungsführung*, 6th edition. Heidelberg, pp. 75–104.

Liebrecht, H. (1988): Systematische Erschließung von Auslandsmärkten, in: Henzler, H. A. (Hrsg.), *Handbuch Strategische Führung*. Wiesbaden, pp. 183–195.

Lobis, Eduard (1998): Italien, in: Mennel/Förster, *Steuern*, 35th delivery, 1998.

Lockheed (1997): Inco-press release. Internet.

Lewis, T. G. (1994): *Steigerung des Unternehmenswertes – Total Value Management*. Landsberg/Lech.

Luck, L. (1997): Wertorientierte Anreizsysteme, unpublished undergraduate thesis from the Otto-Beisheim-Hochschule. Vallendar.

Machin, S.: Are the fat cats getting fatter? Internet.

Manor, Ch. (1995): Lockheed Martin implements guidelines for stock ownership by key employees, in: *Lockheed Martin News & Information*. Internet.

Marakon Associates (1981): The Marakon Profitability Matrix, in: *Commentary*, April, pp. 1–12.

Marston, C. (1996): The Organization of Investor Relations Function by Large UK Quoted Companies, in: *Omega International Journal Management Science*, Vol. 24, No. 4, pp. 477–488.

Mellwig, W. (1989): Die Erfassung der Steuern in der Investitionsrechnung – Grundprobleme und Modellvarianten, in: *WISU*, pp.35–41.

Moxter, A. (1983): *Grundzüge ordnungsmäßiger Unternehmensbewertung*, 2nd edition. Wiesbaden.

Müssener, Ingo (1997): Vereinigtes Königreich von Großbritannien und Nordirland, in: Mennel/Förster, *Steuern*, 32nd delivery, 1997.

Mullen, M./Mayes, C. (1997): Shareholder Value Management – a critical Board issue which is often not addressed. Internet.

O.V. (o.J): *Investor Relations*. Düsseldorf.

O.V. (1998): Beta-Faktoren der DAX-Unternehmen, in: *Handelsblatt*, 30.03.1998, p. 26.

O.V. (1992): Spanien, in: Mennel/Förster, *Steuern*, 27th delivery, 1994.

Pellens, B./Rockholtz, C. (1997): Konzerne müssen sich neuen Marktgesetzen anpassen, in: *Handelsblatt* No. 201, 20.10.1997, p. 16.

Pellens, B./Rockholtz, C./Stienemann, M. (1997): Marktwertorientiertes Konzern-controlling in Deutschland, in: *Der Betrieb*, issue 39/Vol. 50, pp. 1933–1939. Bochum/Münster.

Perkins, A. G. (1995): Director Compensation – The Growth of Benefits, in: *Harvard Business Review*, January-February, pp. 12–14.

Perridon, L./Steiner, M. (1995): *Finanzwirtschaft der Unternehmung*. Munich.

Porter (1988): How Competitive Forces Shape Strategy, in: Quinn, J. B./Mintzberg, H./James, R. M.: *The Strategy Process*. Englewood Cliffs, pp. 58–65.

Porter (1989): Wettbewerbsvorteile. Frankfurt am Main.

Prahalad, C. K./Hamel, G. (1997): The Core Competence of the Corporation, in: Hahn, D./Taylor, B. (Hrsg.): *Strategische Unternehmungsplanung, strategische Unternehmungsführung*, 6th edition. Heidelberg, pp. 969–987.

Prognos (1996): Franzen, D. et al: World Report 1996, Emerging Countries. Basle.

Prognos (1997): Eckerle, K. et al: World Report 1998, Industrial Countries. Basle.

Rall, W. (1997): Strategie für den Weltmarkt, in: Hahn, D./Taylor, B. (Hrsg.): *Strategische Unternehmungsplanung, strategische Unternehmungsführung*, 6th edition. Heidelberg, pp. 523–541.

Rappaport, A. (1986): Creating Shareholder Value. The New Standard for Business Performance. New York.

Rappaport, A. (1986): *Creating Shareholder Value*. New York

Rappaport, A. (1994): *Shareholder Value – Wertsteigerung als Maßstab für die Unternehmensführung*. Stuttgart.

Raster, M. (o. J.): Shareholder Value Management – Ermittlung und Steigerung des Unternehmenswertes, in: *Gabler Edition Wissenschaft*, pp. 191–207.

Reimann, B. C. (1990): *Managing for Value: A Guide to Value Based Strategy*, 2nd edition. Oxford/Cambridge.

Schierenbeck, H. (1993): *Grundzüge der Betriebswirtschaftslehre*, 11th edition. Munich/Vienna.

Schmitz, W. (1997): Die Kapitalkosten wurden nicht verdient, in: *Handelsblatt*, 02.12.1997, p. 14.

Schneeloch, D. (1994): Besteuerung und betriebliche Steuerpolitik, in: *Betriebliche Steuerpolitik*, Vol. 2. Munich.

Schuster, J. R./Zingelheim, P. K. (1993): The new variable pay: Key design issues, in: *Compensation & Benefits Review*, March-April, Vol. 25, No. 2, pp. 27–34.

Siegert, T./Böhme, M. (1997): Marktorientierte Unternehmensführung im Lebenszyklus, in: *Zfbf*, May, pp. 471–489.

Stewart, B. G. (1990a): Market Myths, in: *Journal of Applied Corporate Finance*, pp.6–23.

Stewart, B. G. (1990b): The Quest for Value – A Guide for Senior Managers. o. O.

The National Centre for Employee Ownership (1995/1996): Employee ownership companies pay less for workers' compensation costs.

The National Centre for Employee Ownership (1997a): Employee stock options fact sheet.

The National Centre for Employee Ownership (1997b): The stock options book.

The National Centre for Employee Ownership (1997c): Home page. Internet.

Tillmanns, Wolfhard (1998): Frankreich, in: Mennel/Förster, *Steuern*, 36th delivery, 1997.

Titzrath, A. (1996): Erschließung internationaler Kapitalmärkte durch deutsche Emittenten, in: Schmalenbach-Gesellschaft, Deutsche Gesellschaft für Betriebswirtschaft (publisher): *Globale Finanzmärkte*. Stuttgart, pp. 91–104.

Ulrich, P. (1977): *Die Großunternehmung als quasi-öffentliche Institution. Eine politische Theorie der Unternehmung*. Stuttgart.

UNCTAD (1996): *World Investment Report 1996, Investment, Trade and International Policy Arrangements*, United Nations. New York and Geneva.

VEBA AG (1996): Presentation for investment banks/analysts.

Waadt, M./Bruns, G./Schweiger, A. (1998): *Vergütungsstudie 1998 Fach- und Führungskräfte, geva-Institut*. Munich.

Weltbank (1997): *World Development Indicators*. CD-ROM.

Wiezoreck, H./Wallinger, A. (1997): *Wachstum mit Gewinn, 20 Methoden für die systematische Expansion*. Frankfurt am Main/New York.

Zimmerer (1993): Unternehmensakquisition, in: W. Wittmann (publisher.): *Handwörterbuch der Betriebswirtschaft*. Stuttgart, pp. 4294–4306.

Zwätz, D. (1998): Negativrekord, Handelsblatt, 19.02.1998, p. 25.

Index